THE AMERICANA REVOLUTION

Roots of American Music
Folk, Americana, Blues, and Country
June Skinner Sawyers, series editor

In recent decades American roots music has experienced a revival in popular performance and critical attention. Rowman & Littlefield's series Roots of American Music: Folk, Americana, Blues, and Country seeks to explore the origins of these musical genres as integral parts of cultural experience and shared musical history. With dynamic biographies of musicians responsible for enduring traditions in these genres, the series introduces accessible scholarship to expose the significance of these musicians to a wide audience. Stylistic and cultural investigations into the genres provide contextual anchors for broader understanding of trends which continue to influence music today. Just like the musical traditions investigated, this series looks to music's past in order to understand its future. The series welcomes projects which seek to explore the reaches of folk, Americana, blues, and country traditions as they were formed in the past and as they continue to evolve in the contemporary music scene.

Titles in the Series

THE AMERICANA REVOLUTION

*From Country and Blues Roots
to the Avett Brothers, Mumford &
Sons, and Beyond*

Michael Scott Cain

ROWMAN & LITTLEFIELD
Lanham • Boulder • New York • London

Published by Rowman & Littlefield
A wholly owned subsidiary of The Rowman & Littlefield Publishing Group, Inc.
4501 Forbes Boulevard, Suite 200, Lanham, Maryland 20706
www.rowman.com

Unit A, Whitacre Mews, 26-34 Stannary Street, London SE11 4AB

British Library Cataloguing in Publication Information Available

Library of Congress Cataloging-in-Publication Data

Names: Cain, Michael Scott.
Title: The Americana revolution : from country and blues roots to the Avett Brothers, Mumford &
    Sons, and beyond / Michael Scott Cain.
Description: Lanham : Rowman & Littlefield, [2017] | Includes bibliographical references and index.
Identifiers: LCCN 2016040784 (print) | LCCN 2016056504 (ebook) | ISBN 9781442269408 (cloth :
    alk. paper) | ISBN 9781442269415 (electronic)
Subjects: LCSH: Americana (Music)—History and criticism.
Classification: LCC ML3512 .C35 2017 (print) | LCC ML3512 (ebook) | DDC 781.640973—dc23
LC record available at https://lccn.loc.gov/2016040784

Printed in the United States of America

As always, for Helene

CONTENTS

SERIES FOREWORD

This is the second volume in the Roots of American Music: Folk, Americana, Blues, and Country series. Each book in the series examines the influences on and of the music from a cultural context. Moreover, the books are written by authors who are knowledgeable and authoritative in their field but who are still able to communicate to the general reader. The series examines the body of work by particular artists in folk, Americana, blues, and country, and their offshoots; explores the various influences and roots of these artists, both major and lesser-known artists who warrant closer examination; and studies musical trends within these genres in an attempt to understand, and reveal, their historical influences.

As a genre of music, Americana is its own worst enemy. It incorporates many different types of music under its broad umbrella, which makes it difficult to categorize. But, ironically, that is also its greatest strength. The Tennessee-based Americana Music Association (AMA), which hosts the annual Americana Music Festival and Conference in September, defines Americana as "contemporary music that incorporates elements of various American roots music styles, including country, roots-rock, folk, bluegrass, R&B and blues, resulting in a distinctive roots-oriented sound that lives in a world apart from the pure forms of the genres upon which it may draw. While acoustic instruments are often present and vital, Americana also often uses a full electric band."

Americana is nothing if not fluid. Many varied artists fall under its fold from the obvious (the Carter Family and Emmylou Harris) to representatives of the so-called New Folk Revival (the Avett Brothers and

Mumford & Sons). Artists don't even have to be American to be Americana (think of, say, the great English guitarist Richard Thompson or the Australian singer-songwriter Kasey Chambers).

In *The Americana Revolution: From Country and Blues Roots to the Avett Brothers, Mumford & Sons, and Beyond*, Michael Scott Cain discusses the origins of Americana as both a genre and a movement; explores the historical and cultural role that African Americans played in the development of American popular culture; and examines the international dimension of Americana, among many other topics. He also offers intimate portraits, which he calls interludes, of particular Americana artists (Roger McGuinn, Rosanne Cash, Kris Kristofferson, and Jim Lauderdale). He concludes with an annotated list of recommended recordings.

Whatever label you decide to hang on to these artists, Americana is a music that demands to be listened to. Cain calls it the Americana Revolution, which somehow seems appropriate.

June Sawyers
Series Editor

ACKNOWLEDGMENTS

So many people contributed to the creation of this book that it is safe to say that without the time, effort, and help from dozens of people I'd never met, *The Americana Revolution: From Country and Blues Roots to the Avett Brothers, Mumford & Sons, and Beyond* could not have been written.

Kevin Welch spent hours of his time talking to a stranger on the telephone, informing me, filling me in on background, and giving me leads that paid off with more in-depth background. One of the men he led me to, Al Moss, was in on the creation of the Americana Association and is the only man to have served on the association's board from the beginning until now, a position he still holds. Al devoted an entire Sunday afternoon telling me the story of the association's beginnings, not just what happened but also how and why it happened and precisely who caused it to happen. He also provided me with other sources, including Dennis Lord, another veteran of the formative years of the Americana Association who was able to fill in some very big blanks in my research.

In addition to Kevin Welch, other performers gave time and energy to my project. I want to thank Jennifer Knapp, who spoke generously about her career and her travels from contemporary Christian music to Americana. She was also able to clear up a question that had been bothering me for some time and to which I hadn't been able to find a satisfactory answer up until that point: the difference between religion and spirituality.

Henry Paul, who has led more successful bands than most people have even heard, was kind enough to take me through the journey from hard rock to Americana and was able to emphasize what he sees as the most important aspects of Americana: its honesty and authenticity. Henry spoke with his own authority, that of a man who, in his youth, fought to be admitted to the party, finally got in, and discovered the party was nothing like what he'd expected it to be. Wearing his maturity like one of Mr. T's gold necklaces, Henry Paul talked about the importance of the music not the musician—a factor common to Americana but a sign of insanity in most other genres.

Nitty Gritty Dirt Band drummer and harmonica player Jimmie Fadden enlightened me not only about music but also about an approach to life itself, demonstrating the alignment between the music and the values of the musician. Again, what was scheduled to be a thirty-minute conversation became a two-hour ramble through the band's history and guiding philosophy.

And that's how it went. Nearly everyone I spoke with seemed to recognize how important it was to get a vivid and real picture of this music across and went out of their way to be helpful. Even those who objected to being categorized, such as Ian Hölljes of Delta Rae, were anxious to talk about the southern tradition and the literary aspects of Americana. Maura O'Connell, who has fought being categorized as a singer throughout her career, still spoke with me several times, giving me valuable information about the need for individuality, the importance of being a singer instead of a vocalist, and why, even if she objects, the very nature of being a singer on the road forces one into a category.

Mary Chapin Carpenter, the Hello Strangers, and the Steel Wheels all discussed the inclusive nature of Americana, the fact that it is a movement as much as a genre and gives artists a community to be a part of.

I owe a special debt to Jimmy Carter, the last founding member of the Blind Boys of Alabama. He was eighty-two when we spoke, and he educated me on the history of gospel music—and the Blind Boys' part in it—from the perspective of one who has lived it. He also educated me on how a genuinely good person can make his way through the world.

Buffy Ford Stewart shared extensively the songwriting techniques of her late husband, John Stewart, one of the men credited with creating Americana. From her, I learned much more about John, and his approach to life and career, than his published interviews revealed. Without her help, the section on his work would be much weaker.

Eileen Ivers, Mary Black, Joanie Madden, and Maura O'Connell all showed me the international side of Americana, driving home the point that though it is named for this country, it is indeed a worldwide phenomenon. Despite being Irish, they are all Americana artists, bringing their own backgrounds and culture to the music and proving it is big enough to accommodate them.

I also want to thank Zenas Sears for giving me a place to go in order to find the music when I was a kid in Atlanta, and Piano Red for allowing me to hang out in his studio while he played it. I was twelve, heard Piano Red on the station Sears owned, WAOK, and hypnotized by the music Red was playing live on the air, immediately hitchhiked downtown to the studio and walked in, as though I had been drawn there by a beacon. For some reason, Zenas Sears and Piano Red made a big, dumb white kid welcome, and the radio station became my second home. That was my first live encounter with Americana music, and it helped turn me into the person I am.

I also want to thank Rebecca and Dahlia for tracking down and gifting me with Harry Smith's *Anthology of American Folk Music*, a set I'd longed to hear all my life but had never encountered until my daughters bought it for me. My other children, Gabe and Shannon, gave generously of their time and energy and put up with much more talk about Americana than they would have otherwise chosen to hear.

All of the people, some of them complete strangers, who shot me e-mails with facts, details, ideas, and suggestions, need to be thanked, as well as everyone who corrected my errors. All of the sources worked so hard to help me deserve credit for whatever strengths are in this work; the weaknesses are mine.

All of these people confirmed what Dennis Lord said: Americana is a movement, and it is a welcoming one. I started out talking to strangers but wound up feeling as though I'd made a new circle of friends.

Most of all, I want to thank Helene, who encouraged this work from the beginning, peppered me with ideas and suggestions, gently pointed out to me that I was drifting off track whenever that happened, and made sure my enthusiasms led me in the right direction. She never gave up on my work, even when I was tempted to. *The Americana Revolution: From*

Country and Blues Roots to the Avett Brothers, Mumford & Sons, and Beyond would be a radically different work without her contributions.

INTRODUCTION

When I first began this book, I had very little idea what Americana music actually was. The best I could come up with was that it was a term made up to hide the fact that what the musician was playing was folk music; since everybody knows as a matter of faith that folk music doesn't sell, folk singers, record companies, and promoters wanted to cover that up. Either that or it was a conspiracy to extend the careers of artists who could not get played on the radio anymore.

All I could be certain of at that point was that more and more of the music I loved and had listened to all my life was being labeled Americana. What had once been called garage rock, folk music, soul, bluegrass, or even jazz was now being offered up as Americana. It was confusing. How could so many things be one thing?

Going to see actual Americana shows did not clarify the issue. The first concert billed as Americana that I attended consisted of a jam band from North Carolina, a blues guitarist-singer from New Jersey, and a well-known veteran southern rock band from Atlanta. It was fine music, but I couldn't find a common denominator.

Finding that denominator proved to be tough. When I began hearing the names of Hank Williams Sr., Hank Williams Jr., and Hank Williams III, Dion, Bob Seger, John Fogerty, Solomon Burke, Mavis Staples, Waylon Jennings, and Johnny Cash all described as Americana singers, I could only wonder when Renee Fleming would make the list.

As a result of newspaper and website writing assignments, I embarked on a fairly rigorous series of interviews and secondary research, and when

I began to discover what the artists who carried that label had in common, I was like the man who discovered he'd been speaking prose all his life; it was as though someone had said, "Let's name a genre after all of the different types of music that Cain likes." That appeared to be the common denominator: I loved the music and had been listening to Americana all my life without ever being aware of the fact. I had thought I just liked a wide variety of music, but it turned out that all of the stuff I loved shared one thing: it was roots music, music that had a link to the past and shared a mood and tone with the songs that had come before it.

Still, other than the fact that it was rooted, I had little idea what Americana really was. When a newspaper I freelance for asked me to cover an Americana festival, I centered my piece on trying to define the form. I asked a dozen or so artists in the field what Americana was, and while their answers, along with others, are discussed in detail later in this book, let's just say no two of them saw the same thing when they looked at the music.

Americana appeared to be a category that everyone participated in but no one could identify. Some were delighted to be included, some less so, and some objected to the whole idea of categories, but no one could say exactly what this category consisted of. As we will see, even the men and women who started the association to promote this music weren't always sure what they were promoting. And as we will also see, the singers and musicians who make up the Americana world all see it differently. And, finally, this divergence of vision is an advantage: a strength not a weakness.

This book came out of my exploration. I began seriously searching for a definition and just as quickly saw that defining the genre wasn't enough. To understand it, I was going to have to go back in time and examine where it came from and how it came about. Perhaps it is hard to say what it was, but maybe if I traced the various elements that made up the music over the years, sort of concocting an informal social history, it would lead to a stronger sense of certainty. *The Americana Revolution* is the result. Only that approach can encapsulate the complexity of this category.

A FORMAT SO HARD TO CAPTURE

Americana is the music of artists such as John Hiatt, John Fogerty, Mavis Staples, the Avett Brothers, Emmylou Harris, Johnny Cash, Roger McGuinn, Eileen Ivers, Pete Seeger, Sonny Terry and Brownie McGhee, Sonny Boy Williamson, Muddy Waters, Jennifer Knapp, Mary Chapin Carpenter, Kathy Mattea, Suzy Bogguss, Arlo Guthrie, Mumford & Sons, and Brandi Carlile—artists from all over the spectrum. What makes all of these people Americana artists? Among the most important factors is that their music simply does not fit comfortably in any other category.

A quick look at the career trajectory of a band that has been called the inventor of Americana, the Nitty Gritty Dirt Band, will serve as an illustration, as well as create a road map for the journey we are about to embark on.

The Dirt Band was formed in 1966 in Long Beach, California. Three of the founding members, Jimmie Fadden, Jeff Hanna, and John McKuen, are still with the band, and the "new guy" Bob Carpenter has been there for nearly a third of a century. From the beginning, they were that rare band that, instead of playing what was popular and would get them on the radio, played what they loved. As Jimmie Fadden, who discussed the band's work with me in a lengthy telephone interview, says about their origins, "We were a jug band that played a lot of different kinds of music. We didn't just do jug band music. We played swing, big bandish kind of things, bluegrass, some fancy string band music. We did it on jug band instruments. We played things in a sort of illegitimate way. We were playing Cab Calloway with a washtub bass."[1]

In the days when the band formed, experimental music was a norm; there was no strong need to name or categorize the music. "Back in the sixties," Fadden told me, "format didn't seem to be a very big problem, especially in FM because they were far more open to exploring different things and allowing them to be what they were without calling them something."

The free-form FM stations created an openness to expression without categorization. According to one of the early free-form stations, WFMU in New York City, free-form radio is defined as "an approach to radio programming in which a station's management gives the DJ complete control over program content. Free-form shows are as different as the personalities of DJ's, but they usually have a feeling of spontaneity, a tendency to play music that is not usually heard."[2]

In the 1960s, AM radio was the establishment, and FM was the scrappy band of outsiders trying to be heard. Since AM had a reasonably strict playlist, FM competed by adopting a free-form approach. The first free-form station was the Pacifica community-sponsored radio KPFA-FM in Berkeley, California, which broadcast Jon Leonard's *Nightsounds* program.[3]

Leonard's success caused the free-form movement to spread through the country like weeds through a lawn. Soon, every major city had at least one free-form FM station, and most had more than one competing against each other. Ironically, the very success of the free-form format led to its downfall. As more young people—the favored demographic of radio— tuned in, station managements tried to maximize profits, which led to the installation of playlists and other restrictions on DJs and programming. When that happened, free form was no longer free. At this point also, the conglomeration of radio and the rise of consultants began. Free form as a format lost to tightly controlled playlists. It survives now only on a few college stations and the growing chain of independent stations that program Americana music.

The founding members of the Dirt Band were all listeners to free-form radio for a couple of reasons. One, it was where good music was played, and two, free form was the format that created a sense of community among the young people who felt alienated from the mainstream society of the time. Jimmie Fadden remembers, "I think that so many of us are experiencing that same thing by the fact of being excluded. When I was young, I always thought of myself as an outsider. I was always drawn to this music that was always outside the norm and I fit into that group."

The newly formed Dirt Band played Los Angeles clubs, and on the basis of their live shows were signed by Liberty Records. Their first few albums reflected their free-form, old-time jug band approach, featuring collegiate songs, vaudeville tunes, jug band music, a little rock, and some bluegrass. To critics and record buyers alike, the albums were seen as unfocused attempts at showcasing everything they could do. As a consequence, the records didn't sell.

After four albums that had the dual effect of confusing critics by offering so many different styles of music and failing to draw a mass audience, the Nitty Gritty Dirt Band rethought their approach and broke through to critical and commercial success with their fifth release, *Uncle Charlie and His Dog Teddy*, the first album considered to have created Americana. While *Uncle Charlie* was more focused than their earlier albums, it continued to develop their adventurous spirit, featuring everything from rock to bluegrass, humor, folk, and country, all wrapped in an experimental package that crossed boundaries and blended genres. It also contained their first major hit single, "Mr. Bojangles," which stayed in the top ten for thirty-four weeks.

The creativity and originality expressed on the album was not something the band carefully planned. According to Fadden, it was simply a result of the way the band works. "We've got that 'inquiring minds want to know' kind of feeling. We've got a bunch of guys that say 'what if' in a group setting. We sit around and talk about the possibilities of things," he said during our interview.

> That's the nature of who we are. We've always been interested in combining influences and forces, to remix them, to put them into a shaker and see what comes out. It's like, okay, we're doing this rock thing, why don't you put a mandolin in here and see how it works out. You have to believe there's a process which by combining influences will take you to the outcome you're looking for. We're like kids, messing things up to see how it looks. "Oh, here's some green, let's put some orange on it and see what happens." It's exploring sounds and textures, how they seem to fit. There's been a lot of failure along the way, but we're always interested in trying things.

Among the reasons *Uncle Charlie* isn't hailed by everyone as the first Americana album is because their second release after *Charlie* often claims that title. Twang Nation declared *Will the Circle Be Unbroken* the first and most influential Americana album.[4] So did Juli Thanki in the Nashville *Tennessean*, who added that the Dirt Band was "one of the first Americana acts, though that term wouldn't come into use until nearly forty years after the genre-blending band's inception."[5]

The real story of how the *Circle* album came to be recorded has been lost in time. Many different variations of the tale have been published, offering different narratives of how the three-record set came about and who was responsible for what. Fadden himself says the truth of it has been lost to the narrative but remembers it this way: the band members had been hanging out and jamming with Gary and Randy Scruggs, the sons of the legendary banjo player Earl Scruggs, the inventor of the three-finger banjo technique.

John McKuen asked Earl Scruggs about performing on an album that would feature the Dirt Band with all the old-time country and bluegrass players whose music they loved. According to Fadden,

> The reason Earl said yes was because Randy and Gary had taken note of the music we were playing, which at that point was *Uncle Charlie.* The fact that Gary and Randy took note of what we were doing and shared it with their father allowed this to be a family process with Earl and the kids. The fact was that it already was a family process with John and Bill McKuen, John's brother who managed the band, and it became a family process with Earl and the kids. It took everybody to get it done. It happened really quick. It didn't take very long after everybody was lined up to get done. Without Earl I don't believe it would have happened. He talked to everybody involved at some length and in some way to gain their participation. In the meantime we were hanging out with Gary and Randy and Jody Maphis playing music together and playing Ping Pong together and cemented a relationship. It was a project in which friendships flourished and music was made.

Contributors included country music veteran Roy Acuff, bluegrass legends Jimmy Martin and Oswald Kirby, Mother Maybelle Carter, acoustic guitar master Norman Blake, Doc Watson, and Merle Travis, not to mention the Scruggs family. Nominated for two Grammy Awards on its release, the album is now in the Grammy Hall of Fame and the Smithsonian Museum of Arts and is still available in all formats.

The Nitty Gritty Dirt Band's creative restlessness and insistence on genre bending, on following the music where it leads regardless of category, makes it a model of Americana and moves us closer to a definition. Again, to quote Fadden,

> I think it [Americana] was an attempt to group together a lot of unexplainable forms of roots music in a way that it could be encapsulated, presented to an audience, with an understanding of it having a name. I think all along radio had had a need to call it something in order to have a format. In every sense of our lives we've had somebody trying to put a label on something so that we understand it a little more easily or a little more quickly, to a point we are idiots for trying to know more about it. Americana was a really good choice of words to explain

what it is so many of us do because we've been influenced by so many forms of American or roots music and expressed it in our own individual ways.

WITHOUT A LABEL, HOW WOULD WE KNOW WHAT SHELF TO STORE IT ON?

Fadden suggests that Americans don't simply need to categorize his band's music; they need to categorize everything, because of our deep-seated belief that by putting a label on it, we understand it. As our discussion so far has shown and as we will continue to show, understanding is not that easy. To put something in a box is not to come to terms with it but, in many cases, to oversimplify it, to hide its complexity.

Willie Nelson serves as an example of category hiding complexity. Though he is still looked upon as a country singer, his recorded output suggests that he hasn't actually been a country artist for a long time now, at least since the early 1970s. As far back as 1963, he identified Frank Sinatra as the biggest influence on his singing; Sinatra was a lot of things, but country was not one of them. Nelson's 1978 album, *Stardust*, for example, produced by R&B musician Booker T, is an album of pop standards, fusing elements of jazz, pop, country, and folk. Its focus, techniques, and intention lay far outside the country field. Nelson has made jazz albums, reggae albums, sets of folk and gospel music, and pop; in 2016, he even released an album of George Gershwin standards.

Nelson takes into the studio whatever music happens to move his creative needles at the time. The fact that after a sixty-year career he continues to experiment and is not afraid to fail suggests the adventurous spirit that is also demonstrated by the Nitty Gritty Dirt Band and is such an important part of Americana. Although he is one of the artists responsible for the growth in the popularity of country music, he is not currently welcome on contemporary country radio because his music doesn't fit their format. That an artist whose work played a major role in creating the current audience for country music is banned from its stations demonstrates the power of radio's reliance on categories.

Mary Chapin Carpenter is another artist who has bent genres as though she were Uri Geller with a fork. She began as a folk singer, was adopted by country music, and after her commercial peak passed and she too was perceived as having worn out her welcome on country radio, she spread her wings beyond the scope of the country genre. Her 2014 album, *Songs from the Movie*, rearranges her songs for a symphony orchestra, and she has toured with symphonies. In today's country or folk music worlds, an album such as this one is inconceivable. It rips apart the established formulas. It fits Americana, though. In fact, both Arlo Guthrie and Brandi Carlile did arrangements of their songs for symphony orchestras and recorded with them before Carpenter took her project on.

As we've seen, Americana can, on the one hand, be thought of as music that is made by people who, as the Allman Brothers, who have been repositioned from southern rock into Americana, say, "are in it for the music," music where the commercial motive, while present, does not dominate. Again, as Jimmie Fadden explains, artists might not get rich playing Americana music, but they can make a living with it.

> Americana doesn't pay as much as some fields, but we've always been able to work and make money at a level that has made us somewhat comfortable. There's always been people who wanted to see us play, and that's given us enough to be able to have homes and cars and put our kids through school. Nothing exorbitant but enough. We're able to continue to create and play music for the people who want to hear it.

Most Americana artists have traded the dream of major money for the freedom of expression and exercise of creativity that the field offers, choosing to make their music in listening clubs instead of stadiums. As Ellis Paul once said about being rich and famous, "I'm not famous and I gave up on being rich a long time ago." So Americana is not only defined by its characteristics but also by its attitude, feelings, assumptions, and values.

Consider it this way: In addition to the acts discussed above, the Indigo Girls, the Carolina Chocolate Drops, Ralph Stanley, Mavis Staples, John Mellencamp, the Blind Boys of Alabama, the Allman Brothers Band, the Marshall Tucker Band, the Outlaws, the Green Fields of America, and Maura O'Connell are all considered Americana acts. What do these artists have in common except their creativity, feelings, assumptions, and values?

And what other musical format can encompass all of these varied talents?

TWO WAYS OF LOOKING AT A WORK OF ART

There is always the central question: when we're looking at a work of art, what are we looking at? For many of us, the answer would be, who cares? As long as it pleases me, I'm happy. Others, though, need to know, to understand. In order for us to do that, we need to put things in categories. We must do this because as humans with limitations, we can only know things in terms of their opposites. Can we know anger without knowing calm? Can we know green without a knowledge of red? Dividing things into opposites does not allow us to see the whole in all of its complexity, but it does help us understand the particular aspect we are examining. This division applies not only to objects created by the culture but also to the culture itself. For convenience, we can isolate three different types of culture that operate in the United States: popular culture, mass culture, and elite culture.[6] Elite culture is beyond the scope of all popular music and need not concern us here. Mass culture is the term that refers to products designed to appeal to a huge mass audience. Popular culture also aims for an audience, but it offers something unique to most members of that audience. For our purposes, popular culture is the most important. One key to the emergence of Americana, in fact, lies in the basic concepts of pop-culture studies.

John Cawelti, the scholar most closely associated with the field, states that all cultural products contain a mixture of two kinds of elements: conventions and inventions. Conventions are the formulaic aspects. He describes them as "elements that are known to both the creator and his audience beforehand."[7] In literature, formula refers to the favorite plots, stereotyped characters, commonly known metaphors, and closed symbols, while in Americana music it is the stuff we expect to be present: melody, harmony, vocals, and a blend of electric and acoustic instruments used to deliver elements of roots music styles are all part of the formula of Americana. We expect to hear songs that employ elements of country, folk, rock, blues, bluegrass, and R&B to build their melodies, harmonies, and vocals. Invention refers to the new elements the artist brings to the music. It is the unique qualities that the artist brings to the music, the stuff you won't hear in every song of its type. Formula is what makes it sound familiar; invention makes it sound new. Conventions represent familiar shared images and meanings, Cawelti says, and they show us an ongoing community of values. Inventions, on the other hand, show us new perceptions. Conventions belong to the culture; invention belongs to the artist. Conventions are outside, invention inside. Popular art lies in the right balance of these two elements. Cawelti sees formula as one of the most important ways to study artifacts of popular culture.[8]

Mass culture, on the other hand, refers to a set of values and ideas that arise from sameness, the common exposure to the same products and ideas, the same music, the same art, and the same notions. It is mass produced for mass consumption and is mass marketed. Its intention is to meet a demand that already exists in the mind of the audience. Corporate radio is an example of mass culture.

Mass art, then, is very high on formula and low on invention. The idea behind mass culture is to make every unit as close to every other unit as possible. Take collectible plates, for example. Each one of them is the same. Pop music, at least that aspect of it represented by corporate radio, is misnamed; it should be called mass music. The Disney preteen girl singers and the boy bands are mass art, since each one has numerous clones, all cut from the same bolt of cloth. The fact that these groups can be and sometimes are assembled from choices made on reality competition TV shows indicates the mass qualities they share. They are the collectible plates of music. Granted, there are exceptions, but for the most part, conventional pop as mass culture and Americana as pop culture holds up.

If mass culture is high on formula and low on invention, pop culture is the opposite. It offers enough formula to keep its audience comfortable, but it emphasizes invention, using the old to fashion something new and unique. That newness does not have to be something brought into the world for the first time. A variation, a personal take on a universal subject, an archetype used differently, and a conventional symbol given new meaning as Americana uses them can all qualify as new. To understand this notion, we'll take a look at a song of John Hiatt's. First, though, we need a short look at Hiatt himself.

John Hiatt has been a singer-songwriter for over forty years, and for most of that time, although he's a strong and dynamic live performer, he's been better known for his writing than for his performing. Bonnie Raitt, Three Dog Night, Eric Clapton and B. B. King, Bob Dylan, Willie Nelson, Rosanne Cash, and Bruce Springsteen have all recorded his songs. Hiatt's own recordings of his songs have not only charted but also found their way into some very popular movies, including *Alone in the*

Dark and *True Lies*. "Tennessee Plates" was used in the Ridley Scott classic *Thelma and Louise*; "Across the Borderline," in *The Border*; and "The Usual" was sung by Bob Dylan in the film *Hearts of Fire*.

Like many young singers and writers, Hiatt went to Nashville in 1970, where he landed a staff job in a music publishing house. He picked an excellent time to be there. For many reasons we'll discuss later, there was a great songwriting explosion going on in Nashville. The people who would make up the Americana explosion were settling into place there: songwriters such as Kris Kristofferson, Mickey Newbury, Townes Van Zandt, Guy Clark, and David Allan Coe were all scrambling to get their careers off the ground, writing songs all day and getting together to play the resulting music for each other every night. It was a very fertile and creative environment for an artist, and Hiatt did well enough in it to place some songs on other artists' albums and then to be signed as an artist by Epic Records in 1974.

Hiatt released *Hangin' around the Observatory*, an album that was ahead of its time, since it blended rock, soul, and country. When the album and its follow-up both tanked, he was dropped from the label. For the next few years, he struggled, playing out the same pattern that had happened with Epic: releasing good, well-received albums on a number of labels that were loved by critics and overlooked by the public.

Everything changed in 1987 when Hiatt released *Bring the Family* on A&M Records. With support from Jim Keltner, Nick Lowe, and Ry Cooder—all fine and well-known musicians who would help create Americana—Hiatt offered up his best songwriting to date. He turned to his own life for inspiration and came up with songs that explored love and loss, both the sustenance and difficulties of family life. It is a grown-up album that became an early Americana classic. By now the public was ready for Hiatt's work, and *Bring the Family* became his breakthrough disc.

Hiatt followed it with a series of brilliant discs that demonstrated his ability to mix genres as smoothly and interestingly as English guitarist Richard Thompson, fusing rock, soul, blues, country, and a touch of jazz into a new whole. In 2008, he won the Americana Music Association's Lifetime Achievement Award for songwriting.

As an example of what Hiatt has contributed to Americana, consider his song "Buffalo River Home," which is about the feeling of being stuck in one psychic place, the inability to move or make progress. The song uses standard garage rock instrumentation—guitars, bass, and drums—but it sounds nothing like contemporary rock. It has a timeless quality to it, with a chord structure and melody that could have been written in 1956; it is not so much roots music as it is rooted. Its themes, though, are current and not often found in pop music. The ideas in the song are mature, likely to elude the young kids who make up the pop audience. They are philosophical in nature; you listen to them instead of dancing to the beat. The symbols and images used in the song are purely American but totally unique: loneliness is compared to a fogged-in airport, and the attempt to find oneself is described in terms of American geography, such as cotton fields, bus shelters, the Delta country, and Times Square. Like most Americana and almost all of Hiatt's work, "Buffalo River Home" is a complex work in a simple wrapper.

I've spent some time on this song to show that the pop music of mass culture and the offerings of pop-culture Americana differ in the messages they send. Mass culture tries to figure out what its audience is already thinking and sends messages that reinforce those previously held beliefs. Its maxim is that a thing becomes a hit when the picture it presents matches the picture already held by the audience. Pop culture, however, delivers a picture of reality that its creator believes to be true and accurate. Mass culture's messages then are always simplistic, while pop culture's messages are simplistic only if the artist is simple.

GOALS OF THE BOOK

This book has its origins in the article I wrote trying to find an adequate definition of Americana. After talking to a dozen artists working in the field, I discovered that no two of them looked at the music the same way and that none could offer a definition of the form that matched any of the others. The best conclusion I could arrive at in that article was a paraphrase of Robert Frost's famous definition of poetry: Americana, I said, was the type of thing Americana artists wrote and performed. That was a mostly facetious definition, facile and satisfying enough for a newspaper piece perhaps but superficial enough to cause me to keep thinking about the problem of definition long after the article was published. When I read attempts by others to define the category, I was frustrated; none seemed adequate. Everyone could define the aspect of Americana they carried in their heads, but none could offer a comprehensive statement that looked at the music as it existed outside their heads. One idea that will guide this book, then, will be the search for an inclusive definition that will actually encapsulate the idea of Americana so that when two people discuss the genre they will be talking about the same thing.

In his discussion of non-Aristotelian logic, the general semanticist Alfred Korzybski formulated his statement that A is not B, which has become one of the guiding principles of general semantics. Song A is not song B, guitar A is not guitar B, and definition of Americana A is not definition of Americana B. Perhaps we will discover that Korzybski is right and that an inclusive definition cannot be found. Still, the journey will be worth the try.

A second idea is that this book will examine the way the whole idea of genre, especially Americana, affects our music. I will try to discern what the formulas are and where the invention comes in. Even in a genre-breaking category such as Americana, formulas are present. These can be as simple as the thirty-two-bar pop-song structure, where we have verse, chorus, verse, chorus, bridge, instrumental break, verse chorus, and coda. The formulas can also be as complicated as the artists writing the songs. Kevin Welch, whose songs have been recorded by such artists as Johnny Cash, Waylon Jennings, Roger Miller, Jimmie Dale Gilmore, the Highwaymen, the Judds, Patty Loveless, Reba McEntire, Randy Travis, and Trisha Yearwood, emphasizes that coming up with good songs is both an art and a craft. He thinks there's too much craft emphasized. Songwriting texts are full of rules. Song structure, the books say, demands that the major key switch to a minor for variation. "This is a good example of rules that have to be tested and frequently broken," Welch told me when I observed a songwriting workshop he conducted. "For example, you only need a bridge if it makes a song stouter or if it offers a needed release. My song 'Kicking Back in Amsterdam' is a very simple song, only two chords and a repetitive structure. It has a developing tension, though, and a bridge would just wreck that."

In pop music, Welch's ideas would constitute invention of the highest order. In Americana, though, they are simply part of the formula, a rule that might be stated as "break it if it isn't already broken." This rule is noted by Jimmie Fadden's remarks about the Dirt Band talking about what they can do in the arrangement of a song to make it unusual, a mandolin in a rock song, for example.

Along with formula and invention, the book will examine the notion that Americana music is both a genre and a movement. This idea is important because, as we discussed, Americana is almost indefinable; this can be because some people are defining it as a movement; others, as a genre. Again, as Fadden noted, like many others, he was drawn to the music because he felt like an outsider and this was the music of outsiders. Gathering of like-minded people who feel they are in some way outside the mainstream is how movements originate.

Many of the people quoted or discussed in this book are coming at the idea of Americana from a movement perspective, although sometimes they are not aware that this is what they are doing.

A final idea governing this book is a metaphor I will use to clarify the difference between contemporary pop and country and Americana. Contemporary pop and country are Newtonian physics, while Americana is quantum mechanics. This idea will be developed later in the book, but let me briefly discuss it here.

To oversimplify a little, Newtonian physics deals with objects that have a nonzero size, that is, objects that can be seen and measured. Now, these objects can have complicated movements, that is, a baseball can spin while moving forward, but those movements are limited, measurable, and predictable. Therefore, Newtonian physics has as a basic assumption the notion that matter and energy have definite, knowable qualities, such as where an object is in space and its speed. Newtonian physics also assumes that these objects can only be influenced by their immediate surroundings.

Quantum mechanics, on the other hand, plays with objects that can't really be seen, zero-sized objects such as atoms and photons. If Korzybski's non-Aristotelian logic claims that A is not B, then it is operating on a Newtonian level. In quantum mechanics, A can be B, as it often is, at the same time. Light, for example, is both wave and particle. It turns out that subatomic particles and electromagnetic waves cannot be declared either simply particle or wave because they contain properties of each. Quantum physics also recognizes the "observer effect." It seems that, like people, zero-sized objects behave differently when they are being observed.

What does this have to do with music? Pop and contemporary country deal with the known. With their reliance on familiar ideas and formulaic structures, they are the Newtonian physics of music: interesting perhaps but only useful with visible, known objects and taking place in a framework we have explored before until it has become obsolete.

Americana is quantum physics. It is capable of incorporating Newtonian physics but goes well beyond it into a universe where objects can be and are more than one thing, a universe where the unknown becomes familiar and where complexity and authenticity are valued beyond a superficial understanding or the full understanding of the very simple.

THE PLAN FOR THE BOOK

If we're going to find out just what this force called Americana is, we're going to have to explore three areas: where it came from, where it is, and where it's going, that is, the past, the present, and the future.

Chapter 1 explores where the music came from. We begin by taking a look at the formation of the Americana Music Association. The Rashomon-like memories of the founders explain both why they felt an association was essential and how they went about putting it together. If by the end of the discussion, exactly what Americana is still is not clear, at least we'll know why the concept is muddied.

In the second chapter, we'll see how the beginnings of the nascent recording industry caused a talent search that sent Ralph Peer to Bristol, Tennessee, where on the same field trip, he met the man who would lay down the template for country music and the family who would invent folk music, Jimmie Rodgers and the Carter Family. Even though these artists would establish the pattern for Americana, the chapter will show that the music existed before they got hold of it, packaged it, and offered it up to mainstream and America.

Since many people believe that Americana is a synonym for alternative country (alt-country), in chapter 3, we'll discuss that idea and show why it is an inadequate term, insufficient to grasp the nuances of Americana. We'll see how alt-country began as a reaction to the Country Music Association's attempts to widen the popularity of country music by blending it with middle-of-the-road pop music, leading to the creation of a new genre that opposed mainstream country's march into oblivion. This new genre gave rise to the descriptive cliché "Too rock for country, too country for rock."

Next, we'll take a look at the rise of the blues and see what impact it had on Americana. After briefly discussing where and how the blues originated, we'll talk about how the old masters were forgotten and then rediscovered, bringing their music to a new generation that used it to create Americana.

Periodically through the book, I've provided interludes. These exist to give more information or to highlight an idea, an artist, or a side of Americana that might not be obvious. The first takes a look at the work of Roger McGuinn. It shows the music industry's reliance on labeling and categorizing, pointing out how categorization affects marketing and the way the highly individualistic mindset of musicians sometimes sabotages categories for the sake of the music.

The next chapter takes a look at the process that gave us white rock and roll, demonstrating that there was not all that much that was white about it in the beginning. The music that became Americana crossed racial lines very early, becoming one of the major integrating forces in America. The chapter shows how artists such as Buddy Holly and the Everly Brothers were creating and playing Americana long before we had a name for what they were doing.

Then the examination turns to the historical and cultural role that African American music played in the development of American popular culture. The chapter begins by looking at the minstrel shows and how they melded into vaudeville and then created a circuit for African American performers that spread their music to audiences, white and black, throughout the United States, making it a powerful force in American culture and a distinct part of Americana.

Next we'll look at the way Irish music captivated the nation, exploring the international aspect of Americana. We'll see how Irish folk music grew out of Irish culture and was a reflection of the lives the people led. It was the authentic truth about the hardscrabble, adverse, and difficult lives of the Irish that became a part of the Americana Revolution.

The next chapter dips back into the historical influences on Americana, this time a look at the contribution made by gospel music. Gospel is a mood, an attitude, and a worldview as well as a musical genre. Its artists, because they are artists, get restless and want to stretch themselves creatively. From the time the seventeen-year-old gospel singer Clyde McPhatter moonlighted as the lead singer of Billy Ward and the Dominos, gospel singers have been stretching their way into Americana.

Chapter 9 looks at the noncommercial aspect of Americana, and chapter 10 introduces a necessary component for understanding the complexity that characterizes the genre: the dichotomy between dead records and live ones. A dead record is one that comes out with a blast of promotion and publicity, often sells a huge number of copies all at once, and is, in a few months, dead and forgotten. For example, after he won an Academy Award playing an alcoholic country singer in *Crazy Heart*, Jeff Bridges released an eponymous album. It reached number twenty-five on the pop charts. Well reviewed, the album had Bridges's name being floated as the next big Americana star. That album cannot even be found at flea markets now, and its 2015 follow-up did not even chart. Regardless of its quality, that's a dead record. A live one, on the other hand, will come out quietly, sell a few copies this year, a few next year, and continue selling for years, going its quiet way and having a profound effect on those who bought it. The importance of this idea should be obvious.

If there is a major difference between mass-market music and Americana, it is in the writing. Several people I interviewed in the course of putting this book together emphasized that the key to Americana was its authenticity. Contemporary pop and country songs can be many things, but generally authentic is not high on the list of what they are. Salability is prized, not authenticity. Americana writers try to write songs that are real and true, that speak to who we are as individuals and as a culture. To show how this idea operates, in chapter 11 we'll take a close look at the work of two of Americana's best songwriters, Joe South and John Stewart. And in chapter 12, we will see how Americana music reflects adulthood and is not aimed at teenagers or preteens.

At this point, in chapter 13, we need to take a closer look at the influence southern rock had on Americana. In the 1970s, when "Disco Duck" ruled the airwaves, southern musicians simply could not participate; their musical heritage grew in roots too deep to be interested in disco, novelty or otherwise. Since the present was so weak, they went to the past for inspiration and created a new form of rock that opened up the road to Americana. This movement led to Americana swallowing genres as though they were M&Ms, as we will see in chapter 14. Elements of soul, rock, country, blues, jazz, and folk were drawn into the Americana orbit as if they were metal, and it was a magnet.

We will then, in chapter 15, concentrate on Americana as a movement. It has created a sense of community among its musicians and industry advocates. A form where cooperation trumps competition and where it has become a club, a place where artists who share values and artistic principles can find others like themselves.

Yet not every artist who finds himself or herself in this particular camp is thrilled to be there. In chapter 16, many raise the questions of why they should be categorized at all, feeling that grouping into genre causes their music to be listened to through a particular focus. It isn't that they object to the Americana category; it's that they do not want to be categorized at all. Before wrapping the exploration up, we'll hear from these people.

After looking at some Americana archetypes in chapter 17, we'll finally arrive at some conclusions in the last chapter.

That is the plan for the book. So, to get started, let's begin at the beginning of the formal aspects of the Americana genre, the creation of a trade association.

NOTES

1. "A Brief History of Freeform Radio," *Lowest Common Denominator* 21 (1998), http://www.wfmu.org/.

2. Ryan Bry, "How the Face of Independent Music Changed in 120 Minutes," Consequences of Sound, March 11, 2016, http://www.consequencesof sound.net/.

3. "Brief History."

4. "The Most Influential Americana Album: *Will the Circle Be Unbroken*," *Twang Nation*, July 8, 2013, http://www.twangnation.com/.

5. Juli Thanki, "Nitty Gritty Dirt Band to Kick Off Americana Music Festival and Conference," *Tennessean*, July 28, 2015, http://www.tennessean.com/.

6. M. Elite McClellan, "Popular and Mass Cultures: The Politics of Culture," Prezi, October 21, 2015, http://www.prezi.com/.

7. John Cawelti, *The Six Gun Mystique* (New York: Popular Press, 1972).

8. Ibid.

I

ORIGINS OF THE
AMERICANA MOVEMENT

In 1995 two radio executives, Rob Bleetstein and Jon Grimson, decided they'd had enough; something needed to be done about the trends that were driving their favorite artists off the radio, and they realized that unless they themselves made it happen, nothing was going to happen. If they wanted action, they'd have to create it themselves. Bleetstein and Grimson were aware of a few small independent stations, operating as an alternative to the sterile programming the corporations favored. These stations had begun playing a wider range of music. Mostly small-market mom-and-pop operations, these stations had been quietly gaining favor and developing an audience. Bleetstein and Grimson named the music they'd been programming Americana and, together with a small group of industry professionals who had been championing independent music, formed the Americana Music Association.

Al Moss, an album promoter, was there from the beginning and tells how it happened. He had been working album rock to radio stations and was burning out on that for two reasons; in a series of phone interviews, he told me his story.

> First of all, it was in the 1980s, and that was the worst decade for music since the forties. So I didn't like a lot of the music. That was one reason. The other was it wasn't always about the music. It was about cutting deals with radio stations. Labels might pay five hundred dollars to get a station to add a record. It wasn't payola because it was open, nothing under the table. I didn't like that. I also didn't like it because

the station might take the money and play the record overnight, so you really didn't gain anything. It offended my values, and I wanted out. So while I was a rock radio consultant in Atlanta, I heard Bleetstein was putting together an Americana chart in San Francisco, and I thought this is right up my alley music wise. So I called Jon Grimson, who had come up with the name Americana, to just say hi, introduce myself, and seek his blessing. I told him I was going to do Americana promotion, and he was open to that.

He dipped his feet into the Americana river slowly. For three years, he continued to do album rock, working Americana at the same time. During this time, he mostly talked to stations about music. "It was more of a conversation than about charts and what the label can do for them. They really wanted to talk about music; they played music for the sake of music. It was sort of ironic that the last records I worked on rock radio were Steve Earle's 'I Feel All Right' and the first Son Volt record."

After Americana developed enough that he could work it exclusively, he did, making some sacrifices to be able to. "Not that the money was the same," he laughs. "It still isn't. With Americana, I'm working harder, making less, and enjoying it more than I have in years." Still, he just let rock go by the wayside and continued with Americana. He started in about spring 1995 and, by 1998, was doing exclusively Americana. He was there maybe two or three months after things got started—not at the embryo stage but close.

Bill Gavin, a consultant to radio stations who published the influential Gavin report, had a big convention every year, which was all formats.

At one, we got a little too rowdy for the hotel, and Gavin moved it to other locations. So, one year, we were at Lake Tahoe on the California side. Brad Paul was at Rounder Records for twenty-nine years and had just left because Rounder began to make changes. Brad and I were having a conversation, and Brad said, "We should really do for Americana what Gavin's doing." It was a niche market then. We should get an organization together, incorporate the radio, the craft, the touring side, get all those people together and form an organization. I was moderating a panel, and one of the panelists was Dennis Lord, from SESAC [Society of European Stage Authors and Composers, an organization protecting music rights for writers]. I mentioned to him what Brad Paul had said. All I was, was the catalyst that took what

Paul had said and gave it Dennis Lord and he ran with it. I would say Dennis Lord was responsible for getting the ball to first base.

At a South by Southwest (SXSW) meeting in 1999, a group of people got together and expressed interest in Brad Paul's ideas. A more formal meeting was set up for the fall of 1999 in Nashville to establish an organization, to bring all of the elements of Americana together. Thirty to forty people were at that meeting. All of the founding members were there.

> The biggest elephant in the room was not knowing what to call the organization. We got organized, established a board of directors, [and] didn't know what to call it. There were two people on that first board who have served continuously from that first day, and that's me and a lady named Jessie Scott. A lot of other people have been part of it most of the time, but Jessie Scott and I are the only ones still on the board from the original board of directors.

The last thing we did—we had the board, we had the committees set up, had it going in the right direction—we got everything else out of the way and then it came down to what are we going to call the organization. Jon Grimson had come up with the name Americana and owned the copyright as it pertained to radio. There were other people who weren't comfortable with using the term—it was obvious it should be called Americana, but a lot of other people were uncomfortable with a term for an organization run by a bunch of people and set up to benefit a lot of other people, that one person owned the sole copyright of. Anyway, we're having all the discussion and Jon Grimson turned over the copyright to the organization. He said, "I don't own it anymore, the organization will own it." When he did that, everyone else went, "I think we've got our answer."

HOW AMERICANA WAS ALMOST NAMED WESTERN BEAT

At this point, singer-songwriter Kevin Welch, who was also present at the creation, takes over the birth of Americana story.

"I remember Marc Germino, an underground Nashville songwriter, saying to me, 'You know what we need? We need a name. We need something to call our music. If we call it country music, people will think we're mainstream country, and that's not what we are. So we need a name to show that we're not Nashville,'" he told me in another conversation.

> Later on, I'm flying into Switzerland to play the Montreaux Jazz Festival, and I told the Warner Brothers publicity guy about my conversation with Germino. When we landed, the promoter said we needed a name. He couldn't call us country because the last year he'd had some Nashville country acts and had gotten torn apart for it so he didn't want to use the term country. The Warner Brothers guy said, "Call it Western Beat," and he did.
>
> Back in the states, we all had a meeting. We named our music Western Beat, thinking it showed the real side of roots music. When I put out my second album, I called it Western Beat.
>
> Not long after that, we formed Dead Reckoning Records. We'd all left our major labels and instead of walking across the street and signing with another major the way we always had in the past, we decided to take our destinies in our own hands and have our own record company. We'd been at it about six months when we got a phone call from a PR guy who said "We're starting a new genre. We're going to call it Americana. Can you come down to New Orleans, have a discussion, and find out what Americana is?" At that meeting, we had folk, roots-rock, country, all kinds of genres, all adamantly claiming that what they played was Americana. . . . I see all kinds of people trying to define to fit it into a slot. It's the opposite of that. It's unlimited, hard to pin down. Jimmy Dale Gilmore says, "Americana is whatever me and Kevin Welch like." We made a case for Western Beat, but Americana won out and that's a good thing.

A careful examination of both the association's definition and Kevin Welch's tale of its origins reveals that Americana is actually music that defies categorization. It is not alt-country, but it includes alt-country. It is not rock, although it encompasses rock. It isn't folk, but folk is there. It isn't Celtic but is woven with Celtic threads. It is a blend of forms, music that draws on a wide range of influences.

IF IT WEREN'T FOR THE GRAMMYS, WE STILL WOULDN'T KNOW HOW TO DEFINE THIS MUSIC

The collection of qualities that Americana manifests makes it hard to define, a situation the founders of the association were aware of from the beginning. Al Moss said, "Of course, we resisted for the longest time putting a definition on it; nobody wanted to put a definition on it, [and] we resisted for ages. But when we went after a Grammy category, we failed the first time. Part of the application for submitting for a Grammy category is you had to put down a definition. We had to try to define it in order to get a Grammy category." The fact that Americana is created from so many other genres made it difficult to satisfy the Grammy organization's requirements. "One of the criteria for getting a Grammy category is you had to serve or cover a kind of music that isn't covered anywhere else," says Moss. "The problem with Americana and the reason it took so long to get a Grammy category was that Americana was the opposite of that. It wasn't that Americana was getting covered anywhere else; it was getting covered everywhere. Americana artists were getting nominations in blues, they were getting nominations in folk, in country, everywhere."

Moss believes there was some behind-the-scenes help from executives in other categories in getting the Grammy category.

> I know the country people weren't really happy when people like Lyle Lovett were winning country Grammys because he really wasn't one of theirs. I bet the blues people and the folk people felt the same way. I think there was some help behind the scenes from one or more of those groups of people that helped the Americana people, hoping that it would take the Americana people out of their category so they could make it their own. When we got the Grammy category, it was about the same time that Webster's dictionary listed Americana. That sort of legitimized it.

Dennis Lord is the executive vice president of SESAC, an organization that works to protect performer's rights. He is also an entertainment lawyer and has worked as a songwriter. In that role, he has had many songs published and recorded, including Travis Tritt's first big hit, "Country Club." Before joining SESAC, he led the Washington, D.C., delegation of the Nashville Songwriter's Association. He is also a huge

Americana fan and, as such, was one of the people who helped start the association.

"I was there before the creation," he says. At the Gavin convention in New Hampshire, the one that Al Moss described, "a lot of Americana folks were there and we had concerts and conversations. We could see the vibrancy and the life of the music. So twenty or thirty of us sat around and talked about the possibility of forming the AMA."

"Why did we feel we needed an organization?" asks Lord, who is fond of using rhetorical questions in conversations.

> I can only tell you my feeling about it. I was very much in favor of it. The thing about Americana, it's a bunch of people who go in their own direction. It's always been more of a movement, like songwriters, who notoriously go their own direction. Americana wasn't sustaining itself, wasn't even recognized outside of a small group of folks in the genre. People were telling us it was considered dead, it would not survive. From my perspective, we were creating a market, a vehicle to legitimize Americana and put it out to the world by combining views.

Lord saw a situation where, in some cases, people had to be protected from themselves. "Some people in Americana," he says, "if you sell one record, you've sold out, and there's others that are heartthrobs, you know? These extremes were the hardest to overcome. The goal was to create the marketplace and create legitimacy for a group of artists who were going it alone and without the benefit of a combined effort."

"It's like a technology," he says. "You put together a company that combines six or seven little technologies, you have something that creates something useful. We combined the forces of many, many, many individuals who'd been going it alone without the benefit of a combination. Americana is a group of record labels, artists, publicists, managers, [and] marketing people, all the elements of the music."

The association, with Lord installed as the president of the first board of directors, met with success from the beginning. "We began seeing articles immediately, instantly. The moment we hung out the shingle, we began seeing articles. That started the legitimizing process," he says.

The Americana Music Association (AMA) did not have to invent themselves from scratch. They had a model: the Country Music Association (CMA) had begun in 1968. "To me," Lord says, "the AMA is the same as the CMA. There's no reason why it can't make the music grow and grow and grow."

Dennis Lord sees a major difference between the two organizations, however.

> You see, the key is that Americana is not really a genre, it's more of a movement. It's the art and integrity in the business, no matter what the pressures are and it's always been that way because the people involved insisted on it. For me it's more than a genre because for a long time nobody wanted to be on TV. That was because if you look at the other awards shows, the networks insist on what's going to be on there, who's going to appear for ratings. Nobody wanted that. We wanted to take care of ourselves. The AMA said "No, no, no, this is about art."

Lord notes that the AMA's early progress was held back because of the lack of one important variable: money.

> The board had no staff, no money, and there were a lot of agendas in the room. The great thing was that everybody in the room was willing to park their agendas at the door. The people in that room represented every sector of the music business, and they'd all determined to do something for the greater good.
>
> We struggled along. Everybody had different ideas, there was dissension between commerce and art, something we had to overcome. In order to be successful, everybody had to embrace commerce at least a little.

The organization had no source of money other than the membership. It had no recognition by the recording academy; it took several years for that to happen. It had to deal with artists they were trying to promote that did not carry the automatic press interest of a Lady Gaga or a Katy Perry. Americana didn't have big-selling artists; it had no radio and no full-time radio stations. The organizers of the association realized quickly that they had to do an awards show. They had to have the convention to bring everybody together, had to have the awards show to bring in some revenue, and of course, when they first began exploring the convention and awards show, tension between commerce and art hit a couple of hard times. Lord declares, "We had a lot of people who fell into the Americana bucket who had a lot of fans, and we had to get those people involved."

The ultimate task of the Americana Music Association was to create an infrastructure, a foundation if you will, that would support the art form as it continued to grow. The men and women who created the organization were well aware that without such an infrastructure, the music would be, as a champagne bottle at the dump, buried under the sheer weight of contemporary pop.

There is another danger, though, which I discussed with Dennis Lord; what if the association does too good a job promoting the music and the music outgrows the infrastructure?

> It's possible that's the case. I don't know what sales are and what radio looks like. I really think that if that's the case, it's because Americana embraces so many different things. Everybody talks about Jason Isbell and Chris Stapleton; they're both Americana artists, but to me it's really about the growth of the music. Who cares if it grows the infrastructure. We're already seeing it, you know. Outside the AMA, there's festivals, AM triangles, concerts, TV, all of that. There's growth, and if the growth takes place outside the association, so be it. That's the whole point. The whole point is for the music to be out there.

In these pages, we'll see how the music is getting out there. First, of course, we'll have to see where it came from. To do that, we must briefly dip back into American history.

2

WILL THE CIRCLE BE UNBROKEN?

As the previous chapter established, Americana is not a single thing. As a mash-up of various styles, the genre takes many different forms of music and fuses them together into a new whole. It can therefore be as hard to get a grip on as mercury; the moment we think we grasp it, it slides away. We can easily generalize about the format, we can stereotype it and trivialize it by creating the same sort of category that Americana tries to escape, but we must keep one important idea in mind: it is impossible to fully understand anything without understanding where it came from. The past holds clues to the present and the future, so we must know the past if we are to know the present and future. For that reason, we will look at some of the forms that led to the emergence of this sort of music and some of the ideas that emerge from it. In that way we'll be able to, in a sense, write its biography. As we look at these factors, however, we have to keep in mind one of the contributions of quantum physics: the observer effect, which says simply that a thing changes when it is observed. It is possible, then, that by describing Americana, we will change it in at least small ways.

We know the names of the radio executives who isolated the genre and named it, but as the discussion of the Dirt Band shows and as this chapter will reveal, the music was there before it ever had a name. Not only was the music there, but also it was there in many forms. Its relevant musical history includes the English and Scottish ballads of the Appalachians that became American folk music. The music was there in early country music, the blues, early rock and roll, and the jazz of New Orleans. We'll look at each in turn and then see how they fused into what is now known as Americana. Instead of a survey that drops a lot of names and lacks context, we'll discuss the genres that contributed to it by discussing the life and careers of many artists while concentrating on an iconic name or two in each genre. This chapter will concentrate on folk and country.

FOLK MUSIC CROSSES THE OCEAN AND MOVES INTO THE MOUNTAINS

It is well known that the Caucasian strain of folk music arrived in this country with the early settlers from the British Isles, who brought their songs and instruments with them. Settling in the southern Appalachians, the immigrants sang the songs of their homelands that, over time, became transformed and altered into songs that reflected their current circumstances. Old songs became new songs as the tunes and the lyrics altered over time to reflect the situations the settlers faced in the new land. Many songs were altered beyond recognition, but others hewed close to their English, Irish, and Scottish roots.

At that time, before the invention of phonographs and wax recorders, collecting folk songs and their variants was an academic undertaking confined to folklorists affiliated with universities. As soon as the word spread about the treasure trove in the Appalachians, collectors swarmed over the land like alcoholics over free whiskey. In the late nineteen-teens, the noted English folklorist Cecil Sharp made the first big noise when he came to the mountains in search of what he called "Old World" songs, by which he meant songs that retained their native character despite having been wrenched out of their native environment and brought like slaves to this land. Sharp found hundreds of examples of Old World songs, the best of which he published in a pioneering book, *English Folk Songs from the Southern Mountains.*[1]

Actually, the American folklorist, collector, and folk singer John Jacob Niles went to the mountains first, beating Sharp to the Appalachians by about a decade, arriving there for his first collecting trip in 1907. However, Niles, having a protective nature toward his work that bordered on paranoia, refused to publish any of the songs he discovered until 1960, when he brought out *The Ballad Book of John Jacob Niles*, which contained not just the songs but also the stories behind their collection and their history.[2]

Every forward movement in music is connected to technology. When Thomas Edison created the music industry by inventing his wax-cylinder recording machine, he showed the way to the future. Other engineers quickly improved on his machine, creating primitive machines that could be hauled up into the mountains. As a result, it was no longer necessary for a collector to try to transcribe a song by hand as it was being sung. The singer's voice could now be captured in wax. This innovation allowed the songs of the Appalachian players and singers to spread widely beyond the immediate area as the field recordings of the early 1920s made by such musicologists and folklorists as Charles Seeger, father of Pete, circulated. Among the artists who found themselves being captured on these field recordings were Fiddlin' John Carson, Bascom Lamar Lunsford, Frank Proffitt, and Dock Boggs, all of whom went on to record professionally.

SCHOLARSHIP LEADS TO COMMERCE

Seeger, John Lomax, and the other people making field recordings were scholars working from a home base of universities and supported by grants. They were not overly concerned with financially profiting from their work, seeking primarily the academic prestige that came from being known as the people who brought these songs to light and seeking to convince the American public that the folk song, instead of being a primitive wailing, was a legitimate art form. It took the emerging record companies, who were looking for products to be played on the new record players that the public had become enamored with, to see that money could be made from mountain music.

The man who led that particular charge was Ralph Peer. Peer differed from the ethnomusicologists in one important respect: he was a professional record man. He worked for OKeh Records, where he had previously produced Mamie Smith's "Crazy Blues," the first blues "race music" record, that is, a record aimed at the emerging African American audience.[3] He knew something about making and selling category records.

His experience with "Crazy Blues" taught him something, and Peer was savvy enough to pick up on the lesson immediately and to run with it.

What he learned was this: money could be made by selling records to African Americans. But where would he find the talent? Salable artists couldn't be located in big enough numbers in New York City, a fact that led Peer to conclude that if he wanted to record these artists, he had to go on the road and find them. He started making field trips to the South.

He was smart enough not to confine himself just to race artists, though, as African American singers and players were called in those days. A man who recognized talent, wherever he found it, Peer also recorded what is believed to be the first country record, Fiddlin' John Carson's "Little Old Log Cabin in the Lane" backed with "That Old Hen Cackled and the Rooster's Going to Crow."[4]

As hard as he mined those mountains, though, Peer didn't really strike gold until August 1927 when he went to Bristol, Tennessee, where a sort of musical miracle occurred: he discovered Jimmie Rodgers and the Carter Family on the same day at the same recording session. Although he didn't realize it at the time, both American country music and folk music were born as commercial entities that day.

JIMMIE RODGERS CREATES COUNTRY MUSIC

Jimmie Rodgers never wanted to be anything but a singer.[5] Born in Meridian, Mississippi, in 1897, he began singing as a child. Demonstrating incredible initiative for a kid his age, by the time he was thirteen he had put together two separate traveling shows and had taken them on the road. Both times his father came after him and hauled him home.

Forced to stay at home for the moment and not wanting to stay at home at all, Rodgers got a traveling job. He went to work on the railroad as a water boy—a job his father got for him. There he learned to play guitar from his workmates. A few years later, he became, courtesy of his brother, who was a conductor on the New Orleans and Northeastern Railroad, a brakeman, a job he worked until he was twenty-seven. He was forced to give it up when he discovered he had tuberculosis. The disease made it impossible to continue working on the railroad, so Rodgers turned a problem into an opportunity by going back into show business; he resumed touring the country with traveling tent shows that he organized and produced himself. He expanded into radio, doing his own show on WWNC in Asheville, North Carolina, until July 1927, when Rodgers and his band, hearing that Ralph Peer was coming to Bristol, Tennessee, went there to audition for him. Passing the audition, they were invited to record the next day. That night, however, Rodgers got into a huge argument with his band over billing, which led him to dissolve the band and record as a single artist.

He made it through the session easily and was signed to the Victor Talking Machine Company. The first recordings he released, "The Soldier's Sweetheart" and "Sleep, Baby, Sleep," netted him one hundred dollars and were modestly successful, but the record that followed those songs, "Blue Yodel No. 1" (also known as "T for Texas") sold half a million copies and made Rodgers the nation's first country music star. He toured incessantly—until, that is, pneumonia began getting the best of him. Lacking energy for the road, he moved into radio, hosting a program until his health gave out. He remained the biggest star in the country field until his death during his final recording session in 1933. His entire career lasted six years.

Rodgers did not single-handedly create country music, but he did set the template. Without his work, traditional country music—the type that grew and splintered off into Americana—would not have been what it became. What were his specific contributions? He brought the guitar to the center of the song, sometimes backing it with string band instrumentation, and sometimes using it alone for accompaniment, but always keeping it prominent. Rodgers was also not afraid to experiment. He crossed genres, cutting a record with Louis Armstrong and another with the Carter Family. Like John Hiatt today, he sang in a flexible, gliding voice songs that grew out of his own experiences, exploring his personal feelings and emotions in a series of drinking songs, traveling songs, songs celebrating his mother, and others examining love found and lost. Even though he used his own life as a source of material, he wasn't self-absorbed. Rodgers was a born storyteller, and most of his stories were about working-class people, down-and-out victims of the depression or of their own bad impulses. His lyrics often went against the overblown sentimentality that overwhelmed the pop songs of the day, featuring the sort of down-to-earth truthfulness that is characteristic of Americana. In "T for Texas," he writes about getting a shotgun as long as he is tall, so he can shoot old Thelma just to watch her fall, a lyric about as far from the conventional sentimentality of the pop music of his day as a heartbeat is from a stone. It was a lyric that much later resonated strongly with Johnny Cash, a great Rodgers fan, who in "Folsom Prison Blues" sang about a guy who shot a man in Rio just to watch him die.

Rodgers pioneered the use of the guitar as a lead instrument, the use of raw and plaintive vocals, the idea that the singer's personal life is material for a song, and that the singer's true feelings are worth exploring. If country music is three chords and the truth, as Nashville tradition states, Jimmie Rodgers is the first man to offer those things up. He created that archetype. He also provided the pattern for the simplicity and sincerity that traditional country music traded in. Rodgers created a trail that ran from the singing cowboy of the 1930s through the honky-tonk music of the 1940s, and paved the way for artists like Lefty Frizzell and Hank Williams who brought country music to the southerners who had moved north and west because of the war, thereby making country a national genre.

If Jimmie Rodgers had not shown up in Bristol that day, there would still be country music, but it might have taken a very different form.

THE CARTER FAMILY TAKES A ROAD TRIP AND CREATES FOLK MUSIC

We can also declare that if the Carter Family hadn't gone to Bristol, folk music might also have grown up to become a very different creature than it is now. Consider the songs "Wabash Cannonball," "Can the Circle Be Unbroken," "Wildwood Flower," "Keep on the Sunny Side," "Jimmy Brown the Newsboy," "John Hardy," and "Bury Me under the Willow"— all folk standards, and all Carter Family songs. These are songs that created the folk revivals of the 1940s and 1950s; these titles had a lot to do with making folk music what it is today. In fact, four Carter Family songs—"John Hardy," "Little Moses," "Engine One-Forty-Three," and "Single Girl, Married Girl"—appeared on Harry Smith's influential set *Anthology of American Folk Music*. Smith's anthology—which will be discussed in more detail later—was issued by Moses Asch's Folkways Records in 1952 and is credited as being the album set that created the folk boom of the early 1960s. The Carter Family's songs played a big part in that revival.

The Carter Family—Alvin Pleasant ("A.P.") Carter; his wife, Sara; and sister-in-law Maybelle—sang around their hometown of Maces

Spring, Virginia, and didn't see themselves going anywhere beyond the immediate area. They were amateurs, and the women at least figured to stay that way. But A. P. Carter had bigger plans. When he learned about Ralph Peer's impending visit to Bristol, he talked the women into making the trip to Tennessee to try out. The audition was successful, and Peer recorded "Wandering Boy" and "Poor Orphan Child," which the Victor Talking Machine Company released in November 1927. When the songs turned out to be modestly successful, the company released a follow-up, "The Storms Are on the Ocean" and "Single Girl, Married Girl," both of which struck a receptive chord among record buyers. The Carter Family had a double-sided hit record and discovered that while they had been talking about going home and raising crops and children, they'd become stars.

Their music followed a formula that appeared full blown on their first records, and the group rarely varied from it: Sara sang lead, Maybelle provided the harmonies and played lead guitar, while A.P. wrote (or just as often, found and adapted) the songs. Most of the time, A.P. didn't perform on the records, but occasionally he'd sing a lead or, more often, toss in a bass line.

Jimmie Rodgers chose to tour himself to death, crushing his health by being constantly on the road. The Carter Family took a different route: radio. While it is true that Rodgers used radio to extend his career when he was no longer able to tour, he never saw it as the foundation for a career, as did the Carters. The Carters pioneered the use of border radio, operations that were also known as border blasters. These were stations located in Mexico whose broadcast signals were much more powerful than those used by American stations.[6] A single station in Mexico could be heard all over the southern, western, and midwestern states. Often they were powerful enough to overpower the signals of American stations. One of those border blasters, XERA, signed the Carter Family, enabling them to be heard all through their natural market without having to tour.[7]

They took to the road occasionally, but their success on radio allowed them to control their time on the road so they could still maintain a family life and not have to tolerate the terrible touring conditions of the time. In an age before the interstate highway system and comfortable tour buses and hotel chains, touring mainly consisted of packing everything in a Cadillac—musicians used them because they were big and dependable—piling the band in, and driving hundreds of miles to the venue, playing mainly what were known as school shows because they took place in a town's high school auditorium. They'd do an hour show and then pile back in the car and try to get some sleep while whichever band member had the driving duty piloted them through the night to the next stop.

It was a hideous life, and many people in show business claim it still is, even with contemporary comforts. Few people who do not tour for a living can understand how horrible the experience is. The comedian Rocky LaPorte, who is on the road forty weeks a year, once told me, "On a tour, we ran into the Rolling Stones once. We talked about the road, how hard it was. They said at every stop on the tour, somebody can't take it anymore, some crew member, some musician, they just can't do it anymore and have to go home."

The Carter Family members, by relying on radio for most of their career building, were able to maintain some sanity when it came to touring. Broadcasting also allowed them to keep their families intact. As they came along, the women's children joined the radio show, performing with their parents.

The family act stopped being genuine in 1936, when A.P. and Sara divorced. They continued performing together, though, until 1944, when Sara remarried and moved to California. At that point, Maybelle—by now universally known as Mother Maybelle—brought her daughters June, Anita, and Helen into the act and kept the band alive even after A. P. Carter's death. They continued to perform as the Carter Family, mostly as a part of the Johnny Cash touring show, into the 1970s.

What did the Carter Family contribute to folk music? Most obviously, they contributed a repertoire. When the family first started out, A.P. realized they needed a constant flow of material. In order to generate the material they required, he became a song seeker, going out into the Appalachian hills looking for melodies and lyrics his family could use. As a result, he discovered and brought to prominence many traditional songs that, as shown by their use in Harry Smith's anthology, became a standard part of the repertoire of the folk revival.

Their songs were sung from the 1930s straight through the revival of the early 1950s and into the folk renaissance of the 1960s. Joan Baez's early years were spent singing Carter Family material: "Wildwood Flower," "Gospel Ship," "Little Darling, Pal of Mine," "Little Moses," and others fill her early albums. The Nitty Gritty Dirt Band's epic *Will the Circle Be Unbroken* three-album set contains not only the title song but also Mother Maybelle herself performing on the album, and several of the other guest artists cover her songs. Woody Guthrie, Pete Seeger, and the other artists who spurred the folk revival had their styles and repertoires formed by listening to the Carter Family. Guthrie even credited his guitar style to Mother Maybelle.[8]

Perhaps more importantly, though, Mother Maybelle changed the way folk guitar was played. The famous Carter Family lick, which is also known as the Carter scratch or, as Woody Guthrie called it, the church lick, is derived from her guitar style. In this style, the melody is played on the bass strings using a thumb pick, while the rhythm is maintained by simultaneous chord strumming by the fingers on the treble strings. The effect of this style was to turn the guitar into a lead instrument. Instead of simply strumming to the beat and providing the rhythm—chopping fours, as the jazz and pop artists called it—the instrument played the melody, accenting it with brushed strums.

The technique provided a way for a single guitar to play both accompaniments and solos within the song. It also provided the basis for bluegrass styles and the flat-picking style of playing. Bill Monroe adapted it when he put his first bluegrass band together, while guitarists such as Norman Blake, Doc Watson, and Dan Crary built their styles on Maybelle's.

It is safe to say that without the Carter Family, the folk music strand of Americana would not be what it is today.

NOTES

1. Zubeida Malik, "Cecil Sharp Folk Diaries Released," BBC, http://www.bbc.co.uk/. 2009..

2. John Jacob Niles, *The Ballad Book of John Jacob Niles* (New York: Dover, 1981).

3. Barry Mazor, *Ralph Peer and the Making of Popular Roots Music* (Chicago: Chicago Review Press, 2014).

4. Maryland Public Television, *American Roots Music*, aired October 2001, http://pbs.org/.

5. Bill Wynne, *In Tune: Charley Patton, Jimmie Rodgers and the Roots of American Music* (Baton Rouge: Louisiana State University Press, 2014); Ted Ownby, "Jimmie Rodgers: The Father of Country Music," *Mississippi History Now*, July 2004, http://mshistorynow.mdah.state.ms.us/.

6. Beth Harrington, *The Winding Stream: An Oral History of the Carter and Cash Family* (Georgetown, MA: PFP, 2014); and Mark Zwonitzer and Charles Hirshberg, *Will You Miss Me When I'm Gone? The Carter Family and Their Legacy in American Music* (New York: Simon & Schuster, 2004).

7. Gene Fowler and Bill Crawford, *Border Radio: Quacks, Yodelers, Pitchmen, Psychics, and Other Amazing Broadcasters of the American Airwaves* (Austin: University of Texas Press, 2002).

8. Joe Klein, *Woody Guthrie: A Life* (New York: Delta, 1999).

3

WHEN THINGS GO WRONG, BLAME THE RADIO

This is a book about the development of a category of music that no one can define, a format, in fact, that no one among its creators even wanted to define. And that fact has been an issue in Americana music ever since the form moved into a prominent place in the music scene. From the very moment that Americana leaped into existence, it seems, the people who play, program, publicize, or write about the music have squared off in a serious and sometimes overly academic debate over the question of exactly what Americana is anyway. The genre is made up of music from so many other categories that simply describing it can be confusing. For example, the term "Americana" would seem to imply American—and many musicians in the field use that as a basis for their own definitions—but at this writing, the trade papers are carrying ads for a new CD described, without irony, as "Irish Americana." Whatever it is, the music evidently crosses borders.

We're not even sure of its origins. Some writers trace it back to the 1980s, when a group of Southern California bands, heavily influenced by what Gram Parsons had done as a musician with the Byrds, the International Submarine Band, and the Flying Burrito Brothers, began playing a mixture of traditional country and punk, which quickly became known as alternative country or alt-country. As the style spread, bands such as Jason and the Scorchers and the Long Ryders brought in influences from bluegrass, rockabilly, and folk rock. When Uncle Tupelo released the album *No Depression* in 1990, alt-country took a couple of giant steps toward becoming a trend. A fanzine, named after the album, grew into a national newsstand magazine, and No Depression music, as alt-country was also called, was officially born.

What made alt-country alternative? In truth, many things did so, not the least that it was for the most part very good music. If we're to understand the rise of alt-country, though, we have to understand the fall of establishment country. That happened in the late 1980s and early 1990s, and the members of the Country Music Association were plunged into a deep depression. They could see the end in sight. Country music had fallen so far down in sales and listener interest that the Country Music Association was seriously worried not about what would happen in the future but whether or not the music had a future. Neither buyers nor radio audiences were responding to what the industry was offering. Nothing was selling. Country music has become a plague upon the land, and no cures that the Country Music Association (CMA) could come up with were working.

A period of extraordinary and exponential growth had just ended. During and immediately after World War II, country music expanded far beyond the South as southerners moved north to take jobs in war plants and factories. Like immigrants coming to the Appalachians, they brought their music with them. Country music followed the great migration, and artists such as Hank Williams, Kitty Welles, and Eddie Arnold found themselves enjoying new popularity in new markets. A period of high creativity and increased sales happened, fueled by songs such as Bill Monroe's "Blue Moon of Kentucky"; Tex Williams's novelty song "Smoke! Smoke! Smoke! (That Cigarette)"; "New San Antonio Rose" by Bob Wills and His Texas Playboys; "Smoke on the Water" by Red Foley; "Lovesick Blues" by Hank Williams; and Eddie Arnold's "Bouquet of Roses." All of these songs were chart toppers in the late 1940s.

The good times couldn't last, though. The music became too formularized, shifting from pop culture to mass culture, and audiences, ever restless, suddenly began to reject the material that the record companies released. Nothing the companies threw was sticking to the wall. A huge percentage of the sales of singles, which was the market then, sold because of men and women shoving nickels into jukeboxes. Radio stations took their cues from the boxes and programmed the songs that were widely played, but suddenly and without warning, the boxes lost their allure; people had better things to do with their coins.

Something had to be done to get people to buy the product again, and the record companies responded the way they always had: by changing the music. To move the numbers, the labels smoothed out the corners, burying the music's rough-and-ready naturalism under a bed of polished production that substituted violins for fiddles and used choirs of female singers for smooth backup vocals. Horns—tastefully played—were suddenly acceptable on country records. The CMA named this new country countrypolitan because it had surgically removed the pedal steel guitars and fiddles from the records, adding in their place lush strings, horns, and platoons of pleasant backup singers, who sang pop harmonies instead of country. The music sounded about as much like country as Katy Perry sounds like garage rock.

The industry took out ads welcoming countrypolitan music and spent a lot of money convincing America that smooth country was what they wanted. The movement succeeded. This bastardization of country music caused the industry's market share to rise again and kept the form in the public view. Countrypolitan extended the life of the genre, but it contained a built-in problem: it brought no new fans to the party, since it only appealed to people who were already fans. The young people they had lost were not coming back. Worried about the aging demographics of their audience, the CMA tried to win back the younger record buyers by resorting to gimmicks such as hiring choreographers to make up line dances to be done along with the songs. To watch the country music cable TV channels that existed at the time was to watch a demented version of *American Bandstand*. It was music and dance that appealed to no one, and as a result, the young abandoned country music, preferring to listen to music that was alive and that they perceived as speaking to them.

TOO ROCK FOR COUNTRY, TOO COUNTRY FOR ROCK

Alt-country captured the young and created new fans by offering something unique and creative that the newly won fans could embrace. It rejected the smoothness, choosing to use a lo-fi roughness that symbolized authenticity. The punk elements were as familiar to the young as they were horribly new and discordant to older listeners. The work of the alt-country performers was a creative advance, but despite their soulful playing and deeper lyrics, the movement could not penetrate country radio at all. Nor did these bands find much success on rock radio stations. It was during these days that some anonymous radio station manager declared a record "too rock for country, too country for rock," inventing a cliché still used to keep good music off the radio. (The phrase became so popular that it was used as the title of a song by Lonnie Mack, a song that received no airplay because it was too rock for country, too country for rock.)

All of that changed when the Coen brothers made the movie *O Brother, Where Art Thou?* which featured an all-Americana soundtrack put together by roots-rocker and producer T-Bone Burnett. Burnett used old-timers such as Ralph Stanley and the Stanley Brothers, the Fairfield Four, the Cox Family, and John Hartford, along with current artists such as Gillian Welch, Alison Krauss, and Emmylou Harris. The soundtrack was a huge success, and for a while, Americana stepped out into the mainstream.

Why, we might ask, was a movie soundtrack loaded with old-time, traditional songs done by older and forgotten artists, and a group of performers few people had ever heard of, a multiplatinum success? It succeeded mainly because of those factors. It presented the old music to an audience that had never heard it before, so the old sounded new. It also sounded real, not fake like most of the music heard on the radio. It was music meant to communicate instead of simply being product to generate money. Even though all of the participating musicians would love to make a few dollars off their work, those dollars were not the primary factor when it came to creating and disseminating their work.

The exception may be the Coen brothers. We also have to consider that the Coen brothers are masters of marketing, and they used the soundtrack very cleverly to sell the movie. They succeeded; *O Brother* became an event. And because of the work of the alt-country bands, fans of the soundtrack discovered they had somewhere to go to hear more, to get deeper into this "new" music.

Most importantly, though, the alternative music it presented was attractive because of its honesty. It was more real, more vital and alive than the commercial product filling the airwaves. Still, no matter how authentic it was and no matter how well it sold, the new music still could not be played on commercial radio, which during the 1990s was locked in fiercely determined and unwavering categories. By the time Chris Hillman told *Sound Waves Magazine* that the music he was recording with his Desert Rose Band was unacceptable to both country and rock radio, saying, of course, that programmers and station managers say that the songs are "too rock for country and too country for rock," the phrase had become the most often-used rejection slip for alt-country by radio stations across the nation.

As we will see in these pages, the alt-country to Americana journey leaves out quite a few twists and turns. The music had a much more complicated journey than that. Still, it is true that the locked-in format rigidity in the radio stations was a major factor in the rise of Americana. We will follow the trail down all of its many forks.

THE FOLK PROCESS: ART OR COMMERCE?

Pete Seeger once said that folk music changed forever the first time a folklorist hauled a recorder up into the Appalachians and recorded a singer. Seeger was right; the music changed because of the observer effect: once the singers heard the playback of their songs, they became self-conscious, recognizing that what they had thought of as a mode of self-expression was actually a performance and that a performance, as well as the material being performed, could be altered and molded for artistic purposes. Using a term his folklorist father had coined, he called this decision to alter and change the material the folk process. The folk process allows the artist or folklorist to change the song to fit in with the times and circumstances in which it will be sung. These alterations can be to the lyrics, the melody, the arrangement, or all of those.

Originally, the alterations were a natural and organic result of technology; as stated, once performers heard their performance, everything changed. With modern copyright laws, though, the altered version of the song could be copyrighted as a new work in the name of the person who had changed the song. In his book *The Ballad Mongers*, Canadian folk singer Oscar Brand describes how he rewrote the lyrics of an old traditional song, "A Gob Is a Slob," changing it to "A Guy Is a Guy," which Doris Day recorded. With Brand credited as author, it became a huge hit and he collected royalties.

Dave Guard of the Kingston Trio explained their participation in the folk process by saying that the band had nothing in common with the life or circumstances of Leadbelly, so how could they sing his songs without making them true to their own experience?[1]

Just as the original singers of mountain folk songs were slapped in the face by the folk process, so were the instrumentalists. When the banjo picker listened to his song being played back to him, he heard the mistakes and the missed opportunities. So, just as when the singers sang their songs again it came out different, so did the picker's next take on his tune.

When men such as Ralph Peer began cutting records of these artists' performances and releasing them commercially, people who once sang and played for their own amusement began professional careers performing for money. And amateurs, long sought after by folklorists, now had a model they could follow in the recorded voice. Their performances became more studied, mannered. At this point, a duality that folklorist Richard Dorson later named fakelore came into being.[2]

FOLKLORE AND FAKELORE

Fakelore is the real made unreal. According to the believers in the concept, the original work is authentic and all copies are fakes. Any changes or alterations simply destroy the integrity of the work. So when a singer hears the audience reaction to her song and realizes that a change in the lyrics will improve its reception, she has, according to this theory, shifted from authentic to inauthentic, from folklore to fakelore. At its most extreme, fakelore refers to any change from the original, which is one of the main reasons the term isn't used very much anymore. The major question raised by the term remains: when music goes through the process of change brought on by technology and becomes transmitted to the people through mass media, is it genuine or inauthentic? The question matters for several reasons. For one, when the Desert Rose Band could not have its songs played on either country or rock radio, that refusal to play the music was an example of fakelore accusations. Neither category of radio station would accept it as authentic.

The question also matters to our investigation because the early 1900s, when our story begins, was a time of technological explosion: in just a couple of decades, telephones, recording devices, radios, and phonographs all entered the homes, while clubs and theaters entered the neighborhoods, bringing the entertainment industry with them.

While radio became the way new music was heard, record shops and department stores sold 78 rpm records and sheet music for home play, while nightclub and concert tour appearances became a way for musicians to make money. Where once people made their own music, now they listened to professionals. For business reasons, the growing music industry found it necessary to categorize the music they marketed. It was more efficient to distribute country records to "hillbilly" audiences, jazz to those listeners, and blues to "race" audiences. Performance determined category. Category determined audience. Radio existed to deliver category to listening audience, and the familiarity gained from hearing the song on the radio drove listeners to the shops to buy the records.

COMMERCIAL RADIO CHOKES THE LIFE OUT OF THE MUSIC

Regionalism ruled in radio. Music aimed at the South was different from that programmed in the Northeast as each region had its own stations operating independently of and in competition with each other. Since each station had its own distinct audience, programming differed on each station. As late as the 1970s, it was possible to drive from coast to coast and hear different music in different regions of the country. That system died when the Reagan administration lifted the regulations that determined how many stations a corporation could own and conglomeration replaced independence.

During the 1980s and early 1990s, American pop music went through huge and dramatic changes, changes that altered both the way we listen to music and the music we listen to. Major corporations such as Clear Channel (now I Heart Radio) swallowed radio stations as if they were bowls of grits, and as a result, playlists tightened. Top forty became the top fifteen, because consultants insisted that the way to higher ratings was to play only the songs that the majority of listeners wanted to hear. As stations became more tightly formatted, they played fewer songs and those few songs were rigidly categorized.

On the corporate stations, in order to save money, an ever-increasing number of stations were programmed from a central location, using technology that enabled digitally recorded DJs to be heard on dozens of frequencies in different areas of the country simultaneously. This development caused regional differences to disappear as a certain standardization set in. Everything sounded the same. Radio in Little Rock was now the same as radio in Los Angeles. Stations in Los Angeles sounded exactly like stations in Atlanta. It was not a good time for listeners who craved variety in music.

As technological advances enabled music downloading, record companies saw their profits plummet. They responded by stripping their lists of artists who were not delivering blockbuster albums, while simultaneously narrowing both the types and numbers of albums they released. Since they still relied on radio for exposure, and since the music being released was increasingly superficial, commercial radio listenership declined. The music audience members asked themselves why they should rely on the radio when they could download everything they wanted to hear. The corporate-owned stations responded by tightening their playlists even more. Not satisfied with playing less music of lower quality, the stations began bowdlerizing the songs they played. In 2015, for example, consultants to country stations, armed with research that said listeners found them boring, began recommending to their client stations that they edit the guitar solos out of the records they played. Many stations adopted this practice. Record companies, who naturally wanted their music played on commercial radio, geared their product to the needs of the corporate stations and cut the solos before the stations could do it. In an attempt to be radio friendly, they became self-censors.

The labels came to rely with a greater intensity on tried-and-true formulas in the music they released. The songs heard on the radio more and more resembled songs that had already been heard on the radio. The singers of those songs more and more resembled already established singers. The pop culture that had made radio became mass culture, which destroyed it.

A cycle emerged: Radio limited what they would play, so the major record companies tried to feed radio by limiting what they released. Listeners reacted by departing, and as listeners and record buyers disappeared, artists were dropped by their labels. In those days, according to singer-songwriter Kevin Welch, if you were dropped by your record company, you could walk across the street and sign with another one. Your records on the new label, however, would be no more likely to gain airplay on the radio than your old ones were—unless you geared them to the formulas the stations were playing. Many artists were forced to do just that. Before the Sky Kings, an alt-country supergroup featuring former members of Poco and the New Grass Revival, could be signed to Warners, they had to promise to "chase hit singles." When they didn't get them, the two albums they'd made were shelved, remaining unreleased for more than a decade before they were issued in a limited edition by a collector's label.

All of this happened in the days of the record supermarkets, with huge chains such as Tower Records, Peaches, and Planet Music operating in every major city, so that the records, if released, could still be available to buyers.

But they were not available on radio. Artists who created challenging, original music found themselves blocked from the commercial airwaves. Willie Nelson, Merle Haggard, Johnny Cash, and the other pioneers who developed today's country music could no longer be played on country stations. Rock disappeared from the playlists and was replaced by the vapid pop of rigidly formatted boy bands and teenaged-girl singers. Where just a few years before, some deviation from playlists was accepted, now the charts ruled. When Johnny Cash died, a program director in a midmarket corporate-owned country station told me that she asked her DJs to pay tribute to him by playing his music. Within minutes, she got a call from corporate headquarters, which had been monitoring her station, ordering her to resume playing the playlist, which did not include Cash's records: Johnny Cash was no longer considered an asset.

NOTES

1. William J. Bush, *Greenback Dollar: The Incredible Rise of the Kingston Trio* (Lanham, MD: Scarecrow, 2013).

2. Richard M. Dorson, *Folklore and Folklife: An Introduction* (Chicago: University of Chicago Press, 1982).

4

DON'T DRINK FROM A BOTTLE IF YOU DIDN'T SEE IT OPENED

Country and folk, as important as they are, are simply two of the threads that make up the quilt that is Americana. The blues is a third. While white southerners were busy transforming the English and Scottish ballads into folk music, African Americans, whose origins and culture in the United States were radically different from the white experience, used the instruments, rhythms, and attitudes of their culture to create a new form of musical expression, the blues.

As it is with every other form of creative expression, much of what we know about the origins of the blues is questionable. At this point, the best bet is that it formed in the Deep South at the end of the nineteenth century. A blend of African music and traditional folk music, it incorporates the sounds of African American forms such as spirituals, work songs, and field chants, using a call-and-response format, a special blues scale, and the use of blue notes, which are third or fifth notes of the scale. These notes, flatter than the others, create the special sound that makes the blues instantly recognizable. Most commonly, it uses a twelve-bar musical pattern in which a line is sung and then repeated. At that point, an answer line is sung and an instrumental lick called the turnaround is played, creating a verse that contains twelve bars of music. This verse structure is known as the AAB pattern. As an example, Big Joe Turner's "Shake, Rattle and Roll" is a twelve-bar blues. In it, his voice presents the call, and the trombone issues the response. In Robert Johnson's "Cross

Road Blues," his voice lines out the call, and a riff on his guitar gives us the response.

Like folk, the blues is played on portable instruments that were available to the newly freed slaves and poor black people who created it. The guitar is the major instrument, along with the harmonica, banjo, and jaw harp. In the cities, a piano was often an important addition to the sound patterns.

Today, we refer to the acoustic blues that sprang up in the rural areas of the South as the country blues or folk blues. After its birth, it fanned out among the African American communities throughout the South, where the regional styles that led to its incorporation into Americana were born.

One of the most important forms was the Delta blues, so named because it originated in the Mississippi Delta country, a region of the South bordered by Memphis, Tennessee, to Helena, Arkansas, in the west; Vicksburg, Mississippi, on the east; and the Yazoo River on the southern end. It was largely farm and plantation country, and the Delta blues was born among the field hands who worked the land.

We can learn something about its origins by looking at one of its greatest practitioners: Robert Johnson, who became known after his death as the king of the Delta blues singers.

THE LEGEND OF ROBERT JOHNSON

As with other figures that have attained mythical status, we really don't know much about Robert Johnson. Like all myths, his has obscured the truth because over time the legend always becomes greater than the truth. The myth has a power that a literal retelling of the actual events cannot capture. And Robert Johnson is shrouded in myth. With Johnson, we don't even know exactly when he was born. We believe his birthday was May 8, 1911, but that date isn't conclusively documented. We know that as a child he was shuttled between various relatives, a roundabout journey that might have led to the restlessness, the searching for a place to belong that characterized his life. We don't even know his real name, only that his given name was not Robert Johnson. During childhood, he was known by many different names. It appears that each household he became a part of renamed him. By the time he married his first wife, however, he had become Robert Johnson; that was the name he signed on the marriage certificate.

The documentary film *The Search for Robert Johnson* reports that his wife's relatives claimed that her death in childbirth was one result of Johnson having sold his soul to the devil, which perhaps was the origin of the legend that he made a pact at the crossroads, gaining his great skill on the guitar in return for signing over his soul to Satan.[1]

It's a story that holds traction to this day, even among people who should know better. Whenever Johnson's name comes up, the soul-selling myth surfaces with it. It has become an archetypal story, one that many people believe and a great many more want to believe, despite their tendency to disbelieve. Did it happen? Did Robert Johnson sell his soul to the devil in exchange for guitar skills? To be charitable, let's say we cannot really know. What we do know is that he went on one of his rambles with a reputation as a mediocre guitarist. When he returned a short time later, he was a master of the instrument. The contrast between his old playing and his new level of skill was so striking that the people of Johnson's time had no problem believing he'd traded his soul for it. The legendary blues singer and guitarist Son House, who worked and traveled with Johnson and, as a result, knew him well, told a *DownBeat* interviewer that the Satanic transaction had indeed taken place,[2] but other interviewers could never get House to repeat that quote. He never denied having said it, but he also refused to ever repeat it. Like House, though, many of the other bluesmen in his circle felt that his progress took place way too fast, so that there had to be an element of the supernatural involved.

In 1936, Johnson met producer Don Law, who recorded him for Brunswick Records in a three-day session that produced sixteen selections, including his classics "Come On in My Kitchen," "Dust My Broom," and "Cross Road Blues." The first song released, "Terraplane Blues," sold five thousand copies, becoming a regional hit. A second session, again produced by Don Law, took place in Dallas, Texas, in 1937, where Johnson cut the rest of the twenty-nine songs that would make up his entire recorded output.[3]

Johnson's death is as clouded in mystery as was his life. We know he died at the age of twenty-seven on August 16, 1938. He'd been working a dance near Greenwood, Mississippi, when he died, and while we still don't know the cause of death, as is always the case with Robert Johnson, several myths and legends have grown up around his demise. Sonny Boy Williamson, the blues harmonica player who was there when it happened, said that Johnson had been carrying on with a married woman—which would not have been uncharacteristic behavior for him—and her husband slipped poison into a bottle of whiskey the woman gave Johnson. As Johnson went to drink it, Williamson slapped the bottle out of his hands, warning him never to drink from a bottle he had not seen opened. Johnson didn't appreciate the tip, and when another bottle was offered to him, he poured down a huge swig. It too was poisoned, and Robert Johnson took sick. A few days later, he died.[4]

Is the poisoning story true? Journalist Robert "Mack" McCormick claims to have tracked down the man who poisoned Robert Johnson but has never made his name public, thereby undermining his own claim.[5] The county registrar on the case examined the circumstances of Johnson's death after it happened and managed to undercut the whole poisoning story by claiming that Johnson died of syphilis. Her opinion was stated in a handwritten note on the back of Johnson's death certificate, which tends to undermine its credibility as a part of the official record.

Among the many things we don't know about Johnson is where he is buried. Several possible gravesites exist, all claiming to be his. We can't be certain which is legitimate. What we do know is that after his death, he almost disappeared from the musical discussion altogether, having to wait until 1961 to have his reputation restored. That was when Columbia Records released a two-album set called, not inappropriately, *King of the Delta Blues Singers*. That album immediately established him as one of the founding fathers of the Delta blues.

If Robert Johnson had never made his contribution, the Delta blues would still exist, of course, but neither the Delta blues nor the electric Chicago blues would exist as we know them today. What are Johnson's contributions? There is a straight line from Robert Johnson down to Muddy Waters, who heard Johnson's music while working the Mississippi cotton fields, learned to play guitar in the Delta blues style, and brought the music north to Chicago, where he amplified his guitar and created the Chicago style of electric Delta blues.

Additionally, Johnson contributed significantly to the sophistication of rock; the British Invasion bands of the 1960s were far more fascinated by American blues than were Americans. They knew the work of Muddy Waters and the other Chicago players and were curious enough to trace their music back to its roots, picking up on Johnson's music when the reissues made it available again. Eric Clapton described Johnson's singing as "the most powerful cry that I think you can find in the human voice." Clapton also said that what Johnson played was far beyond his own level of skill; he himself could not play the blues anywhere near as well as Johnson did. He could, however, play rock and roll versions of it. As we shall see, Clapton and the other British Invasion players contributed to the development of Americana by merging Johnson's finger-style blues with rock.[6] Johnson's music showed contemporary rockers how to get beyond the vapid teen-centric love songs that characterized most rock of the time and create a music with substance instead. Indeed, when the Rock and Roll Hall of Fame put together its exhibit of five hundred songs that shaped the form, Johnson had four songs among them: "Sweet Home Chicago," "Cross Road Blues," "Hellhound on My Trail," and "Love in Vain."[7]

After the 1961 reissues rescued Johnson from the obscurity he had fallen into, recorded examples of his guitar style became available to study, and the students of his style revolutionized blues and rock playing. Rock and blues musicians such as Clapton, Keith Richards, Muddy Waters, Jimmy Reed, Honeyboy Edwards, Robert Plant, Mike Bloomfield, and Jimmy Page have all said Johnson's playing influenced them.

THE COUNTRY BLUES OF MISSISSIPPI JOHN HURT

Many writers consider country and Delta blues to be interchangeable terms. They are not. The two genres come from the same sources, but there are subtle distinctions. The difference between Delta blues and country blues is the difference between an entrée and a menu. Delta blues is one choice from the smorgasbord that is country blues.

Country blues is largely a fusion of blues and folk music. Like most roots music, it originated in the American South and spread throughout the nation as the African American population left the southern states and moved north and west in search of a better life.

The list of country blues masters is a long one: Blind Boy Fuller, Big Bill Broonzy, Sonny Boy Williamson II, Texas Alexander, DeFord Bailey, Blind Blake, Reverend Gary Davis, and others. All of these men— and a bunch of talented women, such as Etta Baker, Lucille Bogan, Ida

Cox, Hattie Hart, and Victoria Spivey—spread the music across America, making it one of the most important contributing factors in the rise of country and folk music. Among the giants, although his original influence was based on a small handful of records followed by a decades-long silence, was a man that few others can match in importance in the long run: Mississippi John Hurt.

Mississippi John Hurt was born in either 1892 or 1893; as is the case with many southern African Americans of his generation, Hurt's birthday is a matter of disagreement. In his birthplace, Teoc, Mississippi, records were spottily kept. As a young boy, he moved to Avalon, where he grew up. By the age of nine or ten, depending on which birthdate you accept, he had taught himself to play guitar in the syncopated fingerpicking style he pioneered and was playing out occasionally, picking up an extra couple of dollars while making his living by working on a farm. In 1923, he teamed up musically with fiddler Willie Narmour, who, when he got a chance to record for OKeh Records five years later, recommended Hurt to producer Tommy Rockwell.

Hurt did two sessions for OKeh, one in Memphis, the other in New York City, and for a time, things were looking good for Hurt—until the records didn't sell and OKeh, which wasn't doing well financially, declined to issue further sides. When the record company folded not long after, Hurt waved good-bye to a musical career, went home, and resumed his old life as a sharecropper. For thirty years, he worked the land in obscurity.

HARRY SMITH EDITS A RECORD AND SAVES FOLK MUSIC

Had it not been for a Greenwich Village wild man in the 1950s, that might have been the end of the story. Harry Smith was that man. Smith, who had a reputation as one of the most eccentric men in New York, was a collector but not necessarily of music, although his acquisitions of 78 rpm recordings were vast because he often bought up whole libraries at a time. According to Moses Asch, who owned and operated Folkways Records, what Smith really collected was information:

> He bought up thousands of records. He knew what he was doing because all the time he kept track of when the records were recorded and

who recorded them. In those days, they issued catalogs that gave the date, the matrix number and the place of the session. In the early Victor and Columbia days, the dealer had all this information. [8]

And that information was what Harry Smith wanted. He was a sponge, soaking up this sort of data. Asch was not the only one to speculate that the data meant more to him than the music. He was aware of what he had, and while the music he documented was completely unknown in the major cities and largely forgotten in the rural areas, Smith knew how important it was; he was sitting on several thousand examples of the history of folk music in the twentieth century. Today we would say he had thousands of individual pieces of Americana and complete documentation on where it had all originated. This stuff had to be made public, he decided.

In 1952, Smith went to Asch and suggested he put out the *Anthology of American Folk Music*, a multirecord set of the old 78 rpm records, complete with a sourcebook, all drawn from Smith's collection. Asch had begun Asch Records in order to issue folk music on 78 rpm records. In 1948, he saw the coming of LPs and changed his operation to Folkways Records, so he could specialize in folk albums and other esoterica, such as poetry readings. When Smith came to him about the anthology, Asch jumped at the idea and issued the set, and as we will see in a later chapter, American folk music was transformed forever.

For the moment, though, what counted was that the work of Mississippi John Hurt was represented in the anthology. Two of the songs he'd recorded for Tommy Rockwell, "Frankie" and "Spike Driver Blues," were included in the set. His music was heard again by a new generation. In fact, it was heard by a whole new audience that was made up primarily of college-aged white kids. The music was working its magic on a brand-new population, listeners who had never heard of this man and were, therefore, stunned by the mastery of his playing, the way his picking sounded so simple but was actually so complex and sophisticated. Who was this man? Virtually nothing was known about him, not even if he was still alive.

TOM HOSKINS LEARNS A LESSON ABOUT GEOGRAPHY

In the early 1960s, a folklorist by the name of Tom Hoskins decided to find out if Hurt still lived. Searching for clues to his possible whereabouts in his music, he heard the song "Avalon Blues" and thought the answer might lie in that town. However, he had no idea which state contained Avalon. A map told him Avalon was in Georgia, so he went there and discovered he was in the wrong state. Later, he found out about the tiny farming community of Avalon, Mississippi, and, on an impulse, went there. This time the trip paid off. He found Hurt sitting on the porch of his house, still working as a sharecropper. Hoskins gave him a guitar and told the old farmer that he'd be back soon. Going back to Washington, D.C., Hoskins found a couple of backers, returned to Mississippi, and brought John Hurt north, where the old former bluesman must have been shocked to find himself a star of the then flourishing folk revival.

It was 1963, and Hurt was able to resume the career he'd abandoned thirty years earlier. He landed a recording contract with Vanguard Records, who assigned folk singer and huge Mississippi John Hurt fan Patrick Sky to produce the records. Sky, incredibly sympathetic to Hurt's music, was the perfect producer; he knew enough to stay out of the way and let Hurt play and sing while the tape rolled. The resulting albums led Hurt to become one of the most influential country blues players. Today, listening to the blues, folk music, bluegrass, or rock, you'll hear traces of Mississippi John Hurt. Listen to the playing and singing of Bob Dylan, Doc Watson, Jerry Garcia, Taj Mahal, Arlo Guthrie, all of the current crop of country bluesmen, and dozens of other musicians, and you'll hear his songs, his vocal phrasing, and his playing style.

His guitar style is especially influential. He plays finger style and is said to be the inventor of what Hamilton Camp called "the educated thumb style." Instead of the thumb playing the melody, as in Mother Maybelle Carter's style, Hurt uses his thumb on the low strings to play a steady bass rhythm. He alternates playing the sixth and fifth strings, keeping up a steady thump on the bass line, while his index and middle fingers play a melody line on the treble strings. Instead of playing the melody line directly on the beat, he syncopates it, floating just ahead or behind the beat. All of the fingerpicking styles that characterize contemporary folk, blues, and Americana music emanates from his playing.

It is safe to say that Americana would not be what it is without the work of Mississippi John Hurt.

MUDDY WATERS DISCOVERS ELECTRICITY AND CHANGES EVERYTHING

It might seem odd that Robert Johnson, an acoustic guitarist, could be so influential in the development of electric rock and blues, but we have to consider the changing times and the population dispersal that World War II brought. During the war years, defense plants began operating in the major cities, and with the younger generation of Caucasian men drafted and fighting, jobs opened up in these plants for African Americans, jobs that were previously closed off to them by segregation. The great migration from the rural south to the big cities took place at that time. Among the plantation-raised Mississippi men who took the plunge and moved to Chicago was McKinley Morganfield, better known to us today as Muddy Waters.

The significant dates in Morganfield's background are, as is the case with so many southern African Americans of his generation, muddled in poor record keeping and the casual racism of the day. He was born either in 1913 or 1915 in Jug's Corner, Mississippi, or maybe Rolling Fork in the same state. Some documents suggest he was born in 1914. He grew up working as a field hand on Stovall plantation in Stovall, Mississippi, where he learned to play harmonica and guitar. By the age of twenty, he was playing dances for his neighbors and running a series of juke joints, where he and other traveling bluesmen played.

In 1941, the folklorist and song collector Alan Lomax, who had first recorded Leadbelly and Woody Guthrie, came to Stovall and recorded Muddy Waters (by now he'd adopted that name) playing two songs. When he received copies of the records in the mail from Lomax, Waters put them on the jukebox that was in the shack from which he operated a juke joint, playing and singing for the other workers on the plantation. Hearing his voice emanating from the box, Waters decided that his future was as a professional musician, so he moved to Chicago to make it happen. When he first arrived in Chicago, Waters was playing an acoustic guitar. However, the listening environment altered his approach. When the blues master Big Bill Broonzy, impressed with Waters's talent, allowed him to open for him in the clubs, Waters recognized that if he was to be heard in the loud and rowdy bars, he would have to plug in and play an amplified guitar, a move made from necessity that had the effect of creating a new form of blues. Soon, every urban blues musician played amplified. Waters formed his first band, which included Roy Rogers on second guitar, Little Walter on harmonica, Otis Spann on piano, and Elgin Evans on drums. That instrumentation became standard for blues bands and still is. Until he died in 1979, Muddy Waters was the most prominent electric bluesman in the world. He is still the archetype for the blues.

You can't overstate his significance on Americana; he influenced nearly every genre of music. In addition to the blues, his basic sound can be heard all over R&B, rock, folk, and jazz—even country musicians have stolen his licks.

Waters is directly responsible for the British Invasion blues bands of the 1960s that gave us such musicians as Eric Clapton—whom Waters called his son—the Beatles, and the Rolling Stones, all of whom admired Waters and gave him credit for awakening their interest in the blues. When he made the first of his regular tours of England and Europe in 1958, he found a ready audience of young musicians who recognized his genius much more than Americans did and who, after seeing him, began modeling their music and even their lifestyles after him. These British youngsters included not only the aforementioned Beatles, Stones, and Clapton but also the American Jimi Hendrix (who was living in London at the time), Led Zeppelin, Foghat, Paul Rodgers, Van Morrison—who, like so many Irishmen, had moved to London to get his career off the ground—and the Animals. These British and Irish musicians took the American blues of Muddy Waters, made it into rock, and brought it back to the United States when they toured here. As Waters always sang, "The blues had a baby and they named it rock and roll."

He was the father, and his grandson is Americana.

NOTES

1. *The Search for Robert Johnson*, dir. Chris Hunt (London: Iambic Productions, 1992).

2. Pete Welding, "Robert Johnson: Hellhound on his Trail," *DownBeat Magazine* 66 (1966).

3. "Blues Wizard's S.A. Legacy," *San Antonio Express News*, November 30, 1986.

4. *Search for Robert Johnson.*

5. *Search for Robert Johnson.*

6. Elijah Wald, *Escaping the Delta: Robert Johnson and the Invention of the Blues* (New York: Amistad, 2004).

7. Rock and Roll Hall of Fame, *The Roots of Rock and Roll: Blues, Gospel, Country, Folk, Bluegrass, and R&B*, exhibit catalog (Cleveland: Author, 2016).

8. Harry Smith, *Anthology of American Folk Music* (New York: Folkways Records, 1952), catalog (33).

Interlude: Roger McGuinn: Respecting Tradition while Transforming It

Americana is about keeping the tradition alive even as artists extend it, bending and twisting it like a balloon animal so that it comes out with a totally different shape. Roger McGuinn is one of the musicians who definitely extended the tradition. Henry Paul, leader of the Outlaws and Blackhawk, sees the Byrds, especially the famous jungle-jangle, twelve-string guitar played by leader McGuinn, as one of the primary influences that led to Americana. Echoes of McGuinn's playing are present in almost every folk, pop, or rock record released. With his Rickenbacker electric twelve-string guitar, McGuinn created one of the basic sound patterns of Americana music and, in so doing, contributed vastly to the spread of Americana as both a movement and a genre.

The Byrds' contribution to the movement was actually a simple but very important one. A few bands had followed Bob Dylan's lead and begun playing an electric hybrid of folk and rock music. The Byrds made it work; they successfully put folk rock over the top and made it an important and chart-topping form. By doing rock-based versions of Dylan and Pete Seeger songs, as well as traditional folk songs, the Byrds showed that folk music could be successfully updated and broadened so that instead of being the music of the hip few, it could be mainstream, accessible to anyone with a radio. An entire phenomenon sprang from their work as rock bands by the hundreds began mining the folk world for commercial gold.

Although the band lasted almost a decade and had many members pass through its ranks, a case can be made that the Byrds were Roger McGuinn. A founding member of the group, he was the only one who was aboard for the entire trip, from launch to reentry. He was also the acknowledged leader of the band; the Byrds' vision was McGuinn's vision.

How does a rock band qualify as a major founding influence on Americana music? It helps if the band in question is not actually a rock band at all. The fact is that although marketed as one, the Byrds were more an electric folk band than a rock group. They did for folk music

Figure 4.1. Roger McGuinn. Photo by John Chiasson

what the Clancy Brothers had done for Irish music: gave it a beat, ener-
gized it, and found a new audience for it.

To understand the band and what it contributed, it's important to remember that all of the members of the group came out of folk music
backgrounds. Roger McGuinn studied at Chicago's Old Town School of
Folk Music where he sharpened his guitar skills and learned to play the
five-string banjo. While still in high school, he studied guitar and banjo at
the Old Town School and played in Chicago's folk clubs and coffeehouses. After hours at the Gate of Horn—Chicago's premier folk music
club, which he was too young to legally enter—he was invited to jam
with Theodore Bikel, the Limelighters, Odetta, and other giants of the
folk revival. These jam sessions led to a job offer from the Limelighters,
which he had to postpone until his graduation from high school. By the
time he was in his early twenties, he had been the banjo and guitar
accompanist for both the Limelighters and the Chad Mitchell Trio and
went on to serve a stretch as both Judy Collins's and Bobby Darin's
musical director.

David Crosby was a touring coffeehouse minstrel for years, working
his way across the country and back playing coffeehouses and small
clubs, touring often with his older brother, Ethan, accompanying him on
bass. In Greenwich Village, he met the folk singers Fred Neil and Vince
Martin and followed them down to south Florida, where a thriving folk
scene, presided over by Martin, who had moved there, flourished. He
became a regular at Coconut Grove's Flick and the other Miami and Fort
Lauderdale coffeehouses, where he became friends with a local folk singer named Bob Ingram. When Ingram went to Los Angeles to join the Les
Baxter Balladeers, a folk group the bandleader put together, he invited
Crosby to come out and join the band. Crosby returned to his hometown
of Los Angeles to sing with that group and continued to work the coffeehouse circuit there after the group folded.

Gene Clark was singing in a folk trio, the Surf Riders, which had a
regular gig at a Kansas City club called the Castaways Inn, when the New
Christy Minstrels, in town for a concert, dropped by after their show.
They heard Clark sing and play and offered him a job on the spot. He
stayed with that group for more than a year, making two albums.

Clark became a founding member of the Byrds when, after he'd left
the New Christy Minstrels, he met Roger McGuinn, who was performing

at Los Angeles's Troubadour club, and suggested they write some songs together.

Chris Hillman, the Byrds bass player and harmony singer, discovered folk music when his sister came home from college and played some records for him. He was determined to learn guitar. Hillman began studying guitar, but when he was in his early teens, Hillman heard bluegrass bands and fell in love with the sound of the mandolin. He began riding the train from his family's home in Los Angeles to Berkeley, where he studied mandolin with Scott Hamby. He joined his first bluegrass band, the Scottsville Squirrel Barkers, when he was still a teenager. After cutting one album with that band, he moved on to join the Golden State Boys, one of Southern California's best-known bluegrass bands. The Golden State Boys changed their name to the Hillmen and were very popular but, like so many bands, could not manage to stay together.

After leaving their respective bands, these musicians all gathered at West Hollywood's Troubadour nightclub, where McGuinn was working as the house-opening act. Together, they found a drummer, Michael Clarke, and became the Byrds.

Strangely enough, Clarke had never played the drums prior to his joining the Byrds. According to McGuinn's website, he was hired because he resembled the Rolling Stones' Brian Jones. Originally, he didn't even have a drum kit and, during their early rehearsals, practiced on a bunch of cardboard boxes. He developed quickly into a strong drummer and beginning with the second album played percussion with the band on all their recordings up to and including *The Notorious Byrd Brothers*, after which he left the band.

Certainly, the Byrds used electric instruments and played rock and roll versions of folk music just as Eric Clapton was playing rock and roll versions of the blues, but the fact is while they made their reputation as a folk act, they never went far beyond folk music. Folk was their base throughout their entire career. Regardless of genre, though, the Byrds were musicians: skilled, restless, ambitious, and hungry to create.

Each of their albums is an experiment, seemingly born out of a desire not to repeat themselves, to continue to stretch themselves artistically. The first one, *Mr. Tambourine Man*, invented folk rock, mostly by amplifying Dylan and Seeger tunes and writing modern songs that centered on folk themes. McGuinn's guitar parts—he was the only member of the band to play on that first album since at that time it was routine for the record labels to insist that professional session musicians play on the albums—are made up of the same techniques he used as a folk singer, just pushed through an amplifier.

The follow-up album, *Turn, Turn, Turn*, used a Seeger song as its title track, telegraphing its direction. It's a full-bore folk music album, on which all of the members of the group played. Its musical statement appears to be, "The record company wouldn't let us all play on our first album, so let us show you what we can do with the same sort of material those studio guys played last time."

Having made the statement, the Byrds' characteristic restlessness surfaced, and they next recorded *Fifth Dimension*, introducing space rock to their repertoire. Many of the songs are rooted in science fiction—"5D (Fifth Dimension)," "Mr. Spaceman," and "2-4-2 Fox Trot (The Lear Jet Song)," among them. These are anchored by traditional folk songs, such as "Wild Mountain Thyme" and "John Riley." It's as though McGuinn and company want to show us the connection between past and future, that the songs, in mood and structure, are actually the same. The highlight of the album, however, was "Eight Miles High." Deemed controversial at the time for its perceived druggy connotations, it is considered the first psychedelic rock song. It successfully blended all of the Byrds' various influences and interests while containing elements of folk and rock and was constructed around the chord changes that the jazz genius John Coltrane had used for his version of "My Favorite Things."

And so it goes. *Sweethearts of the Rodeo* invented country rock; *The Notorious Byrd Brothers* is their psychedelic album. Each new album goes in a different direction, and since by the time these albums were released, the Byrds' lineup changes were as legendary as their songs, we might say that each album goes in whatever direction Roger McGuinn was interested in. It has been said that McGuinn could take any three players and turn them into Byrds, and that's true up to a point.

As long as he was willing to remain autocratic, to be the benevolent dictator of the band, then any group of Byrds he fronted made fine music. In the later days of the band, though, he became sensitive to the dictator charges and made the creative mistake of letting the other musicians contribute more. Since they sometimes did not share his vision, a couple of the later albums get muddy as the Byrds' records become more of a product—the very plastic wares they complained about earlier in their career—and less of a driving force. The records are still strong but are not as tightly focused or as important as they once were.

But then Clarence White came into the band. White, one of the great bluegrass guitarists and session musicians, was a master guitarist and singer whose vision matched McGuinn's perfectly. He was just the man to join McGuinn in going where he wanted to go: deeper into country rock, folk music, and bluegrass. Playing and singing alongside White, McGuinn sounds renewed, completely reinvigorated, as though his motives had changed and he was once more playing music for the sheer joy of playing, satisfying his creative needs. Together, acoustically or electronically, the two guitars play off of each other, each feeding and challenging the other. *(Untitled)*, a two-record set, presents them in both a studio and a live setting; the live sides are filled with wonderfully joyful singing and playing. McGuinn sounds relaxed and happy, and he toured with this version of the band until Clarence White died.

WHAT DID MCGUINN CONTRIBUTE?

A close listening to the live set on *(Untitled)* makes Roger McGuinn's contribution to Americana easier to assess. In addition to contributing a guitar style, he broke down the barrier between types of music, showing in his writing and his playing the dependence Americana has always had on folk music. Even while the songs he wrote and played were not folk songs, they were strongly rooted in the tradition. Like the music of the minstrel shows, they may not have been traditional folk material, but they were the songs of the people—just a more technologically advanced people.

When Americana is described as roots music, it is helpful to ask which roots and whose roots? McGuinn gives us an answer to those questions.

Perhaps his biggest contribution, however, is the idea of the single intelligence. Music of the mass culture is driven by several intelligences: the producer, the corporate record company structure, the writers and publishers of the songs, and finally, perhaps, the artist. When the corporate labels ran the industry, the A&R man (artists and repertoire), a forerunner of today's producer, was the ultimate power, the point man of the corporate committee, and the man responsible for enforcing all of the decisions the label made, from the hiring of the musicians to the selection and arrangement of the songs the artist would record. Often the singers never heard the songs they were to record until they showed up for the sessions. A professional studio musician, a self-described "studio rat," told me that in Nashville, where ever since country emerged as an industry studio musicians are used extensively, the musicians come in before the vocalist and are given a single page chart of the song, laid out in the Nashville number system, in which each chord is given a number. Using that system, the song can be rehearsed and quickly learned in any and all keys so that when the singer shows up, all the musicians have to do is determine the singer's key and they are ready to accompany his or her vocal. The singer has no input into the choice of song or the arrangement at all.

If the singer is a passive follower and trusts the production people and the record company, the system can be effective. For it to work, though, all parties have to be on the same page. When the system is applied to an artist such as Buddy Holly or, for that matter, any highly individualistic Americana artist, the results can be disastrous.

Roger McGuinn, however, showed that the system is not always right: that power can be taken away from the corporate bureaucrats and given back to the artists. Perhaps that is his biggest contribution to Americana music.

5

"IF I COULD FIND A WHITE BOY WHO SANG BLACK . . ."

If there is any one thing that is true about American popular culture, it is this: it's never the same any two days in a row. Americana music is, like all popular culture, characterized by a blend of formula and invention, but like all of the best, it loosens the formulas and is heavy on invention.

Formula refers to the familiar aspects, the stuff we expect to be present, which in Americana includes elements found in the association's definition, such as melody, harmony, vocals, and a blend of electric and acoustic instruments. These are elements used to deliver roots music styles. We expect to hear the songs utilize country, folk, rock, blues, bluegrass, or R&B licks to build their melodies, harmonies, and vocals.

Invention, on the other hand, refers to the new elements the artist brings to the music, the elements unique to each artist: the Buddy Holly "hiccup," or Bob Gibson's use of the relative minor chord. Invention makes the song belong to the artist who created it, for example, Tom Rush's alternate-tuning guitar accompaniments and Jennifer Knapp's tone of pain and suffering in a faith-based song; each ensures that the artists are unique and individual. Americana, while honoring the formula, is mostly concerned with the invention.

One thing Americana avoids is mass culture, a third aspect of the entertainment and culture field, which is heavily dependent on formula. Commercial radio pop has become primarily a form of mass culture. Its goal is to reach the widest possible audience, and its success is measured by the number of dollars accumulated. In an effort to manufacture a hit, mass-culture artists and producers will attempt to replicate what has worked in the past. Are Disney and Nickelodeon princesses selling records this week? Rush teen princesses into the studio. Is Taylor Swift hot? Find me a Taylor Swift. Are young hunks semi-rapping about beer and girls moving the country charts? Get me a bro-country act.

The goal of every mass-culture product is to resemble a previous mass-culture product that has made a ton of money. Americana artists do not play on that court. Instead, by emphasizing invention, they insist on bringing an aspect of originality to the game.

In the development of musical pop culture and especially Americana, we must also take a look at basic geography and social-political trends. For an examination of the geography, we have to go south. If the South of the 1940s and 1950s had not existed, then Americana would have either not developed or grown into an entirely different animal. Today, mass media has largely erased regional differences in the culture, but in the 1940s and 1950s, the South was its own creature, a sort of Loch Ness monster that people in other areas of the country did not believe existed. It was a land based on the myth of a fallen aristocracy that never really existed, a land whose people were willing to fight a war they knew they could not win to protect a way of life they knew had never existed.

Because the South is like no other place, southern music is like no other.

ZENAS SEARS CAUSES A REVOLUTION

For one thing, the South's popular music—especially that aimed at young listeners—has always welcomed African American musicians and songs into the general arena of pop music. It might strike some people as odd that the most segregated area of the country had the greatest penetration of black music into the dominant white culture, but that's just one paradox about the South.

Much of the credit for the acceptance of black music onto the southern mainstream can go to one man. In Atlanta, in 1945, a young white man named Zenas Sears returned from World War II. Having been exposed to African American music in the service, he had fallen in love with both the music and the culture, becoming so enamored of the culture that most people thought he was black, a notion he did nothing to change. Sears took a job as a disc jockey on WATL but quickly moved to WGST, where he could program a show called *The Blues Caravan*, which aired R&B songs nightly. Since his station was located on the campus of Georgia Tech, an all-white school, he picked up a sizable following among young white people. In addition to doing his nightly radio show, Sears began promoting concerts and managing local talent, helping to develop the careers of performers like Tommy Brown, Chuck Willis, and Little Richard. He also produced the first records of these artists. [1]

In 1954, Sears made his move, purchasing the station that had given him his start, WATL, and immediately changed its call letters to WAOK. His new acquisition became the first station in the country to play African American music exclusively. Almost overnight, WAOK became one of the most prominent stations in the Southeast, and Sears's show, *Digging the Discs*, was nationally syndicated. [2]

Why was WAOK so revolutionary? Sears allowed, indeed encouraged, high levels of invention into the music aimed at young people. At the time, the dominant white stations and many of the black-owned stations were programming artists like Doris Day, Frankie Laine, Patti Page, and Eddie Fisher, who were to young people what spoiled meat is to a sandwich. The young, seeking music that more matched their life experiences and that had some energy, rejected the mass-culture offerings of the stations aimed at white audiences and flocked to the R&B stations, like WAOK, where they heard musicians such as Muddy Waters, Howlin' Wolf, Chuck Willis, Billy Ward and the Dominoes, Clyde McPhatter and the Drifters, Jackie Wilson, Hank Ballard and the Midnighters, Ruth Brown, and Ray Charles, artists who brought energy and creativity to the music. [3] They reached the new audience by taking the formula aspect of the jump blues of the 1940s and adding a strong dose of invention to their efforts. *Jump blues* refers to the music of such bandleaders as Roy Brown, Big Joe Turner, Louis Jordan, Bull Moose Jackson, and Cab Calloway. It evolved from the breakup of the big bands due to the economic changes of the World War II years. It became prohibitively expensive to take a big band on the road, but a small group that played for dancing could still make a good living. Jump blues directly led to rhythm and blues and rock. [4]

HAVING HEARD ENOUGH, NASHVILLE STRIKES BACK

The areas WAOK didn't reach were served by the competition that sprung up, such as Nashville's WLAC, a ten-thousand-watt station whose transmitter accelerated to fifty thousand watts after sundown so that, like Mexico's border radio stations, it penetrated the entire Southeast and much of the Midwest. Since it modeled its programming after WAOK's, WLAC offered the same levels of invention that WAOK did. Most of WLAC's nighttime programming in the 1950s was sponsored by Randy's Record Shop in Gallatin, Tennessee, an outfit that not only played the records on the air but also sold them by mail order, so that the hardcore R&B of artists such as Elmore James, B. B. King, Ike Turner, Lloyd Price, and Wilbert Harrison spread throughout the region. DJs such as Randy's Record Shop disc spinner Gene Noble and his chief late-night competition, Ernie's Record Parade DJ John R. (for Richbourg), became stars, joining Cleveland's Allen Freed who leaped quickly onto the bandwagon. All of these men and others plowed the fields that Zenas Sears planted. Other white DJs, seeing the reputations and stacks of dollars these guys were building up, jumped aboard.[5]

These white DJs, wanting to reach the young audience, learned very quickly that if they wanted these kids to tune in, they needed to program the new, original, and energetic music that came from the small regional labels, instead of the bland pablum offered by the New York–based majors. They had to play Little Richard on Specialty Records instead of the covers of his songs offered up by Pat Boone on Decca-owned Dot Records.

And DJs who were at home with the energy emanating from the emerging rhythm and blues learned very quickly that for a minimal investment they could form labels, record singles, and by spreading a few bucks around to other jocks, get them played on the air. Two hundred dollars could get a song recorded, pressed, and played on the radio. Then, after showing there was a market for the record, they could sell the master to the majors.

SAM PHILLIPS INVENTS ROCK 'N' ROLL

All of this sounded like a good business plan for a Memphis businessman named Sam Phillips. In his recent biography, Peter Guralnick points out that Phillips was a child of the South. Born in poverty, he picked cotton next to his tenant farmer parents and African American laborers. Since familiarity generally breeds sympathy, Phillips, like Zenas Sears and a lot of southern boys at the time, became enraptured with black music and black culture. On a trip to Memphis, he got his first look at the city's live music center, Beale Street, and his life's direction was set.

By the early 1940s, Phillips had become a disc jockey at the Muscle Shoals station, WLAY, one of the emerging southern stations to play the music of both black and white musicians. By 1945, he was at WREC in Memphis where he worked for four years as an announcer and sound engineer.[6]

Then, in 1950, he got the idea that changed the face of American music forever: why play the records when you can create and own them? A cautious man for a pioneer, Phillips began by forming the Sun Recording Service, an operation that made commercials for Memphis businesses to cover the bills. This source of income allowed him to feed his real passion: making records. He would, for a fee of a few bucks, record anyone who walked in the door. Among the people who dropped in were B. B. King, Little Junior Parker, Little Milton, Howlin' Wolf, and Jackie Brenston and His Delta Cats (who were also known as Ike Turner's Kings of Rhythm), a group who recorded one of the major candidates for the first rock and roll record ever, "Rocket 88." Since the Kings of Rhythm were signed to another label, the Jackie Brenston name was used. Phillips recorded all of these artists and then sold their masters to larger labels.[7]

Within a couple of years, he had another thought: why sell the masters to other labels and let them make all the money when he could form his own label and keep the money? Sun Records was born, and musical history was changed.

Phillips knew exactly what he wanted with Sun Records: to make money. The way to do that, he knew, was not by imitating the majors but by offering something common in southern music but missing from the nation's mainstream radio stations and record stores: soul and feeling. To him, the emotion a song generated was much more important than its technical aspects.

In a search for that magic feeling, he signed a roster of artists who, without any conscious awareness that this was what they were doing, helped make Americana music a reality: Johnny Cash, Carl Perkins, Roy Orbison, Jerry Lee Lewis, B. B. King, and Charlie Rich, all of whom became superstars.

And, of course, there was that Presley kid.

Phillips is famous for telling a colleague, "If I could only find a white boy that sang black, I could make a million dollars."

Elvis Presley was that white boy. Legend has it that he came into the Sun studio to make a private record for his mother's birthday at a cost of six dollars. The songs were "My Happiness" and "That's When Your Heartaches Begin." Phillips, so the myth goes, heard him and signed him on the spot, and rock was born. As is the case with all myths, the truth is neither that romantic nor that simple. Phillips heard Presley's amateur recordings and thought the boy had talent but needed seasoning. He let a full year pass before he called Presley in and auditioned him. Then he signed him, put him together with guitarist Scotty Moore and bassist Bill Black, and set him on the road to becoming Elvis Presley. The new singer's first audience was country fans, and that's where Phillips first marketed the records, but to show that Presley wasn't your ordinary country singer, he billed him on tour as "The Hillbilly Cat." The breakthrough to rock fame, however, took awhile to happen.

Throughout the South, Sun Records quickly became a force. As struggling country artists heard the new sounds Elvis, Jerry Lee Lewis, and Carl Perkins were coming up with and heard how Johnny Cash was adding rock to country, they flocked to the doors of the Sun Records Company. Phillips welcomed them all, offering Sonny Burgess, Billy Lee Riley, Warren Smith, Bill Justis, Ray Smith, and Billy "the Kid" Emerson their first (and sometimes only) contracts. [8]

Most of these musicians had been playing country music. Phillips told them that to make it big in the music business, they were going to have to add some power and drive to their work. They were going to have to rock. The result was rockabilly, and driven by the work of Presley, Lewis, Perkins, and Cash, the nation's radio stations began to warm up to it. In Atlanta, a daily half-hour program on a country station was devoted solely to Elvis Presley recordings. Cash and Perkins dominated the country charts, while Lewis was solidly in the upper reaches of the rock charts.

For Presley, though, despite his cult popularity, it was a harder path to travel. He didn't truly fit in either country or rock. Until he broke through to mass national popularity, he toured the South, doing school shows, country-themed bars, and guest shots on the *Louisiana Hayride*. Rock radio, however, though it tried, could not neglect his power and charisma, and he soon won acceptance as both a country and a rock act.

Slowly, the majors lost their stranglehold on the radio and the independents gained market share and influence. When Carl Perkins recorded "Blue Suede Shoes," it signaled that radio had been forever changed; the song became Sun's first national number one hit.

What was Phillips's secret? Why was he able to create a new genre and plug into the hearts of the nation's young people? It was a willingness to experiment, an attitude that said let's try something new and see what happens. Freed from the constraints and the formulas of the majors, Phillips's artists could make their own music their own way. Of course, Sam Phillips guided them toward the salable product, and as a businessman, a former salesman who knew the radio business inside out, he was able to market their material efficiently.

The majors struck back the way they always did, by buying up his talent. Facing a financial crisis, Phillips sold Presley's contract to RCA Victor, while Johnny Cash, unhappy with his royalty rate, went to Columbia. Phillips's blues artists, such as Howlin' Wolf and Little Milton, signed directly with the Chicago-based Chess Records, which had been buying their masters from Sun, and B. B. King went to Modern Records.

Other artists were lost to bad luck and bad behavior. At the height of his "Blue Suede Shoes" fame, Perkins broke his back in a car wreck and was unable to follow up. By the time he was healthy enough to tour again, he had lost his momentum and, as a solo act at least, never regained it. Jerry Lee Lewis's marriage to his thirteen-year-old cousin became public while he was touring in England, and the public outrage that followed drove him out of the country and into the international headlines, which pretty much cost him his career.

These setbacks drove Phillips out of the top spot in southern music. He never held a prominent spot in the record business again. He did, however, get very rich, which was his goal. He invested some of that RCA Presley money in Holiday Inn when that chain was starting up, sold Sun Records to country music mogul Shelby Singleton, and started

WHER, the first radio station in the country to have an all-girl radio format.

In an interview with National Pubic Radio in 2001, Phillips reported that his success was due to a cultural gap that he had noticed: "Teenagers did not have, before rock 'n' roll and rhythm and blues—they did not have any type of music they could call their own once they got over four or five years old until they were well into their twenties and considered adults."

By filling that gap, Sam Phillips became the first man to be inducted into the Rock and Roll Hall of Fame, as well as three others: the Hall of Fame for country, for blues, and for rockabilly.

He died at the age of eighty in Memphis.

BUDDY HOLLY SNEAKS IN THE BACK DOOR

Another pioneer rockabilly artist who inadvertently helped create Americana music built his career in another area of the country that was geographically removed from the centers of the record industry. Charles Hardin Holly (known to his family and friends as Buddy) was born in Lubbock, Texas, in 1936. Falling in love with music early, by the age of thirteen he had become a first-rate guitarist and was playing out professionally. At fourteen he made his debut on local television. Although he didn't know it, he was moving personally toward the creation of what would become Americana; he was doing country but lacing it with the R&B he heard on late-night radio. By 1955, he was opening for traveling acts that came through Lubbock, including, among others, Elvis Presley.[9]

Holly signed with Decca Records and cut several disappointing sides for them. Pushed into the Owen Bradley Nashville country music machine, he was given unsympathetic producers and studio musicians who were locked into establishment country music and actively disliked the rock and roll he was pioneering. The assumption at the majors back then was that only the seasoned label professionals knew how to make records; artists were simply the singers, one more instrument in the producer's mix. For an artist to have a suggestion made about as much literal sense as Mighty Mouse living on the face of the moon. A strong and independent musician as well as a stubborn young man, Buddy Holly knew exactly what he wanted to accomplish in his songs, but he quickly discovered that no one cared.

Holly was not allowed to use his own band or write his own arrangements, so, far from the original sounds he had in mind, his records came out sounding like everyone else who was recording in the country music capital. Bradley insisted that Holly's recordings follow the established Nashville formulas, a questionable move since Holly's music was rooted in generating what John Cawelti called invention, that is, the use of unfamiliar elements and new approaches to the formulaic parts of the music. Holly's first singles went nowhere, so the label dropped him and Holly went back to Lubbock, determined to have full control over his music from that moment on. [10]

Holly connected with producer and musician Norman Petty, who had a studio in Clovis, New Mexico, and went there with his band to record. Making Petty's acquaintance was a fateful meeting. Petty became to Holly what Sam Phillips had been to Elvis: a man who respected what he was doing and allowed the young singer to experiment in the studio until he found the sound he wanted. That sound resulted in "That'll Be the Day," a single that Petty took to Brunswick Records, a subsidiary of Decca, the label that had cast Holly off a year earlier. Seeing the irony, Holly said, "Decca threw us out the front door and we went around and snuck in the back." [11]

Released under the band name the Crickets, since Holly was still signed to Decca as a single act, the record reached number one in the United States and in Britain. He followed it up with "Peggy Sue," which not only reached the top ten on the U.S. and British charts but also reached number three on the rhythm-and-blues chart.

At that time, Holly's music was solidly in the rockabilly camp but was slowly and organically expanding into more original forms. He learned to play down the country aspects, while emphasizing the rhythm-and-blues and rock elements. Then he began to experiment with tenor saxes and string sections. Continuing to grow as both an artist and a musician, Holly became a more complex, more wide-ranging, and, subsequently, much more influential figure. His death in the legendary Winter Dance Party tour plane crash in Iowa did nothing to diminish his influence. In fact, his absence only served to show how badly his music was missed.

It is astonishing to realize that his entire musical career lasted less than eighteen months.

What makes Buddy Holly a pioneer of Americana music? The music he created is the living embodiment of the Americana Music Association's definition: it was and is contemporary. It incorporates elements of country since he first worked in that genre. He moved on to roots rock, another element of the Americana genre, by adding the emerging sounds that artists like Elvis Presley were coming up with while keeping his songs rooted in R&B and the blues—most of his guitar accompaniments are blues shuffles played on the tonic and fifth notes of the chords. He also used both acoustic and electric instruments. All of that adds up to the fact that placed against the pop music of his day, Holly's music sounded as if it came from another, better world; it was highly inventive, creating new patterns while not abandoning the old traditions.

All of that is secondary, however, to Holly's real contribution: his absolute insistence that all of his music be authentically his. It reflects his own mind, his own needs and loves, and his own beliefs. Even a song like "Words of Love," although it sounds like a standard love song, when listened to closely reveals that it is a song about insecurity, more about the need to be loved and reassured than about love itself. "Think It Over" is another multileveled song. In it, the singer has just been dumped and is urging his girlfriend to reconsider the action that she has just taken, which has, he warns, implications she has not thought about. Yet even as he warns her, he reveals his longing and despair. Most of Holly's love songs touch on the fragility of love, our neediness, and our inability to make it without someone to walk through our lives with. His songs appear to take sides when actually they explore dichotomies.

Holly is the insecure, lost person who hides his loneliness and vulnerability beneath a tough veneer. This self-portrait gives his music a universality and an authenticity that has enabled it to last sixty years so far, with no signs of dropping in popularity.

Just as Holly said that none of his music would have been possible had not Elvis paved the way, most of the British Invasion bands of the early 1960s credited Holly as paving the way for them, giving them inspiration and direction. Top American musicians like Bruce Springsteen, Bob Seger, John Fogerty, and the Nitty Gritty Dirt Band have all testified to what Holly's music meant to them.

Without Buddy Holly, American music would sound a lot different.

Despite Holly's considerable importance and influence, though, a case can still be made that one of his contemporaries was truly the first Americana band: the Everly Brothers.

THE EVERLY BROTHERS INVENT AMERICANA

Don Everly was born in 1937 in the site of John Prine's song, "Paradise," Muhlenberg County, Kentucky. By 1939, the family had moved to Chicago, where Phil was born. They spent most of their childhood in Shenandoah, Iowa, where their father, Ike Everly, had a radio show. Billed as Little Donnie and Baby Boy Phil, the Everlys became regular performers on that show.

After they finished high school, the brothers moved to Nashville where family friend Chet Atkins got them a deal to release a single on Columbia Records. The disc flopped, but it led to a contract with Archie Bleyer's Cadence Records.[12] Bleyer had served a long stretch as radio and TV personality Arthur Godfrey's musical director. Godfrey, a former radio announcer with little discernable talent who had somehow parlayed his way into hosting several TV shows, was notoriously controlling and, while he portrayed himself on his various shows as mellow and folksy, actually carried a good deal of the tyrant inside himself. One day he realized that a singer on his show, Julius La Rosa, was getting more fan mail than he was. La Rosa had become too popular, Godfrey decided; people were tuning in to see him instead of Godfrey. Claiming that La Rosa had lost his humility, the host fired him on the air. Since La Rosa recorded for Bleyer's record company, Cadence, Godfrey fired Bleyer also.

For Bleyer it was the best move that could have been made. Freed from his radio and television duties (Godfrey had three programs on the air at the time, and Bleyer had been responsible for the music on all of them), he was now free to concentrate on growing his record company. In 1956, he signed the Everly Brothers.[13]

Songwriting husband and wife team Felice and Boudleaux Bryant were connected to Bleyer's publishing company, so they were charged with writing for the brothers. The Bryants brought the Everlys a song that had been rejected by nearly thirty acts, "Bye Bye Love." They recorded it, and the result was as though lightning had struck a tornado. Their recording of "Bye Bye Love" hit number two on the *Billboard* pop charts, number one on the country charts, and number five on the R&B listings. It wound up selling more than one million copies.

For a while there, the brothers had the golden touch, with every record they released making the charts and selling tons of copies. They had major hits with "Wake Up, Little Susie," "All I Have to Do Is Dream," "Till I Kissed You," "Problems," "I Wonder If I Care as Much," "Hey, Doll Baby," and dozens of others, all written by the Bryants. But the sheer level of success ensured that problems quickly surfaced. Signed as songwriters to Wesley-Rose, an outfit that was connected contractually to Cadence, the Everlys found that the deal they had signed forbade them from recording anything the company didn't publish. When their friend Buddy Holly wrote a song for them that they had to reject, it became galling. When they wrote songs that weren't published by Wesley-Rose, they weren't allowed to record them; they were legally prevented from doing their own material. Phil described the constant arguing over song choice and musical direction with Fred Rose and Archie Bleyer exhausting.

By the time their contract expired in 1960, they had had enough, so the Everly Brothers moved to Warner Brothers, where their music and the sphere of influence that surrounded it like a halo both increased. There they were able to break away from the simple formulas Cadence imposed on them. The first result of the new freedom was "Cathy's Clown," which the brothers wrote and which sold eight million copies. At Warner's they could record blues, such as "Nashville Blues," and cover Little Richard's "Lucille" or Mickey and Sylvia's "Love Is Strange." They did solid country, as in Hank Snow's "I'm Moving On," and paid tribute to their forefathers, with Jimmie Rodgers's "T for Texas." When they wanted, they could go for progressive, semi-avant-garde rock, such as "Lord of the Manor."

In short, at Warner's, they had the freedom to be themselves, to explore fresh dimensions, and they took full advantage of the opportunities. In doing so, they found the pattern for Americana music. With the Appalachian roots to their music picked up from their father—their early album *Songs Our Father Taught Us* is a collection of traditional folk songs—the Everlys always had a strong folk strain to their music that, even as they dug deeper into rock, they never abandoned. They got their start in country music, cutting all of their early records in Nashville with country session musicians and producers. Huge R&B fans, they not only recorded straight rhythm-and-blues songs but also worked soul into their other material while rocking out. They even cut the occasional bluegrass song.

Let's return to the Americana Music Association's (AMA) definition of Americana:

> Contemporary music that incorporates elements of various American roots music styles, including country, roots-rock, folk, bluegrass, R&B and blues, resulting in a distinctive roots-oriented sound that lives in a world apart from the pure forms of the genres upon which it may draw. While acoustic instruments are often present and vital, Americana also often uses a full electric band.

We can see that the Everly Brothers' music fits that definition perfectly.

A full forty years before Americana existed, the Everly Brothers were playing it.

NOTES

1. Georgia Radio Museum and Hall of Fame, "Zenas Sears, 1914–1988," accessed September 9, 2016, http://www.grhof.com/.

2. Ibid.

3. Ibid.

4. A fuller discussion can be found in Robert Palmer's book, *Deep Blues* (New York: Viking, 1981).

5. James R. Lowe, "WLAC-Radio: The Unofficial Web Page," last updated May 15, 2003, http://www.yodaslair.com/.

6. Peter Guralnick, *Sam Phillips: The Man Who Invented Rock 'n' Roll* (New York: Little, Brown, 2015).

7. Ibid.

8. Ibid.

9. John Goldrosen, *The Buddy Holly Story* (Madison, WI: Popular Press, 1978), 42.

10. Ibid., 45.

11. Ibid., 78.

12. "The Everly Brothers," *Rolling Stone*, accessed September 14, 2016, http://www.rollingstone.com/.

13. "Musician Archie Bleyer; Fired by Arthur Godfrey," *Los Angeles Times*, March 22, 1989.

6

APPROPRIATING BLACK CULTURE

Although the product released as pop music might make more of an immediate impact on the mass audience, the fact is Americana is this nation's most important music format. Since it is, as we have seen and will continue to see in chapter 8, the most American of musical formats, it can be surprising to recognize exactly how much of Americana isn't American in origin. Since the United States is, in truth, a nation of immigrants and most everyone has ancestors who came here from somewhere else, it is only logical that American music should originate outside the United States. Certainly its themes are native to this country, and certainly the genre became Americanized as the people did, but the musical forms such as folk and blues, as we've seen, originated in the British Isles and in Africa, respectively, and became Americanized as the cultures that brought them here were assimilated into this country. (Exactly how successful this assimilation has been is a political question that lies outside the scope of this discussion.)

As immigration to the United States continued, each culture that landed on these shores brought with it its own music. The streets of early twentieth-century cities rang out with Irish and Scottish tunes, klezmer songs, jazz, and British music-hall songs—the music of the United States has always been a polyglot of styles that remind us we have always been many transforming into one, a unity in the act of unifying. American popular music has reflected our transformation.

Americana, then, was not born with the founding of *No Depression* magazine in the 1990s, as some have maintained. It has been evolving for as long as this country has been evolving and took its first great step forward during the Civil War era. It has, like matter examined from a quantum perspective, evolved exponentially, rather than sequentially. That exponential growth is one reason casual listeners did not notice. Another reason Americana seemed to have arrived full blown out of nowhere is because it evolved from musical styles and genres that no one associates with it.

BLACKFACE, HIGH-STEPPIN', AND THE APPROPRIATION OF BLACK CULTURE

The minstrel show, an important forerunner of Americana music, was a highly popular form of entertainment in the mid-nineteenth century. Created as a form of low entertainment based on the bastardization of black culture by white people, the minstrel show consisted of song, skits, and dance, generally done by white performers in blackface who made a specialty of lampooning not black people but the popular stereotype of black people. The traveling minstrel shows emerged in the 1830s, and within a decade they had become the dominant entertainment form of the country. They held the top spot until the turn of the twentieth century when the rise of vaudeville did them in. These shows did a lot to drive the stereotype of the lazy, shiftless, popeyed, singing, and dancing Negro into the white mindset.

Historians of the period claim that the white performers had no idea they were stereotyping African Americans. They thought they were presenting an accurate portrayal, even though exaggerated for comedic purposes. Whether this statement is accurate or not is debatable; the casual racism of the day led to a certain level of discrimination by assumption. You can't expect a culture that declares a race of people to be unfit for self-government, and a society that declares these people to be, like Jonathan Swift's Yahoos, more animal than human, not to carry racist attitudes and behave in racist ways. Still, whatever their motivations, the minstrel-show performers took elements of black culture and used them for their own purposes, usually to get cheap laughs from unsophisticated audiences.

That appropriation of the minority culture was not the most significant thing about the minstrel shows, even though it led to the first vocalization of the charge that has been made against white musicians with every type of music from rock to blues, doo-wop, jazz, and hip-hop: the claim that they have ripped off and co-opted African American art forms. As a point of fact, soon after the Emancipation Proclamation and the Civil War freed them, former slaves formed their own minstrel groups and toured the country, doing shows that offered a more authentic look at African American life and music than did the white troupes.

The truth is never as pleasing as the fantasy, however, so the stereotype stuck. It also stuck because of the separation of the races that was a result of both custom and law. Because of the dominance of white culture, the white companies could play many more venues than their African American counterparts. The black companies could only play in the segregated areas of the cities where African Americans were forced to live, while white companies could play wherever they could pay the rent for a venue.

IS THIS ANY WAY TO CREATE AN INDUSTRY?

Whether performed by black or white musicians, the minstrel shows were not only the most popular entertainment form the country had but also the center of the American music industry. It was through them that people heard new songs. In fact, the minstrel shows supported such songwriters as Stephen Foster and Dan Emmett, the composer of "Dixie," a song that made its debut in the shows.

Irish and Scottish music, African songs and dances, and Appalachian folk songs all made their way out of their respective cultures through the minstrel shows, which spread the songs to audiences all over the nation. The shows were America itself: they were raucous, vibrant, loud, energetic, very often tasteless and crude, and decidedly anti-intellectual—all qualities shared by many Americans of the day. And the music? It was decidedly pop, striking a strong blow against the European-modeled elite culture of the day; the troupes might have satirized opera, but they definitely did not bring that elite form to the masses. Instead they brought the popular music to a widespread audience that went on to spread the songs around their communities. The music itself was as threatening to the mainstream culture and as feared by the elites as the possibility of an income tax. Historian Dale Cockrell described the minstrel show songs as "music that jangled the nerves of those who believed in music that was proper, respectable, polished, and harmonic with recognizable melodies."[1]

Cockrell wears his elitism like a cashmere sweater. The minstrel show was musical theater for the working class. It was to the common people what Gilbert and Sullivan were to striving upper middle classes yearning to show their culture, or what opera was to the sophisticated rich. It was music that defined them, showing them their place in the culture and uniting them. The minstrel show, according to Ken Padgett, "evolved from several different American entertainment traditions: the traveling circus, medicine shows, shivaree, Irish dance and music with African syncopated rhythms, musical halls and traveling theatre."[2] All of the traditions that Padgett mentions had one thing in common; they entertained the ordinary people, the workers and their families.

As such, one of the great contributions of the shows was that they showed the people that the folk music they loved and supported, the music that reflected their traditions and their old-country values, was not out of place in this new country. In fact, it could be, rather than just something that warmed their hearths, professionally performed. One could make a living supplying the shows with songs. Therefore, a professional class of thoroughly Americanized songwriters and performers emerged. Alongside the previously mentioned Stephen Foster and Dan Emmett, the minstrel format gave us James A. Bland, Edwin Christy, Joel Sweeney, and Gussie Davis—and the wonderfully named William Shakespeare Hays.

DEATH OF THE MINSTREL SHOWS

The people who created and worked the minstrel shows not only created a totally American art and entertainment form but also inadvertently built the conditions that allowed vaudeville, the form that put the minstrel show out of business, to emerge. We even know the date upon which the death of the minstrel show happened: the minstrel show died on October 24, 1881. That's when New York impresario Tony Pastor featured what he termed "polite variety programs" at the Fourteenth Street Theater in Lower Manhattan. Since his goal was to attract women—who, because of the raucousness of the program, would never have attended a minstrel show—and their husbands, he made the acts work clean and banned the sale of alcohol in the venue. As a further enticement, he gave the ticket buyers free hams.

Pastor's idea of the polite variety show worked, and vaudeville was born. It caught on in New York, but its national growth did not begin until Boston-based theater manager B. F. Keith put together a chain of theaters and developed the Keith circuit, where performers could travel from one of his theaters to another doing their acts. The circuit idea was a blessing for both performers and venue operators; an act could sign for anywhere from a few weeks of work to a season of bookings and pay a single commission. Contracts and paperwork were simplified and set up to guarantee steady paydays for both performers and management. It is a system still used in country music, especially for the summer county fair circuit.

The circuits traveled by the vaudeville entertainers had been paved by the minstrel show artists, who had worn out the road for years before vaudeville began. Medicine shows ripped off the comedy song and dance offered by the minstrel shows, using them to gather crowds to whom opium-based "medicines" could be sold. The medicine wagons also paved the way, as did the touring Wild West shows, which offered employment to the heroes who had tamed the west and, because of the disappearance of the frontiers, no longer had a function in life, leaving men and women who had become well known because of newspaper stories and dime novels that grotesquely exaggerated their exploits with nothing left to do but to become entertainers. All of these entertainment packages helped to create a road map the vaudeville promoters could use to build the stops on their circuits.

By the 1890s, vaudeville had almost totally supplanted the minstrel show, accomplishing its destruction by offering a more rounded and less racially motivated form of entertainment and by co-opting the most popular forms and entertainers that the minstrel shows had to offer. Several competing circuits now existed. In addition to the early pioneers, Pastor and Keith, Martin Beck owned and operated the Orpheum circuit, which, with its accumulation of more than forty-five theaters, was easily the biggest chain. Its nearest competitor, the Pantages circuit, owned thirty theaters and managed sixty more. It wasn't unusual for an artist to travel forty-two weeks a year, playing theaters that were controlled by one circuit. Among the artists who developed and showcased their talents in this way were jazz pianist Eubie Blake; magician Harry Houdini; child singer and comedian Baby Rose Marie; comedians George Burns and Gracie Allen, Bob Hope, Jack Benny, and W. C. Fields; and dancer Bill "Bojangles" Robinson.

How did vaudeville contribute to Americana music? It contributed in primarily the same way the minstrel show had, by bringing to the vast American audience the music and culture of minorities and immigrants, thereby showing how varied and unique American popular music really was and how American popular music was from the beginning a polyglot of songs from other nations and cultures, all put through a particular blender that rendered them solidly American. The music, no matter what culture it originated in, belonged to all of the cultures that made up the Great American Polyglot. It showed Americans what they had in common, helping to create the sense of community that runs through Americana. It contributed to both the genre and the movement.

AFRICAN AMERICAN ARTISTS STRIKE BACK

You might think of vaudeville as an all-white phenomenon. Since segregation was both the custom and the law, it primarily was. Although major artists such as the dancer Bill "Bojangles" Robinson were able to crack the color line, and in the biggest cities, African Americans were permitted to attend shows (although they were restricted to the farthest balconies), the form was still dominated by whites. As a response to this treatment, black entrepreneurs formed their own collections of venues around the country; the famed chitlin' circuit, in which rhythm-and-blues acts toured well into the 1980s, was one of these that lasted the longest and had the most impact.

It wasn't the most prominent African American circuit, though. That distinction went to the Theater Owners Booking Association, created by the black vaudeville comedian Sherman H. Dudley. In 1911, Dudley began buying and leasing theaters, and by the 1920s, his organization controlled more than a hundred venues. By advertising heavily in black newspapers, Dudley was able to build a well-known and profitable organization, despite the fact that many of his artists complained that the profits came from underpaying them.

Although Dudley gave some important artists exposure when they needed it, he never won their loyalty. In fact, he lost his artists to other promoters because he would not pay them what they thought they were worth, even as he was increasing their value by providing them exposure and regular work before many different audiences all around the country. Ironically, he made them so valuable he could not afford to keep them.

Among the people who became stars in Dudley's theaters were Ethel Waters, Ma Rainey, Mamie Smith, Tim Moore, Fletcher Henderson, Fats Waller, Duke Ellington, Cab Calloway, and Count Basie. But though he made these performers famous, the act of turning them into stars pulled them into the orbit of white producers, who stole them away by offering more money than the tightfisted Dudley felt he could give them.

The creators of these vaudeville circuits have been credited with creating the diaspora of many leading African American artists and performers, and the flight of the people out of the major cities into the rural areas of the country. The constant touring of vaudeville performers introduced them to parts of the country they never saw before, and when it was time to hang up their traveling shoes, they settled throughout the land, where, despite segregation, they heavily influenced both American music and culture. The claim might be overstated, but it is true that both American culture and Americana music would be much different were it not for the minstrel shows and vaudeville.

NOTES

1. Dale Cockrell, *Demons of Disorder: Early Blackface Minstrels and Their World* (New York: Cambridge University Press, 1999), 1.

2. Ken Padgett, "Blackface Minstrel Shows," Blackface! August 20, 2014, http://black-face.com/.

Interlude: Rosanne Cash: The Search for Self

Rosanne Cash's story is a familiar one in Americana; it is a well-traveled path, the same trail followed by hundreds of singer-songwriters, one that leads from the wrong genre to the right one, from a place that rejects fierce individuality and a commitment to the music to one that accepts those qualities as an admission badge.

Hers is a story of what Maura O'Connell would call the transition of a vocalist into a singer. When Rosanne Cash began her career, it was sort of something she'd stumbled into, a part of her growing up. By the time she finished maturing, she had figured out what was important to her as an artist and made moves to grab and hold it, moves that were not supported by the people who were supposed to be in her corner.

Looking at how that happened and what it means can be instructive.

After her parents, Johnny Cash and his first wife, Vivian, divorced in 1966, Cash stayed in Southern California with her mother until she finished high school. Then, wanting to get to know her father better, she moved to Nashville to join his road show. Her first job as part of Johnny Cash's team was mending and repairing costumes. A few tours into her tenure, though, she moved up to background vocalist.

A child of the 1960s, always restless and searching, Cash moved to London, but when England did not fulfill her she returned home and enrolled at Vanderbilt University in Nashville as an English and drama major—until her restlessness drove her back to Los Angeles to study acting at the Lee Strasberg Institute. In her memoir, *Composed*, Cash describes herself as too insecure to be an actor: "I knew in my heart that being part of a group of people who were singularly committed to an artistic ideal mesmerized me, but I recognized that I could not make a life as an actor."[1]

Unable to bring herself to go to auditions, Cash withdrew and left Los Angeles, this time for Germany. While in Munich, she signed to record an album that was only to be released in that country. The idea of its restricted distribution appealed to her insecurities, and she returned to Nashville to make the demos.

At a party at Waylon Jennings's house, Cash met Rodney Crowell, who was then best known as a songwriter and the rhythm guitarist in Emmylou Harris's band, and intuiting that his sensibility would be right for her project (and "I also thought it would be a way to get to know him and try to get him to like me"), she asked him to produce her demo. While making the album in Munich, she had her first—but not her last—experience with an unsympathetic and dominant producer determined to have his own way. She fought back, and the album got made but sank in the marketplace.

During the sessions, Bernie Vonficht, the producer assigned to her project by the record company, had demanded that she record a song called "Lucky," which Cash didn't like and couldn't relate to, so she refused. Vonficht, certain that the song would be a surefire hit, sang it himself and had a triple platinum hit with it. He later told Cash that even though it went triple platinum, he'd have never recorded it had he realized he was going to have to sing it every night for the rest of his life.

Johnny Cash played his daughter's record for Rick Blackburn, a Columbia executive who initially didn't like it. When Cash was called out of the room to take a phone call, however, Blackburn turned to another track, which sounded better to him. When Cash returned to the room, the executive told him he wanted to sign Rosanne to the label.

When it came time to record her first American album, Cash again called on Rodney Crowell to produce it. By this time, he had left Emmylou Harris's band to make his own first album but put it on the back burner to work with Cash. During the production, Crowell and Cash got married. The album, *Right or Wrong*, produced a hit, a duet with veteran country singer Bobby Bare called "No Memories Hangin' Around," and drew positive reviews even though Cash was unable to promote it; she had become pregnant.

With her next album, *Seven Year Ache*, Cash hit the big time. The title track hit number one on the country charts and number twenty-two on the *Billboard* pop charts. It was followed by two more songs that reached the top of the country charts, "My Baby Thinks He's a Train" and "Blue Moon with Heartache." *Seven Year Ache* landed Cash her first gold record.

Her life settled into a routine of recording, touring, and raising children. She didn't feel artistically fulfilled. After her biggest country album, *King's Record Shop*, which became her second gold album and gathered four more number one hits, Cash, who had been feeling more and more restricted by being confined to the country category, recorded *Interiors*, a more personal and introspective album that she produced herself and that did not thrill the executives at Columbia: "I delivered *Interiors* to the label and they sent the head of A&R to the studio to listen to a few key tracks with me. After listening to four songs, [he] laughed coldly and said, 'We can't do anything with this.' He looked at me with bemusement. He was clearly flabbergasted that I thought this was music the label would consider commercially viable."[2]

At this point, it is important to note that the major record labels have their own business models to follow, as well as their own goals. They are in business to provide profits to their corporate owners by selling large quantities of records. They advance money to artists to make their records and to tour to promote them, and they expect to recoup that money. While what they do is very often not what Americana artists want or need, it is still what the labels do, and they quite naturally expect the artists they sign to commit to the label's business model. As the Byrds pointed out in their song "So You Want to Be a Rock 'n' Roll Star," the companies "are waiting there to sell plastic ware." Americana artists, as a rule, do not see themselves as providers of plastic ware. Their goals are different from those of the major labels, which is a fact that still takes many artists by surprise when they encounter it.

Rosanne Cash was one of those taken by surprise when Columbia did not receive *Interiors* warmly.

The album meant a lot to her, indicating the direction in which she wanted to go, so when Columbia abandoned *Interiors*, Cash recognized that she and the label were traveling in different directions and she could no longer work with the Nashville pros running her label. She asked to have her contract transferred to the New York division. Columbia granted the request, so Cash moved to Greenwich Village, effectively leaving country music and moving into the newly emerging Americana field. Despite the fact that *Interiors* had been dumped by the label, only released at all because of contractual obligations, its quality was recognized by critics and was nominated for a Grammy in the Best Contemporary Folk Album category (which has since been replaced by the Best Americana Album designation).

Cash's albums became more introspective and personal as, free from the pressure of having to chase country hits, she was able to write and record the music that played in her mind, able to write honestly and deeply about the things that were important to her. Her next album, *The Wheel*, widely considered to be about her 1992 divorce from Rodney Crowell, followed the pattern established by *Interiors*, drawing enthusiastic, rave reviews and few sales.

The Wheel was an ambitious album, dealing thematically with the elements of "fire and water, wind and moon," and Cash wanted the sonics to reflect the elements. When she explained this to John Leventhal, whom she brought in to produce the record, Cash didn't think he fully understood what she wanted, because she was caught up in what she described as "some foggy quasi–New Age mind-set" in an effort to gain some psychic distance from the divorce she was going through. Leventhal told her that since the making of *Interiors*, she should think of herself as a producer but agreed to coproduce with her. The record they made is a masterpiece, a live album that continues to live well beyond its sell-by date.

After its commercial disappointment, she asked to be released from her Columbia contract, and the label agreed to let her go. Moving across the street to another major, Cash signed with Capitol Records, and released *10 Song Demo*, an album that sounds exactly like what its title implies—a stripped down, minimally produced, sparsely arranged collection of songs. After that, she and Leventhal, now married and with Cash pregnant, began work on *Rules of Travel*, but Cash lost her voice due to polyps on her vocal cords. Told that she should avoid surgery because the polyps would heal naturally after she gave birth, she could not sing for two and a half years. During that time, she developed her prose writing skills, publishing a highly regarded collection of short stories and a couple of children's books.

When her voice returned, she and Leventhal finished *Rules of Travel*, which was nominated for a Grammy for Best Contemporary Folk/ Americana album. By now, her early insecurities had been overcome and Cash had found her own voice, her own direction, and her own happiness. As the Americana field grew, her career grew with it, through a series of brilliant albums that pull off the Americana trick of finding the universal in the singular. *The List*, consisting of twelve songs from the list of the hundred greatest country songs that her father gave her when she eighteen, won the 2009 Album of the Year award from the Americana Music Association.

A highlight of her career was the 2006 release *Black Cadillac*, an album about the loss of three important adult figures in her life: her stepmother June Carter Cash, her father, and her mother. Nominated for a Grammy Award, *Black Cadillac* swept the album-of-the-year lists for 2006. In 2014, her album *The River and the Thread* grew out of her trips to the South when she was working with Arkansas State University's Johnny Cash's Boyhood Home project, which was committed to restoring the house where her father was raised in Dyess, Arkansas. The album won three Grammys: best Americana album, best Americana roots song, and best Americana roots performance. It also took the Americana Music Association's Album of the Year award.

Rosanne Cash's journey was not simply from country music to Americana music; it was from record company employee to artist. From her first German album, she was under the thumb of producers and executives, who followed a corporate line and insisted that she follow it also. From the beginning, she was strong enough to fight against directives that opposed her intuitive direction, even when she was not secure enough to be sure her intuition was right.

Early on, she saw that her choice was simple; she could bow to the pressure, let the Nashville heavies guide her career and make a large amount of money, or she could follow her own direction and risk failure and a much smaller bank account. Her father's example probably helped her resist the pressures. He fought back all through the best years of his career and only suffered a decline in sales when he followed the corporate advice. He too had to fight to make the records he wanted to make, and he too saw them neglected by the company, left abandoned by the curb, and thrown away by the people he had trusted to bring them to the attention of the public. Just as was the case with Johnny Cash, when Rosanne fought

Figure 6.1.   Roseanne Cash. Photo by Clay Patrick McBride

to make the albums she wanted to make and make them her way, they didn't chart or sell, a fact that Columbia took as validation for their point of view.

That happens when you operate in a system where popularity equates with quality.

Where many recording artists would go with the company to keep the money flowing in, Rosanne Cash was determined to maintain her vision and her independence; she was willing to sell fewer records in order to make the records she wanted to make. Money wasn't the goal; music was. As soon as she saw that Nashville wasn't going to board her train, she left Nashville in a search for her musical home.

It turned out that her home was in Americana.

Cash also had to turn to independent labels to get her music heard. As soon as she left the formulaic, mass-culture country music she had been recording for Sony/Columbia and Capitol, the major labels lost interest in her. When the Columbia A&R man told her the company could do nothing with *Interiors*, she knew his statement was a death knell, either for her career or for her music. In order to find sympathetic ears and a commitment to the music she wanted to write and play, she had to go to the boutique labels; these are labels owned by the majors but allowed to operate as independents. Her two most successful post-Columbia albums, *The List* and *The River and the Thread*, were released by Manhattan Records and Blue Note Records, respectively. These labels did what the majors had failed to do; they recognized and validated what Cash wanted to do instead of trying to squeeze her into a preexisting box. The result was, in both cases, worldwide hits, with increased and better critical reception and better sales, and a string of major awards.

Rosanne Cash's is the archetypal story of how a singer-songwriter winds up in Americana. The journey begins when the corporation standing between the performer and her audience inevitably grows dissatisfied with the performer's sales record and feels that with their guidance, he or she can do better. Demands are made, sometimes subtly, sometimes directly. Kevin Welch says that his record company kept their hands off his first two albums but then let him know that was not going to be the case with his next one. Choosing control over the help that a major label could be, he asked to be let out of his contract and, along with some friends who were in the same situation, formed Dead Reckoning, their own record company.

John Stewart was told by his major label that he was going to have to record other people's songs, a move he likened to wearing somebody else's clothes. Rather than comply, he left the label.

In their cases, like hundreds of others before and after them, folk rockers wound up as Americana artists.

Rosanne Cash's journey also shows us another aspect of the archetype: as the artists shed the negative influences of the corporation, their music improves. As long as she knew her record company did not like and would not get behind the songs she was writing, Cash could not let herself go, to give herself fully to the song. She had to have full control in order to do that.

It is archetypal for artists to go down the road, and that's why Americana thrives; it is the loosest of categories, the most open and the most welcoming. A movement as well as a genre, Americana gives artists like Cash a place to find support and companionship as they make their way. It is a genre and a movement that encourages you to be who you are.

NOTES

1. Rosanne Cash, *Composed: A Memoir* (New York: Penguin, 2010), 92.
2. Ibid., 121.

7

THE IRISH CLAIM THE BRONX

As immigrant performers settled throughout the land, the Irish planted their flag in the Bronx. And that's where Eileen Ivers grew up, in a culture that ensured her music, though Irish, would be international, and that the interweaving of influences, like a comforter made from the scraps of cloth found throughout a multigenerational home, would be Americana. Her Bronx neighborhood was characterized by music; Ivers learned early that she could not live a life without music.

Before we discuss her contribution to Americana, though, we have to take a look at the rise of Irish music in America.

THE CLANCY BROTHERS LEAD A REVOLUTION

The key date was January 1961, and the prime actors in the drama were the Clancy Brothers and Tommy Makem, who almost single-handedly are responsible for the great revival of Irish music during the folk boom of the 1950s and 1960s. As Liam Clancy tells it in his autobiography, some talent scouts from *The Ed Sullivan Show* saw the Clancy Brothers and Tommy Makem play at the Greenwich Village club the Blue Angel and asked them to do the show:

> On that particular night, the starting act got sick. The producer came to us in a panic.

"We've got a problem. Could you guys improvise three extra songs? That would leave us with about fifteen minutes out of an hour show."

"Sure. That's not a problem."

The night after *The Ed Sullivan Show*, we went to the White Horse [tavern]. We were heroes. . . . A few days later we were walking down State Street in Chicago. We were opening that night at the New Gate of Horn. A passerby stopped us on the street.

"Hey, I saw you guys on *The Ed Sullivan Show*. Fantastic. You guys were fabulous. Can I have your autographs? Martha, look who we've got here. The Clancy Brothers."

"And Tommy Makem," Tommy added.

"The Clancy Brothers," another passerby shouted.

Soon we were surrounded by a mob—signing autographs as fast as we could scribble.

Writing furiously, Tommy looked over his shoulder.

"Hey!" he said. "We're fuckin' famous."[1]

The popularity of Irish folk music in America began that night, when the Clancy Brothers filled the time allotted to a performer who fell ill and wound up doing a fifteen-minute personal showcase on the highest-rated variety show in America.

Of course, it is true that like most pioneers in most fields, the Clancy Brothers popularized Irish folk music, but they did not invent it. The music grew out of the lives and pain of the people, just as the music of the Appalachians grew out of the lives the inhabitants of the mountains were living. With the Irish, the music is as big a part of the culture as is storytelling. It is the way the people made it through the hardscrabble, adverse, difficult lives of being subjects to a foreign power in their own country. Singing and dancing were a way of dealing with their troubles. As Eileen Ivers said when I interviewed her,

Ireland is a place where, when you see the landscape, you see why it is so musical. Music grows out of what the people have been through. The poverty, the emigration—there's no word in the Irish language for immigrate. They did not want to leave, they had to. The famines, the wars, the occupation of the country, the shutting down of their relig-ion. . . . They keep rebounding. It's the spirit of the people, the poetry, the art.

Joanie Madden, the leader of the all-female Irish American band Cherish the Ladies, supports what Ivers says, pointing out that "Ireland is a very spiritual hands-on country. People needed to have entertainment, so they'd sing and play at night. We were growing up in a house where Irish music was the second language spoken."

The key to the power and beauty of Irish folk music, according to Madden, is that it is music written by people who didn't know what note they were playing or what key they were writing in. "They didn't have a clue, but they loved what they were doing," she told me in an interview. "When you play the old, slow tunes, the airs, they're so touching, so beautiful, and usually sad. When you learn the stories behind the songs, they're usually sad ones."

The Clancy Brothers and Tommy Makem led a revolutionary change against the overt and drowning sentimentality that dragged down the songs like a concrete block. Until they came along, professionally sung and played Irish folk music was largely sentimental consolation. The Clancys mangled that tradition. What they did was simple; their revolution consisted of killing the maudlin and mawkish traditional folk music of the island. Before their rise, folk music meant singers such as Paddy Barry, Eddie Butcher, Robert Cinnamond, and Margaret Barry, people who considered the song more important than the singer, men and women who saw their role as artists as keepers of the oral tradition, as keeping the old songs alive. To them, the idea of entertainment had about the same appeal as a head cold. Mixing elements of other genres into the songs and giving them a beat was to them an act of heresy.

The Clancys did away with that approach. As actors, all of whom appeared regularly on and off Broadway as well as working on programs during the first Golden Age of Television in the 1950s, they knew how to bring out the drama and comedy in the songs they sang. Joanie Madden remembers seeing the Clancys with Tommy Makem at a party after a concert. "They recited poetry," she said. "They remembered and recited fifty verses of a poem, and since they were actors, they'd bring out every nuance of the poem." When they sang, they also brought out every nuance.

When the Clancys and Tommy Makem heard American folk and pop music, they knew they could give the music a beat and provide the songs with drive. They called Ireland the land of happy war songs and sad love songs and brought those emotions to the forefront in the music. With a relaxed and informal presentation, the Clancys emphasized qualities that signaled the music was fun, no matter how much the themes dealt with the sadness of the immigrant population, with war and occupations by their native land by the British, and with the quislings who exploited "the Troubles" for their own political gain. They made the music joyful by not overdoing anything, by not taking things too seriously. Their first album, for example, was recorded while sitting around a tape recorder in the back room of the White Horse Tavern in Greenwich Village, singing drinking songs over pints of beer, accompanied only by Liam's strummed guitar and Tommy Makem's banjo and occasional pennywhistle. The music they played and sang was irresistible—not just to Irish immigrants but also to folk music fans of all stripes. They became so much the face of Irish music in this country that the young Bob Dylan, a friend of theirs in the Greenwich Village days, declared that his goal was to become as famous as the Clancy Brothers.

Once the Clancys stirred up the waters, new bands rose up in their wake, bands that responded to the new elements the Clancy Brothers had brought to the music. These bands took from the best of the Clancys but brought their own generation's interests and skills to the mix. The people responded. By the 1970s, as Maura O'Connell says, the folk bands were the rock and roll of Ireland. They made the charts, crossing over to mainstream popularity, and were able to tour worldwide. Bands such as Planxty, the Scottish group the Battlefield Band, the Bothy Band, the Dubliners, and the Chieftains emerged during this time. One band alone, De Dannan, introduced singers Maura O'Connell, Mary Black, and Dolores Keane to the larger worldwide stage. These new musicians grew so popular that they defined Celtic music for a new audience.

EILEEN IVERS DISCOVERS AMERICANA

It was bands such as the Chieftains and the Dubliners and musicians like Mick Moloney that Eileen Ivers listened to while growing up in the Bronx. They led her on a straight path from traditional Irish ballads to Americana.

She wasn't always one of the top promoters of Americana. She had once been the most traditional of stars. Taking up the violin early, she became one of America's best and most successful Irish fiddlers. Before she was out of her teens, she had won nine All Ireland Fiddle Champion-ships, with an additional championship for her tenor banjo work. Today, she has more than thirty championship medals. A former member of such traditionally focused Irish bands as the Green Fields of America and Cherish the Ladies (an all-female, all-star Irish band that she cofounded), she grew restless and joined the rock band of Hall and Oates. She ex-panded her recording range and has played on somewhere between eighty and one hundred albums, with such artists as the Irish musician Joanie Madden and the Irish band the Chieftains, world music experimenters Afro Celt Sound System, Irish rockers Black 47 and Brian Keene, punk goddess Patti Smith, and jazzman Al Di Meola, creating a proficiency in a number of genres and styles. The *New York Times* has called her the Jimi Hendrix of the violin, and the *Washington Post* proclaimed her to be the future of the Irish fiddle.

As Ivers told me in an interview, she was initiated into Americana as a child.

> In the early years, my folks played recordings all the time—Irish mu-sic, bluegrass, and country. My father, especially, loved bluegrass and country music. I fell in love with music at an early age. I don't remem-ber this, but my uncle says he remembers when I was three or four years old, going around our apartment with a pink plastic toy guitar and a wooden spoon, playing some sort of violin.

By the 1970s, bands such as De Dannan, the Fureys, the Waterboys, and the Battlefield Band were all placing hit singles on the charts and found their music spreading far beyond the normal range of Celtic folk music. Ivers heard this music both in the United States and in Ireland, where her family spent every summer. Those summers helped her to fall in love with the new folk music. She kept asking her parents to get her a violin, and finally they did. Getting a violin changed everything and introduced her to a teacher who turned her life around.

The legendary fiddler and teacher Martin Mulvihill was born in Ire-land and began to study the fiddle at the age of nine. Since his mother played the instrument, he learned the Irish traditional style and quickly developed a reputation as not only a fine musician but also an excellent instructor. Later, after adding both button and piano accordion to his set of musical skills, he immigrated to the Bronx, where he played out in various bands and taught. Says Ivers, "My cousin was taking both piano and accordion lessons from him, so I went to him for fiddle lessons."

Through Mulvihill, Ivers met a man who guided her to the music she needed to hear.

> I was a driven kid. When I was playing in fiddle competitions, I met a great adjudicator, Dan Collins—he ran Shanachie Records—who helped me a lot. He said, "you have to listen to all these traditional players," all these amazing fiddlers that I hadn't heard before, had to listen to how they bowed, how they played ornaments, all of that. Irish music being such an oral tradition, there were all these great players who were drastically underrecorded. I had to listen to all of them. It was a great education.

One major thing she learned was that "the violin is an extension of the person." She also learned the traditional styles advocated by Comhaltas Ceoltóirí Éireann but did not totally accept traditional music; to do that would be to reject the American side of her heritage.

Through her training and her early work in bands such as the Green Fields of America and the Hall and Oates Band, she learned to play many different styles. "I have no problem changing genres," she explains. "I love the music, I love the violin. I get goose bumps when we're invited to play with a symphony orchestra. I'm not a great classical violinist or jazz player, but I love going from a traditional reel to an improvised section and bringing it back to the roots." Roots, both musically and nationally, are very important to her. "As an Irish American, I feel close to the roots, so I love to go, say, into bluegrass, where the violin fits comfortably."

PUTTING THE IRISH IN IT

Ivers fits comfortably into Americana because the spirit of Celtic music lies prominently within the music of many cultures. That spirit is what makes Irish music Irish. "It's the joy in the music," she says.

> It's a music of emotion. It is wide and deep and difficult to play. If you're playing it and you're in the zone, you're tired when you stop. But the music is in the people. It is in their lives. It goes where they go. It came over here when we came over here. In this country, Appala-

chian music came out of Irish music. When the Irish immigrants came here, they brought their music with them. Since they couldn't bring instruments, they used homemade instruments: flutes, guitars, drums and banjos.

So what exactly is Irish in it? "It's hard to explain," she begins.

There's a strain of Irish music in bluegrass, but bluegrass isn't Irish. It's hard to pin down. If the spirit of the music is diluted, it isn't Irish. If it isn't diluted, that's Irish. It's in their diaspora, the sadness and the joy. If it's related to the essences, that's Irish and it's very accessible. I walked into a bar in Tokyo, and there was a Japanese musician up there with his bottle of Japanese Guinness, playing Irish music and it was authentic.

Ivers's most prominent venture into Americana to date is her album *Beyond the Bog Road.*

The album is about the way the Irish influences America and America influences the Irish. We have incredible traditional songs on it, railroad songs, some blues—we have a traditional singer and a roots singer on it. Since a lot of Celtic music entered this country through Canada—there's a strong Irish immigration in Cape Breton—we have Canadian Irish traditional songs. There's also a few originals, like "Walk On," which is about keeping the tradition alive within you as you go through life.

What Ivers says about Irish music being born out of the suffering of the culture helps explain why southern music is so soulful, with its deep mythology and current of sadness and sense of weariness with life, its acceptance of integration long before society accepted it. Both southern whites and southern blacks suffered under the laws, traditions, and values of the area. The music of the South, then, that led to every American genre has an association with suffering.

NOTE

1. Liam Clancy, *The Mountain of the Women: Memoirs of an Irish Troubadour* (New York: Doubleday, 2002), 281.

8

BRINGING THE GOOD NEWS

Since it is one of the basic assumptions of this book that most of the forms of music that created Americana came out of the church, we need to spend some time studying gospel music, one of the main tendrils of the Americana vine. Gospel is roots music, personal but universal, being as it is about the relationship between the individual and the supernatural. Drawn from the inner needs of the artist, the form is created from a combination of elements; it contains blues, work chants, prayers, hopes, and dreams, neatly wrapped and bound with a strong chain of soul. It's a reflection of life lived, not imagined, and therefore is the element that blends soul with rhythm and blues, pop, and rock to create nourishment with a unique taste. Gospel is an important aspect of American folk music. For those who emphasize the American aspect of the word Americana and associate the category with the values, norms, traditions, and myths of this country, gospel is not simply an aspect of Americana; it is Americana. And yet, like nearly everything American, it is European in its origins.

We can thank Martin Luther for that fact. Luther, a German professor of theology and a seminal figure in the Protestant Reformation, believed that God's grace and the eternal life that comes with it do not have to be earned or paid for through the purchase of indulgences. Instead, it is God's gift, given freely and lovingly. He taught that the Bible alone is the source of divine knowledge of God, so that interpretation by a priestly class is neither needed nor desirable. People should read the text themselves.

There was, however, one problem with Luther's teachings: most of the population in the 1500s could not read. Therefore, he saw that a participatory mass was needed, one that involved the worshippers and would make up for their illiteracy. If they were unable to read the Bible, they could sing it. Luther came up with the call-and-response spiritual, where the leader would sing out the good news of God, and the congregation would repeat it. Luther's innovation spread throughout Europe, and when the colonists sailed for America, they brought the form with them. It came to permeate the southern church. From the beginning of American history, then, gospel music has been in the forefront of emerging music.[1]

Gospel, whether from the white churches or the African American churches, is a celebration. Originally a church music, the participatory form invented by Luther, it migrated here during the early seventeenth century and became especially popular in the South. The African American strand of gospel was largely improvised and, of course, sung by slaves. Gradually, gospel grew and spread beyond its slave origins to become a dominant music among blacks and whites alike.

A vocal music, often performed a cappella, it was the music of the lower classes, which meant that the main thrust of the music, the praise elements, had to be verbal in order to be communicated. The main statement of a gospel song is lined out by the lead singer and repeated by the harmony singers, who can be either a small group, say a quartet or quintet, or a full choir. The harmonies are generally rudimentary but powerful; feeling is emphasized over smoothness of technique. Once, while discussing singing, June Carter remarked that who had the best vocal chops was unimportant. What counted was who had the most soul. Carter's statement is certainly true when it comes to gospel.

Two elements are central to the music: the call and response and the heavy use of repetition, both of which were pioneered by Martin Luther. As stated, these elements allowed illiterate members of the group to join in.

The music was spread, of course, through the church. It can't be emphasized enough what a force the church is in the South. Southern Pentecostalism covers the nineteenth-century South the way floodwaters cover land. With its emphasis on the direct experience of God, its insistence on the literal truth of the Bible, and its belief in the end times, Pentecostal evangelism perfectly meshed with the stark, hard poverty that characterized the life most southerners lived.

All black southerners and many white ones arrived in this land bound to someone else. To the southern immigrants, freedom was a dream. African Americans, of course, arrived as slaves, while the white southerners who worked the land often arrived here as indentured servants, men and women who contracted to live as slaves for periods of up to seven years before they won their freedom. Ironically, when they finally emerged as full citizens, they learned they were free to live almost exactly the same life that they did as indentured servants. Only now they were sharecroppers. No matter how the laws and customs of the nation changed, theirs was neither an easy life nor a particularly happy one. It was a life characterized by backbreaking work for little reward, a life of existential suffering with no particular hope for relief.

Only the church offered hope. The church held out the promise of two things that the believers could hold onto: a little comfort and, since the church members believed that Jesus was a redeemer, someone who could offer a vision of a better life in the not-too-distant future. All that was required was a public acceptance of the death, burial, and resurrection of Jesus Christ, which would eliminate all our sins and restore us to our natural relationship with the Almighty; and being born again through baptism is seen as an act that will unite us with God. Since the benefits offered by religion were desperately needed by the working-class people of the South, both black and white, Pentecostalism, usually the Baptist brand, triumphed.

THE ORIGINS OF GOSPEL

How gospel became a major force in the South is worth taking a more in-depth look at. Since the white slaveholders saw Christianity as a means for controlling their captives, African Americans were allowed to attend churches. After the services, they'd gather in the church building or in a house on the plantation designated as a "praise house" and continue to sing praises. As Christianity rose to become the driving religious force of the slave population, one day a week to exercise their spiritual nature was insufficient, especially when the white masters controlled what went on at their services, frequently forbidding African instruments and dances.

The answer? Secret camp meetings, where African Americans gathered in unauthorized places and at unauthorized times. There they celebrated in their own way, bringing African drums and dances to the spiritual music, so that it became their own. The Third Great Awakening, a strong revival movement of the 1850s, spread spirituals through the country. The growth of spirituals was also aided by the new black colleges that sprang up all over the South during the period after the end of slavery. Several of them, such as Nashville's Fisk University, raised funds by sending gospel choirs on tour, successfully changing the music from spontaneous improvisation to a formally structured, thirty-two bar song, generally with a series of verses, a chorus, and a bridge.

ENTER GEORGIA TOM

In the 1890s, a blues pianist who went by the name of Georgia Tom found God and wound up changing the entire gospel field. His real name—and the one he is remembered by—was Thomas A. Dorsey, and after his conversion from Georgia Tom he turned to writing spiritual music and ultimately came to be known as the "father of black gospel music." Dorsey, from his days as a blues musician, was able to see new possibilities in gospel music. He changed the dominant structure from abstract praise to personal expression by adding elements of blues and jazz to the music. In fact, he defined gospel as a music that combines praise with jazz and blues. His songs became so popular that for a time newly composed gospel songs were known as Dorseys. He was also known for another contribution to gospel; he made it personal, writing in the first person about himself and his own relationship to the Lord. From his position as music director at Pilgrim Baptist Church in Chicago, a post he held from 1932 to the late 1970s, he wrote not just a steady stream of songs but more like an entire river. Among his songs are "Take My Hand, Precious Lord," "Peace in the Valley," and "I'm Going to Live the Life I Sing about in My Song," all of which were a long way from the blues hits he used to write, such as his 1924 song "It's Tight Like That."

As spiritually oriented Americana artists such as Jennifer Knapp do today, Dorsey, in his lyrics, expressed his own feelings and doubts concerning his personal relationship to God; instead of just declaring God great and praising him, Dorsey wrote dialogues with the Lord, meditations on fate. He dealt with the complications of life and used the choirs to spread his songs through the nation. As Robert Darden wrote in *People Get Ready*,

> And with the changing music came a new style of performance, a style that emphasized movement and improvisation, a style that demanded emotional involvement and personalized expression. Dorsey's model singers—those who initially presented the songs and then coached the young choruses—all came straight out of the sanctified church. Sallie Martin, Mahalia Jackson and Willie Mae Ford Smith each believed in letting the Holy Ghost have Its way; each of them made this belief performatively obvious in their singing. The new choruses, under these vocalists' careful tutelage, thus learned more than just new tunes. They also received training in the freedom and faith of singing in the Spirit.[2]

Dorsey's approach fit the emerging times. In the 1890s, the rise of the Fourth Great Awakening, a Protestant revival spurred on by traveling evangelists, swept the nation, causing an increase not just in fundamental religious belief but also in the way it was expressed and celebrated. New churches grew out of this fertile ground, featuring a new way of praising the Lord. In these churches, African Americans were free to exercise their religion's willful power, whereas before they had been compelled to keep the noise down and the energy low so they would not be discovered and prevented from demonstrating their faith. Now they could— and did—let out their boisterous side with shouts, hand clapping, foot stomping, speaking in tongues, and freewheeling gospel songs. As the popularity of these churches and their singers grew, it became possible for gospel singers to make a living by touring and performing in other churches and singing in secular halls. In the late 1930s, Sister Rosetta Tharpe became a star by accomplishing the four-minute mile of gospel, a feat that, until she did it, had been thought to be impossible: she sang gospel music in a secular nightclub. As a result, a personal statement of belief in the supernatural became an art form.

In both the African American and the white Southern Baptist churches, gospel songs called the people to action, offering them a way to participate and, as Martin Luther had intended by introducing hymns into the service, a way to learn the message of the Bible. Since the church was officially segregated, its music was too. In the black church, gospel music would lead to soul music, while in the white church, it became a form of bluegrass.

CONTEMPORARY GOSPEL SELF-CONSCIOUSLY MERGES WITH AMERICANA

If we want to know how gospel music fits into Americana, we need to take a look at the road the Blind Boys of Alabama have traveled since their beginning almost eighty years ago. Their story tells us a lot about the qualities that led to Americana. In their history, we see the importance of the message and the need to share it, the social and political reasons for its current importance, the fact that it is a deeply personal music that still creates a community, and the way the use of invention leads to new forms.

Jimmy Carter, the last remaining founding member of the band, epitomizes the modern history of gospel music. Carter started his career when he was a child because his ambition in life, his direction, hit him early and stuck like butter to bread. Like most people, he discovered gospel music in the church and, in 1936, formed his first group while he was still a student at the Alabama Institute for the Blind, performing originally in local churches. All he ever wanted to do, he says, was sing gospel music, and that's what he has done for better than seventy years. Now in his eighties, he has received life achievement awards from the National Endowment for the Arts and the National Academy of Recording Arts and Sciences. He is in the Gospel Music Hall of Fame and has won five Grammy Awards for the more than seventy albums he has made. On an interview, he said, "We started out at the School for the Blind and decided we wanted to try to be professional gospel singers. We got our first professional job in 1944, singing on a radio station in Birmingham, Alabama." His goal was simple and straightforward: "We weren't looking for accolades, awards or rewards. We just love singing gospel music, and that's all we wanted to do."

Gospel music, however, is not a simple form of entertainment. It has higher aims. The music exists to bring the word of a supreme being to the people, to change the lives of the audience. Along with the rest of the Blind Boys, Carter has never seen the band's role as simply providing music for people. The group doesn't want to simply provide an audience with a good time. They want to go beyond just entertainment. "We're concerned with the message. Our aim is to touch lives."

Why has the message always been so important in gospel music? Carter's answer goes back to Thomas Dorsey. Like Dorsey, he sees gospel as "the good news of God. It's the news that Jesus died so that we might live." If gospel is the good news of the Creator, then it is only natural that the good news exists to be shared.

The other reason the message is important has to do with the circumstances under which the music was made. The formative time of their career, the first twenty or so years, was spent performing in the South during the Jim Crow era, a time of turmoil, strife, and conflict for the African American people who made up their audience back then. It was a time when hope was easy to lose, a time when maintaining your optimism was difficult, and when a positive message could ease the tension the way ibuprofen eases a headache.

"In the beginning, we could only sing for black folks. We went through the civil rights times, the civil rights movement." During the years of the movement, the Blind Boys participated in marches and demonstrations and sang at benefits for Dr. Martin Luther King Jr. With a chuckle, Carter says, "Those were trying years. We had us a mean old boy down here named Bull Connor who caused us some problems."

Back in the early 1960s, Bull Connor, who became an international symbol of southern racism, was the commissioner of public safety for the city of Birmingham, Alabama. Connor enforced segregation laws with a disregard for individual rights that made Georgia's baseball-bat-waving governor Lester Maddox look like the father on *The Brady Bunch*. Connor turned fire hoses on children and attack dogs on demonstrators. As a public servant, he was always careful to show a high regard for human dignity and life, as long as the life in question was white. Ironically, his actions served as the catalyst for changes for the better; when the excessive use of force that he delighted in using was seen on worldwide television, the revulsion people felt became a major factor in the passage of the Civil Rights Act of 1964.

As a citizen of Birmingham, Carter was present during the Bull Connor years. As an African American citizen, he felt the stings of segregation personally, but as he says, "As the years passed and the times changed, everything else changed too." The positive takeaway? "Now we can sing for anybody. It's much better." He laughs again. "I'm an old country boy. I grew up in the South, and I still love the South. I still live in Birmingham, Alabama."

Gospel grew out of hard times, slavery, and segregation. It was the music of despair, a cry for sustenance in the wilderness. At the same time, it foresaw an eventual triumph, so it was also a music of hope and praise. That double message is where its strength and soul comes from. As a deeply personal music, with songs that explored the dark night of the soul while promising victory over it, gospel offered spirit and strength and had as its mission the bringing of hope and thanks to a people who, because of the political and social issues they faced daily, sometimes had difficulty maintaining positive attitudes.

The end of segregation spread the word of gospel to a larger world. It brought new audiences and offered new opportunities that spread its message to more and different types of people. New doors opened for the Blind Boys, and others like them, and most were happy to accept the changes and the challenges—as long as they didn't have to alter their mission. The turning point for Carter came in 1982, when Lee Breuer, the founder of the avant-garde theater company Mabou Mines, and composer Bob Telson, men Carter describes as "two white boys," came to the Blind Boys with a provocative proposition.

> They came up with the idea of doing a gospel version of Oedipus at Colonus. They wanted a gospel feel, a gospel flavor, so they got the Blind Boys, the Soul Stirrers, and a choir [the Chancel Choir of the Abyssinian Baptist Church] and put it all together. We played off Broadway, and then moved it to Broadway. We toured with it and even took it to Europe. We went to Paris, Austria.

The Blind Boys stayed with the show off and on for eighteen years. "The last venture was in 2000 or so, when we went to Greece." They got to sing their music for a worldwide audience that had never been exposed to it before, and as a result gospel spread to new audiences and new markets and gained new acceptance. "That show changed everything for us," Carter said.

One of the things the show started was the conscious movement of the Blind Boys toward the wider world of Americana, further spreading the power of gospel music by recording with younger, secular musicians. Many members of the newer generations of soul, rock, and blues players began to feel their Americana résumés were not complete without recording with the Blind Boys. This was fine with the Blind Boys, who saw an opportunity to reach further into the pot and draw out another segment of the overall audience. Carter says that the group doesn't alter their style or change their music in any way when they play and record with these younger and more diverse musicians. "Those boys love gospel music, and they love the Blind Boys. When they work with us, we have the last say. They adapt their styles to ours. We love working with the younger people, and they love working with us."

He continues, "We are traditional gospel, and we always will be traditional gospel, but gospel has many faces: traditional, contemporary, solo, group, choir. We want to incorporate all of that. That's why we collaborated with the younger artists, people like Ben Harper, and Peter Gabriel, John Hammond and Van Morrison. It used to be African American music. Now it's anybody's music."

As much as he wants to incorporate all the facets of gospel into their music, though, Carter insists that the Blind Boys are and always will be solidly traditional. He sees no conflict between, say, recording with blues harp master Charlie Musselwhite, acoustic blues musician John Hammond, folk rocker Taj Mahal, or progressive rock star Peter Gabriel, for whose record label the Blind Boys have recorded. No matter whom they record with, Carter says, the core values of the Blind Boys always remain intact.

There are several reasons the Blind Boys' music fits so easily with the music of the younger generations. First, their gospel is roots music to the core, just like Americana. Younger artists recognize their own music in the Blind Boys' work. Because they perceive common denominators, the young are, as Carter says, fans of the Blind Boys and are anxious to make music with them. There is also the fact that rockers want the cachet that is associated with the Blind Boys. When people have dominated your chosen art form for close to seventy years, it is only natural that you would want to be associated with them. It's like Eric Clapton being informally adopted by Muddy Waters: the ultimate compliment.

More importantly, though, rock has its origins in gospel. Not that there is a direct line from gospel to rock. The connection is more subtle: almost every founding father of rock and roll came out of the Pentecostal church. All of the people—Johnny Cash, Jerry Lee Lewis, Elvis Presley, Buddy Holly, the Everly Brothers, the Carter Family, and Little Richard—who created rock came to the music from the church. These artists, growing up in a fundamentalist culture in the South where life, death, and religion permeated the air like fog, could not help but be influenced. In addition, these rock pioneers loved black music, and black music came from the church. Since both the church and the church music formed the very air they breathed growing up, even if they were secular musicians, gospel was in their very blood. The licks, the spirit, the rebellion, the heart and soul, and the very vocal and instrumental style of rock came from the church. When Sam Phillips uttered his famous line about how he could make a million dollars if he could find a white boy that sang black, this is what he was referring to.

In many cases—think of Buddy Holly or Jerry Lee Lewis—rock was a rebellion against Pentecostalism, a rejection of the established values that the church preached, which many of these singers found restrictive. Lewis, especially, suffered from the fear that he had lost his soul by committing his life to playing "the devil's music." Anyone who does not believe he paid a psychic price for his choice need only listen to the *Million Dollar Quartet* recordings where his pain is palpable and obvious.

RAY CHARLES STEALS GOSPEL

While white artists were openly influenced by the church and by gospel music and were able to visit the form when they wanted and ignore it when they didn't, the situation was more complicated for African American artists, who had to make a clear choice. They could sing gospel or they could sing R&B, but they could not do both. Nor could they float back and forth between the two genres. Ray Charles had his first major hit in 1954 with a song called "I Got a Woman," a remake of the old gospel song "My Jesus Is All the World to Me" but rewritten with secular lyrics. (It should be mentioned, however, that some critics claim the source of "I Got a Woman" is "I Got a Savior.") Another song, "Hallelujah I Love Her So," was originally sung in praise of God, rather than a girlfriend. As Charles says in his autobiography, *Brother Ray*, not everyone approved: "I got letters accusing me of bastardizing God's work. A big-time preacher in New York scolded me before his congregation. Many folks saw my music as sacrilegious. They said I was taking church songs and making people dance to 'em in bars and nightclubs."[3] Charles says he was not bothered by the criticism. "I had always thought that the blues and spirituals were close—close musically, close emotionally—and I was happy to hook them up."[4]

Charles was not the only musician to face such criticism. In the early days of modern gospel, people leaving the field to sing secular music were looked down upon by the church and the gospel audience. When the Reverend Al Green sang secular music, he paid a price in popularity; many members of his audience would not follow him. Sam Cooke, who came from the Soul Stirrers, was criticized by his original churchgoing audience for the rest of his life, as were Lou Rawls and the Staples Singers. In the early 1960s, Little Richard left rock to sing gospel and was welcomed by the gospel audience. When he tried to go back to rock, however, both gospel and rock audiences abandoned him. His career stayed afloat but never again reached the heights he had occupied before. All of those artists had to fight to keep their careers alive.

Regardless of the pressures the gospel audience placed on the artists and the music, the creative needs of the rockers and soul artists made sure the gospel music of groups such as the Blind Boys of Alabama blended into the cauldron of boiling folk, gospel, bluegrass, country, and rock that led to Americana music.

NOTES

1. Beth Harrington, *The History of Christianity*, DVD (London: BBC, 2010).

2. Robert Darden, *People Get Ready! A New History of Black Gospel Music* (New York: Bloomsbury Academic, 2005), 143.

3. Ray Charles and David Ritz, *Brother Ray: Ray Charles' Own Story* (New York: Dial Press, 1978), 137.

4. Ibid., 137.

9

THE BATTLE FOR THE SOUL

Of all the things Americana is, one of the biggest is that it is solidly noncommercial. In fact, it is a reaction, a protest, against the commercialization of the nation's mass-media-driven music. As we have seen, its origin lies in the fact that the swallowing of radio by corporate giants killed originality in music programming. In country radio, where Merle Haggard and George Jones were once the vocal standards, now it is Blake Shelton. Where once the Nitty Gritty Dirt Band held the medal for vocal groups, today that medal, tarnished and battered, belongs to Florida-Georgia Line. Waylon Jennings said that when he came to Nashville, every man who came to town wanted to be Hank Williams and every woman wanted to be Patsy Cline. Today, it appears that every man wants to be Kenny Chesney and every woman wants to be Taylor Swift.

It's the same for rock artists. Rock radio no longer exists as a force, and pop radio, which loses 25 percent of its audience per year, is primarily made up of female singers who have very good publicists and are too young to vote. The situation and the music are so bad that many consultants are predicting the end of "over the air" radio over the next ten years or so. Only satellite will survive, these consultants say.

Therefore, Americana is not simply the alternative to today's radio programming. Many people believe it is the antidote to the poison that is broadcast over the air daily. As Trent Wagler of the Steel Wheels put it, Americana aims to recapture American music. As such, it sees its mission as exactly the opposite of commercial radio. Where mainstream radio compresses, Americana expands. Mainstream radio vacations in its basement; Americana travels the world.

That's why Wagler is proud that the Steel Wheels, a contemporary band playing old-time music, is being tossed into the Americana category. He says that if you look at the list of names that are characterized as Americana, names like Lucinda Williams, Ryan Adams, Bob Dylan, Emmylou Harris, the Band, Steve Earle, Bobby Long, the Avett Brothers, Buddy Miller, and T-Bone Burnett, the names on that list are as different as a Cadillac is from a bicycle. Americana offers us dozens of different types of bikes, while commercial pop is the Cadillac.

Americana is an attempt to remind us of the value of bikes. As such, it's an attempt to take back the heart of pop music.

"Commercial pop is about the bottom line: Americana is not about the bottom line," Wagler says when I interviewed him.

> At its best, Americana is about the heart and soul of what a band can do. I want to be free to draw from the Band; I want to pull from the best of a Steve Earle. It's hard to get a handle on. If I say, I'm going to an Americana show, am I going to hear a string band or an electric band? As hard as it can be to pin down, I'm excited about hearing Willie Nelson, who isn't quite country enough, who plays standards, jazz, everything. Johnny Cash, who began as country and moved on from there, excites me also, especially as his music got more complex and more stripped down.
>
> I love Americana both from a player and from an audience standpoint. I love going to a festival and seeing a string band and then a telecaster master, all kinds of music.

That variety, that freedom, is what Americana offers. It is also the reason the genre is of no interest to corporate radio. It is simply too varied, too diffused, and contains far too many unpredictable elements. That is why Trent Wagler and the Steel Wheels are enthusiastic members of the Americana community; the movement they see as an attempt to take back the heart of pop music. Commercial music, he says, is about the bottom line, while Americana is about the heart and soul of what a band can do.

In Wagler's statement, we have the essential dichotomy between Americana and radio-friendly commercial music; it is hardly exaggerating to say we are in a battle for the soul of American music. In this chapter, we'll discuss the implications of the notion that music serves more than one purpose: money and art. Corporate music, or as we might call it, money music, is mass-culture music: highly formulaic and aimed at the biggest audience possible, in order to generate as much profit as it possibly can. And it cooks up plenty of profits. According to *Variety*, the highest-grossing tour of 2015 belonged to Justin Timberlake, which generated $2,115,081 per city, followed by George Strait with $1,596,184. Paul Simon and Sting touring together pulled in $1,467,002, while Elton John took $1,444,916.

Those are enviable grosses by any standard, but if you are an established act playing to the lowest common denominator, it's easier to put bodies into seats. These performers are pretty much presold, and most of them have their tour expenses advanced to them by their record companies. They spend a lot of money on promotion to secure those grosses.

The majority of Americana artists can't afford to play in that park. Most of them don't have major record labels to front the expenses required to make their names big enough to be a major draw on the tour circuit. They also have no one to pay their tour expenses. Mainly, though, they don't have the desire to play music on that level. They're in the game to make music before they make money. Americana music serves more than just a commercial purpose. As Trent Wagler said, among its goals is the saving of the soul of American music. Americana is independent music, where the artists themselves are responsible for the development of the band.

Commercial pop and Americana live in different worlds. Commercial pop takes place in stadiums, arenas, and sheds, while Americana occurs in clubs, coffeehouses, and living rooms. Commercial pop is created by technology, sometimes one note at a time by producers who often have the final say over the product. The producer, from the days when he was known as the A&R man, is the power and wields the authority. It has been that way since Ralph Peer decided which Carter Family records to release and which to shelve.

As an example of corporate control, consider that back in the 1950s, Columbia Records refused to sign any rock acts because their head of artists and repertoire (A&R), Mitch Miller, disliked the genre. He was strictly a middle-of-the-road producer, and he forced his singers to do middle-of-the-road material in a bland and nonoffensive, middle-of-the-road way. Columbia consistently lost market share while Miller waited for that scourge of good music, rock and roll, to just fade away as he was certain it would. It wasn't until the 1960s, when Clive Davis took over as the head of the label and forced Miller out, that Columbia built their stable of rock acts.

Whereas commercial pop is recorded in state-of-the-art professional studios, very often the studio credited on the liner notes of an Americana CD is a rough-and-tumble setup located in someone's living room. Americana is frequently recorded on very small budgets in these home studios. Commercial pop is heavily promoted and advertised, while many Americana performers can't even afford to hire a publicist.

Americana is music that flourishes outside the mainstream music industry and finds its audience by offering quality instead of a huge advertising and promotion budget. Essentially, commercial pop is studio and producer driven while Americana is artist driven.

Music in which the producer is the primary creative element rather than the artist is going to be radically different. Being producer driven, commercial pop is a separate thing altogether from Americana. Americana does not live in the same psychic arena as commercial pop. The amount spent on an Americana recording would not provide the craft services budget for a day in a major studio. As the singer-songwriter Melanie said, "They used to send a limo for me that took me to the studio where a dozen or so musicians and technicians were waiting and we'd spend all night working up a song and getting it down on tape. Now my son calls upstairs and says, 'Mom, I need you to come down here and record.' I go downstairs and lay down my vocal track."[1]

As noted earlier, technology has changed everything. Where once it was very expensive to set up a studio, which required lots of space for the equipment, now the prices are much more affordable and the machines have gotten smaller and portable. The folk singer Carolyn Hester says she gets calls offering recording possibilities from labels, and as a veteran of the broken promises of commercial record companies, she is dubious. Her standard answer is "What do I need you for? I'm looking at a 35 track recorder right across the room."

Of course, mass-culture pop, with its profit motive, will always exist on a much bigger scale than pop-culture Americana. Pop music takes place in stadiums and massive cavernous halls where upward of thirty thousand people can gather. When Miley Cyrus tours, it is an operation involving hundreds of people. The artist, her band, crew, and entourage hit town like an invading army, swarm over the venue, rake the place for cash, and then move on out, headed for the next city. For most Americana musicians, this sort of tour is out of the question.

According to the magazine *Ehow*, touring musicians make more money than their more stationary counterparts, with salaries in the top 50 percent in terms of wages earned. We have to figure, however, that there are three types of touring musicians: independents, who work on a per diem basis for promoters, and make an average of $31.23 per hour; their counterparts who work for arts organizations and average $33.67; and finally, those musicians hired by sporting-event and performing-arts promoters that make about $40.00 per hour. We have to understand, though, that although these are nice hourly wages, musicians spend a lot of time unemployed.

The star of the show, of course, makes a great deal more money.

A young Americana musician friend of mine, however, got an opportunity to take his band on tour backing a well-known singer. He crisscrossed the United States for four months, sleeping in the back of the van, showering in the venues, and eating fast food. He came home with a net profit for four months' work of four hundred dollars.

Indie musician Jack Conte, a member of the band Pomplamoose, wrote an article for the online magazine *Medium*, detailing how the band's expenses for a one-month tour totaled $147,802 and their income topped out at $136,000. Here are their expenses:

$26,450: production expenses
$17,589: hotels and food
$11,816: gas, airfare, parking, tolls
$5,445: insurance
$48,000: salaries and per diems
$22,000: manufacturing merchandise, publicity, supplies, shipping
$16,463: commissions for booking agency, business management,
    lawyer

Here is their income:

$97,519: income from ticket sales
$29,714: merchandise sales
$8,750: sponsorship

Pomplamoose did twenty-four shows in twenty-eight days and actually did very well; Conte says he'll remember the 1,100-person show at the

San Francisco Fillmore for the rest of his life. Still, they came home $11,819 in the hole.

These are in no way Miley Cyrus numbers.

Every Americana musician knows these stories. Most of them have lived it. In my interview with her, Maura O'Connell said, "When you're young and building an audience, you do that sort of thing. It's part of the business. That's the way the touring business is going these days. Expenses are way up, and profits are down. Club owners can't afford to give guarantees anymore, and audiences are aging out, so the clubs aren't what they used to be for a performer."

A touring heavy-metal guitarist, Max Phelps, told me, "I wouldn't do what that kid did. He went out as a backing band for somebody else's music. If I was playing my music, then maybe I'd make that sacrifice, but not to play somebody else's music."

The market is different for Americana performers. A mass artist like Katy Perry might be immune to what's happening in the marketplace for a season or two and rake in killer money. Most Americana artists, however, will never even play in that marketplace.

Most have no desire to. They create music that flourishes outside the mainstream music industry.

Where Katy Perry and Miley Cyrus play stadiums, Americana artists play small clubs, listening rooms, festivals, bars, small theaters, and more frequently, house concerts (shows in people's homes).

The house concert originated as a way to fill in empty dates between "real" gigs. When an artist was driving five hundred miles between gigs, it was a bonus to be able to stop halfway at someone's house and pick up a couple hundred dollars doing a show. Now, though, the house concert has become an established circuit.

The Austin, Texas, singer-songwriter Carrie Elkins says of house concerts,

> They are the bread and butter of our existence because so many of the clubs, like the Cactus Cafe [a music venue and bar on the campus of the University of Texas at Austin, which closed in 2010] and other venues have closed. If you want to go on tour and play every night, the house concerts can fill up the whole run. We're really lucky. It's so refreshing to go to a venue and get a home-cooked meal. The idea has also taken off in England. It's not that big but we've done a few there.

You learn so much more about a place, much more than just showing up at a club and playing.[2]

For many Americana artists, coffeehouses and house concerts represent the main stages upon which they play. Why would professional musicians, struggling to make a living, want to play venues that can hardly afford to pay them? David Morealle, an East Coast singer-songwriter who was promoting a folk-music concert series for his church, told me, "At the end of the night, performers want to take some money out of the venue, sure. But just as important they want to play for good audiences, crowds that listen and appreciate the music. Give a singer-songwriter a knowledgeable and appreciative crowd and they'll take it over a rowdy crowd that pays better."

With Americana, music is more important than the money. Trent Wagler said the Steel Wheels just wanted to play their music live; they became touring professionals almost by accident. As he once told me,

Becoming a musician can't be a simple business proposition. Even with all the changes, even with the fall of the record companies and the radio business as it is today, it's a fascinating industry. The culture still wants to hear new music as much as ever before, maybe more. The touring model is still alive. We've been together for ten years, started playing out in 2004. That was part time, though, just playing locally, wherever we could get a gig. We did that for six years. We had day jobs and never thought we'd become professionals. Live performances offer something. It's the way musicians live now.

Nobody in his right mind would go into the music business as a business. We didn't see ourselves as full time. Our band wasn't formed as a touring model. As I said, we played out from 2004 on, and after a while people would ask us, "Why haven't you recorded?" or "Why aren't these songs on CD?" So we thought that might be fun, and we made a CD.

At some point, though, Wagler says, you have to make that leap. In 2010, they quit their day jobs and became a touring band. They had some lean years early on, but he says, "we've been through the bad gigs, but we got our confidence built up and got our audience built up. Now, I'm grateful to be able to do this, to go out and play music."

And it is going out and playing their own music that attracts them, not making bad music to make good money. To them, as it is to many

Americana bands, taking the music to the people is an ongoing effort to take it back from the corporations that currently control the music industry.

NOTES

1. Melanie Safka, home page, accessed September 15, 2016, http://www .melaniemusic.com/.

2. Jim Caligiuri, "Carrie Elkins and Danny Schmidt Sell Out: Betrothed Songwriters Ready a Wild Weekend at Wyldwood," *Austin Chronicle*, June 19, 2013.

Interlude: Kris Kristofferson

When people talk about sacrificing for their art, they usually mean going through life with a limited income, not being able to afford a few basic luxuries, or having to hold down a day job in order to support their music, poetry, or painting—whatever art form they practice.

With Kris Kristofferson, the sacrifice went far beyond that. He literally sacrificed his family; when he left the military to pursue a music career, his parents disowned him and they never reconciled. Shortly after that, his wife, who had married an army captain and found herself living in a strange city with a man who supported them with odd jobs while he stayed out all night writing songs, took the kids and left.

How did all of this come about?

Kristofferson came from a military family—his father was a U.S. Air Force major general—and his grandfather was an officer in the Swedish army. It was assumed that Kristofferson would follow the family profession. He was, however, in love with the English language and saw himself as moving toward a writing career. After graduating with a degree in literature from Pomona College, Kristofferson won a Rhodes scholarship to Oxford, where he continued to study literature and began writing songs. Under the name Kris Carson, he cut a few singles for an independent British label. Those records went nowhere.

With those early songs, though, he did discover his abiding theme, which he stated in a journal in 1967, writing, "God, help me shoulder the burdens of freedom." Freedom was the desired state; it overrode everything, yet as the chorus of "Me and Bobby McGee" states, "Freedom's

Figure 9.1.   Kris Kristofferson. Creative Commons: Atkins, 2010

just another word for nothing left to lose." An artist (and an individual) must be free, but freedom carries with it a terrible price; you must sacrifice everything, and since that is the case, freedom is ultimately as much of a curse as a blessing.

The romantic nature of Kristofferson's formulation of freedom comes from his other great influence, William Blake, whose life and work Kristofferson discovered at Oxford and never abandoned, according to Mary G. Hurd, who wrote a study of Kristofferson in 2015. The nearly eighty-year-old Kristofferson is apparently still fond of quoting what he considers a key passage from Blake: "If he who is organized by the divine for spiritual communion, refuse and bury his talent in the earth, even though he should want natural bread, sorrow and desperation will pursue him throughout life, and after death, shame and confusion are faced to eternity."[1] This need for freedom regardless of the negative consequences has driven Kristofferson personally and creatively all of his life.

When he graduated from Oxford, Kristofferson was assigned by the army to teach literature at West Point. Instead, he resigned his commission, moved his family to a fifty-dollar-per-month cold-water flat in Nashville, and threw himself into becoming a songwriter, supporting himself with odd jobs, including a job sweeping the floor at Columbia Studios. Eventually he landed a deal with Maryjohn Wilkin's Buckhorn Music Publishing, cranking out songs for her while supporting himself by flying a helicopter down to the oil rigs in Louisiana. He would work a week on the oil platforms, writing songs and flying the chopper. Then he'd go back to Nashville and spend a week pitching the songs he'd written. He broke through in 1966 when Dave Dudley recorded his "Vietnam Blues."

Wilkin dropped Kristofferson as a writer, saying, "I couldn't afford to carry him any longer. He hadn't had a hit." Kristofferson managed to land an audition for Fred Foster's Combine Music publishing company. Foster had a standard policy: "If you came on wanting me to hear your songs, you'd have to sing four. Anyone can luck up and write one. Can't do it four times."

Kristofferson auditioned for Foster by first singing "To Beat the Devil." Foster recalled it: "I thought, well, that's a really interesting piece of material. . . . The next song, I thought, there's no way this guy can be this good. Third song. And I thought I must be hallucinating. . . . Nobody had ever come into my office and laid four classic songs on me. And then he did 'Jody and the Kid.'"[2]

Foster signed Kristofferson to two contracts: a songwriting deal with Combine Music and a recording deal with his label, Monument Records. Monument released the eponymous debut album in 1970. Unfortunately, the record tanked, although songs from it became hits for other singers, and Kristofferson wound up being the only man to win Song of the Year awards from both the Academy of Country Music (for Ray Price's cover of "For the Good Times") and the Country Music Association (for Johnny Cash's version of "Sunday Morning Coming Down") the same year.

By the early 1970s, it seemed that no album was released without at least one Kristofferson song on it. When Janis Joplin's posthumously released "Me and Bobby McGee" became her biggest hit, Monument retitled the Kristofferson album *Me and Bobby McGee* and reissued it. This time it became a hit.

His second album, *The Silver Tongued Devil and I* came out in 1971 and climbed the charts. Kristofferson finally had the success he'd sacrificed so much for. Ironically, his success came at the price of his precious freedom. He found himself almost enslaved by it; all his time was devoted to touring and recording—he was committed to an album a year for ten years for Monument, and those albums needed to be promoted. He had also proved attractive to the movies, and his second career as an actor ate into his writing time and weakened his music. In the tradition of his idols, Hank Williams Sr. and Johnny Cash, he began to rely on drugs and alcohol to keep up with the pressures, and also like them, he became an alcoholic and a substance abuser.

Between his touring, his acting, and his drinking (which was his prime method for dealing with the tensions and stresses the touring and acting caused), Kristofferson had trouble coming up with enough good songs to fill out his album-a-year contract. We must also consider that by now his life experiences changed so that he was no longer writing the type of songs that had made his reputation. Always leaning toward the left, he began exploring political subjects in his lyrics, which led to Nashville giving him the cold shoulder because the songs were less commercial than his early classics.

It should be noted that although he worked in Nashville, Kristofferson was never a country singer. In fact he never considered himself a singer at all; he sees himself as a writer. In terms of vocal style, he was naturally more of a folkie singer-songwriter, and his records sold more to the rock and pop market than to country. He chose Nashville and country music in which to make his mark because of his self-identification as a writer. If you intended to write songs for other artists to record, Nashville was where you went and the country field was what you tried to break into. Rock and pop and folk performers were, by this time, writing their own songs. Only in country music was the professional songwriter still flourishing. And the industry was making a lot of money off of other people covering Kristofferson's songs.

He was still making a lot of money for the country music industry, but when that money dried up, they dropped him. His independent nature, his insistence on freedom and to go his own way, cost him. To the executives at the labels, his albums were collections of demos to be spread out among talent that could take them to the tops of the charts. After his tenth and last Monument Records album, it was eight years before Kristofferson released another solo album. His songs no longer charted; the industry lost interest. His songwriting career was in trouble. It was at this point that his film career tanked also. Although he got a boost from costarring with Barbra Streisand in the remake of *A Star Is Born*, Kristofferson made some odd choices after that. He starred in *The Sailor Who Fell from Grace with the Sea*, an Americanization of a Japanese novel that simply did not cross cultures well and left the few people who saw it dumbfounded. Then he took on *Heaven's Gate*, a five-hour-long western that became famous only for bankrupting its studio, going so far over budget that it drove United Artists out of business, since it was considered unreleasable. In an effort to recoup some of its vast cost overruns, the film was cut to two hours and given a run through the theaters. At that length *Heaven's Gate* made no sense at all, and it disappeared quickly, leaving behind it a stench that infected everyone associated with it, Kristofferson included. Kristofferson was a good actor. His work in *Cisco Pike, Alice Doesn't Live Here Anymore*, and *Pat Garrett and Billy the Kid* testify to that. But for every *Cisco Pike*, there was a *Vigilante Force*. Film offers dried up, and for three years, he could not get a movie deal. He had lost two careers simultaneously.

For Kristofferson, however, the onrush of failure simply made him able to find his freedom once more. His career decline was simply more of the burden of freedom. As far as he was concerned, freedom was an essential condition; his view of the concept was romanticized, coming as it did from William Blake: freedom involved suffering and sacrifice. One did not gain freedom as much as one lost everything else and wound up with it, like a consolation prize. Only freedom, however, allowed creativity into a life; to write, you had to be free, and to be free, you had to sacrifice all of the things that normal people hold dear, such as stability, comfort, family, and career.

He joined with other legendary artists whose careers had faded— Willie Nelson, Waylon Jennings, and Johnny Cash—to form the Highwaymen. For ten years, from 1985 to 1995, the Highwaymen toured and recorded together. Then, Kristofferson returned to a renewed solo career.

Kristofferson always occupied the state that Al Moss said characterized Americana artists; he was wildly independent, determined to go his own way, regardless of the cost. Did the country music industry refuse to accept the protest songs about the American government's nation building and tendency to invade Middle Eastern nations? Too bad. That was what was on Kristofferson's mind, so that was what he had to write and sing. He had no choice; that was where the burden of freedom led him.

Kristofferson's commitment to freedom and his need to follow his gifts wherever they led were the factors that make him a prime Americana artist. Determined to go his own way, to make the music he hears instead of the music the industry hears, and willing to sacrifice his popularity in order to play by his own rules means that if his music is to be categorized, it must be placed in a category open enough to support him, instead of one tight enough to confine him.

Americana is that nurturing category.

NOTES

1. Mary G. Hurd, *Kris Kristofferson: Country Highwayman* (Lanham, MD: Rowman & Littlefield, 2015), 15.

2. Stephen Miller, *Kristofferson: The Wild American* (New York: Omnibus, 2010).

10

AS DUKE ELLINGTON SAID, THERE'S ONLY TWO TYPES OF MUSIC: GOOD AND BAD

The writer Raymond Federman once distinguished between two types of books: dead and live. A dead book was one that came out in a flurry of hype, with a huge print run, sold a whole bunch of copies in a hurry, and when its commercial run was over, disappeared and was never thought of again. The best-seller list is loaded with dead books. Except for the very best ones, most genre books are dead. They have about a six-week shelf life and are gone. Are they entertaining? Absolutely. Some of them would, in fact, become classics if they were treated differently in the marketplace. Others, though, perhaps most, are content to entertain in the way a television sitcom entertains: on a lightweight level, satisfied to bring a grin to your face every once in a while. James Patterson writes (or more often these days supervises the writing of) dead books. They bring fun to his fans, but when you finish one you find it has not stuck in your mind; you forget details immediately, and after a short period of time, all memory of the contents of the book are gone from your memory.

According to Federman,

> The world is far more complex, far more chaotic, far more confusing, far more inaccessible than the false images we are offered daily. And the experiences that create the world for us are far more complex, chaotic, confused and confusing than THEY think. By THEY, I mean those who falsify OUR WORLD for us. OUR WORLD—the one we as writers

deal with every day—is a static-filled screen, a fuzzy image agitated by emotions a hundred times more voluptuous, but also a hundred times more painful than those THEY are trying to make us feel.

THEY are the purveyors of dead books and what THEY do is overlook the complexity of our experience, our world; THEY oversimplify our lives and our reality, purveying for us an orderly universe that unfolds simply and is incapable of taking us by surprise. The dead book says that an event violates the order of the universe and the characters of the book then put things back in their proper order, so that everything is ultimately safe.[1]

A live book not only carries a different set of messages; it exists in a different commercial world. Typically, it is published with much less fanfare, so that it has a much smaller launch. It can be hard to find; Wal-Mart and Barnes and Noble are not interested in live books because, since they usually have little or no promotion budget and since their publishers cannot offer bigger discounts for larger sales, few people other than the fans of the artists have ever heard of them. Live books, then, do not move massive quantities of copies quickly. A live book, though, since it offers something of value to its readers, does not die at the end of the season. It might only sell a few copies per year, but it continues to sell for years and years, building an audience one reader at a time for years, even decades.

The Great Gatsby was never a best seller. A vast commercial disappointment when it was issued, its reception by the public was so poor that it caused F. Scott Fitzgerald to vow never again to write a book less than forty thousand words long. In fact, the poor reception was one of the factors that spiraled Fitzgerald into the decline that he never recovered from. The book, however, sold like a live book: a few copies the year it was published, a few more the next year, growing its readership slowly over time and gathering steam as the decades went by. Today, almost one hundred years later, *Gatsby* is recognized as a classic of American literature and continues to be read by a discerning and receptive audience.

It lives, while all the best-selling books of 1925 are long forgotten. *The Great Gatsby* is alive; they are dead.

WHAT APPLIES TO BOOKS APPLIES TO MUSIC

The point here, obviously, is that the music heard on corporate radio is mostly dead, while Americana is alive. While what remains of the music industry is trying to pull off the mass-culture trick of predicting what its audience wants by searching for the song of the summer, the Americana artists are using the pop-culture model: presenting an original vision, dressing it in a comfortable suit, and offering it to people who feel a need for it.

The problem for the Americana writer is to present the truth to the audience, to be authentic. If we don't, according to Federman, we wind up as a part of the problem:

> How to react? How to reply? How to write today the world in which we live and write? How are we to symbolize differently and more truly (I did not say, more realistically, but more truly) our experience of the world? It will most certainly not be in the mode of an easy, facile, positive literature written in an industrial high-tech prose, it will not be a literature which has sold out to the Spectacle whose rich territory it wants to enter by any means, by compromise or by prostitution, but especially through simplistic cynicism, or with an ostentatious kitsch. This pseudo-literature, which is becoming more and more drab, more and more banal and predictable, more and more insignificant, functions beyond the pale of our anguish and desire.
>
> When literature ceases to understand the world and accepts the crisis of representation in which it functions, it becomes mere entertainment, it becomes part of the Spectacle.[2]

The "Spectacle" is the land of dead music, and if Americana does not refuse a bus ticket to that land, it becomes a part of the existential emptiness that dead music is paved with.

Where dead music finds its themes in common-denominator topics, such as first love, teen life, fashion, the thrill of kissing a girl, or taking your pickup truck down to the river and getting drunk, the themes of live songs are internal; they grow out of the artist's obsessions, obsessions that are as often as not literary. Lucinda Williams used to play shows with her father, the great southern poet Miller Williams. He would read his work and then she would play songs inspired by them, a practice that Billy Collins and Aimee Mann have continued.

Another band finding their inspiration in books is Delta Rae, whose work is steeped in southern literature. "I learned from southern writers," says vocalist and guitarist Ian Hölljes in an interview with me.

> Pat Conroy is a favorite, the early William Styron, some of Faulkner. That combination led to southern tradition. It's a tradition of a kind of beautiful, natural imagery—that what you are is tradition, holding on to a southern tradition.
>
> I always read southern writers. I was born in Durham, moved to Nashville when I was three or so, then moved to California. I never felt at home in California. Then I came back to Durham to go to college. I think I was always looking for some sense of home.
>
> Delta Rae has been criticized for mythologizing the south, but the mythology is its biggest beauty. It's the history and the mystery of the places where we grew up. The literature of the south, myth-loaded and folkloric, always spoke to me.

Because dead music tries to capture the biggest possible buying audience as quickly as it can, it does not spend much time touring the neighborhoods of complexity and controversy, two communities in which Americana lives. Delta Rae, for example, has a strong spiritual streak in their songs, an element you're not going to hear much of on a corporate channel except at Christmas.

Hölljes explains that the band actively seeks the spiritual in their songs and works to locate it.

> We seek the spiritual, but it's also a reflection of my core beliefs. I'm not a religious person; neither are most of the members of the band, but we are spiritual. I think the absence of religion can have an important way of helping us connect with a higher power. Music fills the void in some ways. Music and art. There are complicated feelings there. Whether the spiritual comes from the deep south is an open question. Certainly the southern music and literature reflects a spiritual search.

Dead music has to fit in its coffin, while live music is free to wander where it will. One reason for this freedom is that most Americana is issued on small, independent record labels, which specialize in the genre and understand the music, its makers, and its audience. A large percentage of the labels are owned by the artists who record for them or by other artists; new technology, as we have seen, allows musicians to make their own records and distribute them themselves. Most Americana records, though, are sold directly to the audience by artists at their shows. David Roth, a well-known singer-songwriter and a major-label veteran now recording for a tiny midwestern label, told me, "It's like being on my own label. The only difference is I buy the CDs from them, instead of from the manufacturer. All the sales still come from my shows."

This is not to say that dead music is bad, and live is good. As is the case whenever driven people are given the keys to the studios, some Americana artists who are not quite ready to share their work with the world yet are making records. And certainly, many makers of dead music are coming up with entertaining material, so it isn't a case of good and bad; it's simply a case of different.

The question of quality brings to mind Sturgeon's law. Once, the science fiction writer Theodore Sturgeon was being interviewed by an unsympathetic reporter, who asked, "Tell me, Mr. Sturgeon, why is it that 95 percent of all science fiction is pure crap." Sturgeon answered, "Because 95 percent of everything is pure crap."

Maybe the percentages can be disputed, but the statement is true. Two factors have to be considered, though: one, we need the 95 percent in order to create the 5 percent. In the 1960s, for example, Jimi Hendrix exploded onto the scene, but even at his peak, the made-for-TV group, the Partridge Family, outsold him five to one. The Partridge Family, though, belonged to the 95 percent, and today their work is forgotten. They're remembered only as the subjects of a bad sitcom that was developed as a family-friendly version of *The Monkees*. Hendrix, on the other hand, represents the 5 percent; he is still a respected artist, and like *The Great Gatsby*, his work still sells.

Live records, though they might not create a fire on the sales chart, have one more very valuable aspect to them. Since they last forever, they help their artists last forever also. In 2015, Mary Chapin Carpenter rerecorded a dozen of her best songs with composer Vince Mendoza, doing new and orchestral arrangements that have their origins in movie music. Mendoza's arrangements and Carpenter's vocals give the music a cinematic quality that adds up to a new approach and a new interpretation of the songs. The album is as different from her more mainstream country albums as eggplant is from cheesecake. She says that although it has not sold as many copies as her more mainstream albums, the album, *Songs from the Movies*, has no shelf life. "For the rest of my life," she told me, "I can go somewhere and perform that album."

That is a live album.

While corporate radio chases after dead music, Americana creates music that is alive.

NOTES

1. Raymond Federman, "The Real Begins Where the Spectacle Ends," Raymond Federman, 1996, http://www.federman.com/.

2. Ibid.

11

SPEAKING THE TRUTH TO THOSE WHO HAVE EARS TO LISTEN

As we have seen, the standard definition of Americana is built on its difference from mass-culture pop. It reflects the old Buddhist idea that we can only know things by comparing them to their opposites. To know joy we must have known sadness. Otherwise we will not know that it is joy we're feeling. According to this theory, it is not possible to know courage without a basic knowledge of fear, compassion without anger, or good health without illness. It is a linear system, like Newtonian physics.

The truth, Buddhists say, is more quantum based. Buddha claims that ultimately all things are unified, that all opposites live within us at once. We can't see the unity, however, and so we categorize things in terms of their opposites in order to gain a clearer perception of them, even though we know what we see is an illusion, a term that when the Buddhists use it means a partial truth.

What does the necessity to divide have to do with Americana music?

Being veterans of commercial radio, Rob Bleetstein and Jon Grimson wrote a radiocentric definition of Americana that was designed to satisfy the Grammy people, to set the form apart from commercial pop. That is why the two defined the form in terms of the instruments used, the blend of forms, and the fact that it is roots music.

Their definition is fine for its purpose but does not consider the themes of the songs, which are at one and the same time wide ranging and closely textured. The standard themes—loves won and lost, the search and the outcome, and all of the archetypal ideas—are there, of course, but other themes rooted in the American experience are prevalent. We have seen how Americana taps into this nation's history, its past—both real and mythologized—and into the elements that turned the United States into the nation we have become. But nostalgia is not its major contribution.

When the Band sings about the Civil War, for example, they do not, like the Cumberland Three before them, sing about battles fought, acts of heroism and sacrifice, or any of the standard ideas. Instead, they see the war from the point of view of an ordinary working man, Virgil Caine, who loses his job and scuffles through, trying to make the best of it, as the war rages around him.

As Jim Lauderdale would say, "Now, that's Americana!"[1]

Americana deals in truth. Its lyrics and performance aim to convey genuine emotions. Artists explore and reveal their actual feelings in order to create those same feelings in the listeners. This stance is in contrast to commercial mainstream pop that primarily traffics in reinforcing what the audience already feels. In this genre, artists aim to find the universal in the personal, operating from the assumption that what is true to their experience and is authentic will be true and authentic to everyone; the specifics might be different, but the overall idea will be the same. Americana, then, takes its audience on a journey, while mainstream pop applauds the place the listeners already occupied.

Commercial pop can be clever, funny, ironic, and easy to listen to. What it can very rarely be is deep and true.

To show how Americana deals in deeper issues, issues that are important to the life of the United States, we will take a look at the work of two of the most American of songwriters, both pioneers of Americana.

Americana is a writer's medium; as an audience, we come to it for its meaningful lyrics: the lyrics speak to us. We want to be enlightened as well as entertained. Americana offers us many fine songwriters who take many approaches to the truth. Some stick to an exploration of personal issues; they stay away from the archetypal ideas of social criticism that make the personal universal.

Joe South and John Stewart, though, lived in that larger territory. They wrote about the eternal verities, yes, but they also wrote about the nation, its history, its mythology, and its psychic place in the lives of all of us who occupied it. They wrote to communicate a personal vision that they felt existed, unseen, within all of us.

Joe South always said he played music because he could not communicate any other way. He had a headful of ideas and observations that he needed to share, and since he could not do it directly, he chose the art of songwriting as his medium. He was born in Atlanta in 1940, so he grew up in the middle of the musical maelstrom that was southern music at that time. As his later session work for artists as diverse as Wilson Pickett, Aretha Franklin, Bob Dylan, Gene Vincent, and Simon and Garfunkel showed, the musical environment he grew up in equipped him to play in any genre.

He fell in love with music early in his life, preferring country at first but then branching out to all categories. When he was eleven, his father, an amateur guitarist and mandolin player, gave him a guitar, and less than a year later, South had his own radio show. Shortly after that he moved into local television, joining a country show hosted by Bill Lowery, who became his mentor.

Lowery, one of the most important men in southern music, operated publishing companies and maintained a recording studio. In 1958, Lowery formed a record label, NRC Records, as part of his effort to control all aspects of the record business; he also operated, in addition to the aforementioned studio, a pressing plant and a distribution company.

He hired South, not quite out of high school, as staff guitarist. The remainder of the house band was made up of local Atlanta musicians Jerry Reed, Rick Carty, Joe's brother Tommy South, and Ray Stevens. South played on almost every record to come out of NRC. The poet Bill Morgan, who as a high school student was a member of a band that recorded for NRC, remembers Joe South playing on his records and told me about it in a conversation: "Joe was a very private man, always uncomfortable around lots of people. When he played on our songs, he would sit by himself in the far corner of the studio, surrounded by his equipment, so you could hardly see him over there. With his head down, eyes on the neck of his guitar, he'd play his parts while crying out softly every once in a while, 'huh.'" Here is Morgan's description of a recording session at NRC that South played on. It shows the amount of control producers had over the recording process back then:

> First thing I realized today: he was only six months older than I!
> We arrived at our recording session with our own band—two guitars and a piano—but Lowery wasn't pleased with the sound, so he sent in first Jerry Reed, to "see if you can liven it up." He did, and our

lead guitarist [Nathan Hamilton] got the message and packed up. Shortly after, Lowery brought in his own pianist and drummer. Last to join, as I recall, was Joe, who displaced the last man standing of our band: Von Lambert, guitarist and writer of Divided Heart.

He was young, friendly, and not showy at all. I think I remember his playing posture as rather bent—bent over the guitar with his head down—it looked as if he was cradling the guitar. That was very unlike Jerry Reed's address to the instrument: his head was thrown back and his fingers were flying, as I remember.

I had no idea Joe was a singer as well until he started putting out singles a few years on.

"Don't It Make You Want to Go Home" brought back lots of memories. I always thought I could see the real place in my own memory when I heard "There's a drag-strip down by the riverside / where my grandma's cows used to graze."

I'm pretty sure Lowery was disappointed with the record (NRC 502)—both the sound and the sales—since it dropped out of sight quickly and since he never called us back to complete the contract for a second pair of songs.

It was at NRC that South met other up-and-coming Atlanta musicians, including Freddy Weller, Tommy Roe, and Billy Joe Royal. Together, these musicians played shows all over Atlanta and the Southeast.

He was also writing songs now and, with Lowery as his publisher, began selling them to other singers. In 1959, Gene Vincent recorded two of them, "I Might Have Known" and "Gone Gone Gone." By that time, Lowery, who had always been in awe of South's talent, was recording him as a solo artist. Since he was still a kid, South had not yet discovered his own vision, so he followed Lowery's direction and, looking for hit singles, churned out some pretty good, well-crafted rockabilly that really had no point of view. Listening to the records, you get the feeling that he's searching for not his voice but a hit.

Ironically, he got a hit with his first released single, one of his worst songs, "The Purple People Eater Meets the Witch Doctor," a novelty tune that aimed to cash in on the alien motif that was prominent in pop music at the time. It hit number forty-seven on the charts. Its follow-up, though, a much better straight-ahead rocker called "I'm Snowed," went nowhere, as did the half a dozen singles that came after that. Soon South found himself relying on session work again, a trade he followed until the mid-1960s. He branched out by producing other artists, scoring hits with the

Tams and Billy Joe Royal, among others, but in an interview with Jan Donkers, he said that he found producing others frustrating. "My own ego was crying out," he said. "But I had confidence problems."[2]

Like most session musicians, he went to Nashville where he played on the albums of dozens of major artists, such as Simon and Garfunkel—that's his finger-picking guitar all over the *Sounds of Silence* album—and Bob Dylan's *Blonde on Blonde*; he plays lead guitar on "Sad Eyed Lady of the Lowlands" and does the finger-picking motif on "Just Like a Woman." He was also a regular at Muscle Shoals Studios, where some of the finest rhythm-and-blues records of the 1960s and 1970s were made. He plays the unforgettable opening guitar riff on Aretha Franklin's "Chain of Fools," for example.

Still, even though he was a successful session musician, South longed to make his own records and to make them right. It was Dylan who showed him what he was going to have to do to become the solo artist he wanted to be. South told Dylan about his difficulties getting good records made. Dylan replied that Joe was going to have to quit trying to please producers and audiences. He had to just make the music he wanted to make with no thought about anything but the music. But in order to make his own records, Dylan emphasized, he would have to take total control of the entire process.

South went back to Atlanta and told Bill Lowery what he wanted to do; Lowery negotiated him a contract with Capitol Records. Now that he had decided to take control, he stopped writing for a market, choosing to write for his soul instead. His first Capitol album, *Introspect*, was not a hit, peaking at number 117 on the chart, but it did contain "Games People Play," which reached number 12 and has gone on to become a standard, after winning two Grammies in 1969. Ironically, by the time the single became a hit, Capitol had already given up on *Introspect* and had pulped the album. *Pulp* refers to a process where the unsold and returned albums were literally melted down so that the vinyl could be used again to make other albums. Now, with an award-nominated hit on their hands, Capitol found itself in a bind, so the company hurriedly put out a revised version of the LP retitled *Games People Play*.

South's first major hit was an attack on organized religion, superficial people, the act of lying, and the idea of putting yourself first at the expense of everyone else, making it, for the time, a most unusual song. It won two Grammy Awards: one for Best Contemporary Song and another for Song of the Year. Certainly the lyrics had something to do with the Grammy wins, but the arrangement of the song probably put it over: in addition to standard rock instruments, South used a lush and swelling string section, brass, an organ, and an electric sitar in the mix. In other words, "Games People Play" sounded like nothing else on the radio at the time. Finally, Joe South was making his own music.

But was anyone listening?

He had several minor hits but never again hit the peaks that "Games People Play" reached. "Birds of a Feather," a narrative about an alienated couple, two outsiders, who were able to handle their lack of a place in society because they had each other, reached number ninety-six on the charts, while "Don't It Make You Want to Go Home," a song about the inevitability of rapid, uncontrollable change, went to number forty-seven. "Walk a Mile in My Shoes," a plea for the better treatment of and acceptance of minorities, put him back in the game by reaching number twelve domestically and number two in Canada. It was his last commercial hurrah, though. He kept releasing fine, challenging, and original music, but mainstream success had left him behind.

Ironically enough, though, while South could no longer chart with his music, other artists could. Billy Joe Royal hit the upper reaches of the *Billboard* top one hundred with four of South's songs in a row, on records produced by South. Paul Revere and the Raiders had a huge hit with "Birds of a Feather," while Brook Benton covered "Don't It Make You Want to Go Home." Elvis Presley got hold of "Walk a Mile in My Shoes" and wouldn't let it go. South's biggest cover, though, came from country singer Lynn Anderson, whose version of "I Never Promised You a Rose Garden" was a hit in sixteen countries and became her signature song.

Life on the road took its toll on South, and some of his songs, such as "Redneck," an attack on the boorish behavior that some young southern men exhibited, and "I'm a Star," which criticized the way show business could destroy your identity, became cynical, with a bitter edge. The songs lost the compassionate touch that had characterized his earlier work. He soldiered on, however, until his brother Tommy, who was the drummer in his band and on his producing projects, killed himself. Unable to continue without his brother at his side, South left the music business, living in Maui in seclusion for years. In the 1990s, he tried a halfhearted comeback, but the fire was gone. After that, he returned to Atlanta, where he died at his home on September 5, 2012. He was seventy-two.

His contributions to Americana were many. For one, consider the lyrical content of his songs. Probably influenced by his friend Bob Dylan, his songs had a strong philosophical content and a clever use of social criticism. "Mirror of Your Mind" questions the idea of abandoning your individuality by becoming a part of a group that shares a philosophy, that thinks it's found the way. South says that if you look and listen closely, the difference between what they are and what they say they are becomes apparent.

"Games People Play" is a powerful attack on hypocrisy that resonated so strongly it swept the Grammies when it was released. In it, South confronts people who play games and don't mean what they say, covering everything from personal relationships to guru cultures, academics in ivory towers, and organized religion. Even though the song protests strongly, it is a compassionate attempt to understand and sympathize with the innocent people who are the victims of the hypocrites he skewers. "These Are Not My People" takes on self-destructive behavior, speaking to a woman who has found herself all alone and abandoned by friends and family and by her God because she bought into the lies. The speaker in the song is a friend or lover who has had enough and who feels he has no choice but to abandon her also.

But South's songs were more than the message contained in the lyrics. Having grown up on the wide range of music available on southern radio, where it was not at all unusual for country, rock, soul, and gospel to be played on the same show, South's songs reflected all of these genres, dressing them in original and unusual arrangements that blended string sections and electric guitars, and planting imaginative hooks and clever call-and-response patterns within them. One reason they were not heard much on commercial radio is because, after the fall of free-form FM, there was no place for them.

The songs were also very personal, dealing in themes that were important to South, exploring questions that plagued his mind. His genius resided in the fact that he could interest an international cult audience in the things that interested him. His influence spread to other songwriters who followed.

One of those influenced by Joe South was John Stewart. Stewart, who was reluctant to record other people's material—he described that practice as akin to "wearing another man's clothes"[3] —made an exception for

South and covered "Don't It Make You Want to Go Home" on his *Darwin's Army* album.

John Stewart was born in Southern California and fell in love with music early. He bought a ukulele and learned the songs of some of his favorite musicians—Tex Ritter was an early favorite. But then he heard Elvis and Buddy Holly. Picking up an electric rig, he formed a rock band, Johnny Stewart and the Furies, who toured the college circuit in Southern California and released a single called "Rockin' Anna" on a local label. It became a regional hit.

The rock band lasted until he heard the Kingston Trio. The trio played a popularized version of folk music and, in 1958, changed American music when they released "Tom Dooley," which went to number one and began the folk revival of the 1960s. Stewart told English writer Spencer Leigh, "I heard these great songs that you could play with a guitar and no amp. The songs were about history and, as I love history, were tailor-made for me."[4]

Dumping his electric rig, Stewart began playing acoustic guitar and learned the five-string banjo. Along with Gil Robbins and John Montgomery, he formed the Cumberland Three, a Kingston Trio–like act that recorded three albums for Roulette Records. Stewart indulged his passion for history by making two albums of Civil War songs, one of songs sung by the North, the other by the South. The third album was a collection of folk material and Stewart folk-themed originals.

While with the Cumberland Three, Stewart began selling songs to the Kingston Trio. "I played some stuff in their dressing room and they did 'Molly Dee,'" he told Leigh. "They put it on their album *Here We Go Again!* and my first royalty was for more than my dad made in a year. That set my course."

In 1961, after ten albums and three years of solid touring, founding member Dave Guard left the trio, and Stewart was chosen to replace him. Dave Guard had been very serious, cerebral, and as time went by, driven by a desire to delve deeper into the folk music of the world. Nick Reynolds and Bob Shane, however, felt the trio was on the right track, as evidenced by four albums in the top ten simultaneously, and saw no compelling reason to change. The classic entertainment versus art argument had been wearing all of them down, and it was only solved by Guard's leaving the band. By the time Guard quit, all of the joy had gone out of the band; Reynolds, Shane, and Guard had spent a solid two years fighting over two opposing visions for the band. The addition of Stewart meant that entertainment had triumphed. In fact, Nick Reynolds declared that Stewart's arrival made the trio fun again.[5]

Over the next six years, the Stewart trio would record a dozen albums and a dozen or so hit singles. They would finally break up for good in 1967. By that time, the impulse to hang it up was mutual. They all felt the Kingston Trio had gone as far as it could go; on the farewell concert album, John mentions a possible future playing lounges at Holiday Inns and suggests it is time to pack it in. Their farewell concert at the Hungry I shows Stewart more than ready to leave. While still committed to the trio's music, he performs as if everything the trio had to say has been said several times and now it is time to move on to other challenges.

In his time with the trio, however, he did take the band in a new direction, expanding their repertoire with his original tunes and bringing in work by Tom Paxton, the Dillards, Mason Williams, Rod McKuen, Ian and Sylvia, Eric Andersen, and Bob Dylan. By the time the trio disbanded, though, the folk group idea was dead, killed by the emergence of the Beatles and the other British Invasion bands, such as the Rolling Stones, the Animals, Van Morrison and Them, and the Kinks. Music was changing faster than the Kingston Trio had changed it.

When Tom Rush's *Circle Game* album, containing the first recordings of songs by Joni Mitchell, James Taylor, and Jackson Browne, initiated the singer-songwriter craze, Stewart, who had been watching its emergence, was ready to join in. Forming a duo with Buffy Ford, whom he later married, Stewart recorded *Signals through the Glass*, a collection of history-themed originals that included a song about Lincoln's body being taken back home by train after his assassination, songs about life in rural America, and salutes to archetypal American figures. "Mucky Trucky River" comments on the Vietnam War, antiwar movement, and the hypocrisy of the people who "hold the Hope" and simply "sit and smoke their dope" and "talk of where it's at."

In an interview with me, Buffy Ford calls this the album that began Americana, and she has a point. It is a hard record to categorize, better described by what it is not than what it is. It is not rock or folk, or pop or soul. In fact, it is a complete blend of all of these, mashing up elements of all of our varied genres. It is a totally American album, and if it did not start the Americana movement, Stewart's next one did. Stewart followed *Signals through the Glass* with his first solo album, *California Blood-*

lines, which was named by *Rolling Stone* magazine as one of the two hundred best albums ever made. It contained the best of his history songs, "Mother Country," in which he sings about an old woman remembering the Johnstown Flood and the boys who became men fighting back the waters, men who not only did what was expected of them but also did it "pretty up and walkin' good." The second verse tells the story of E. A. Stuart, an old horse rancher who is going blind and who wants to ride his best horse, the Old Campaigner, one more time while he still can. The song celebrates the heroism of ordinary people, a favorite theme of Stewart's. A tribute to childhood, "The Pirates of Stone County Road" is also included—Stewart is nothing if not nostalgic for a simpler life. The title song discusses both love and a sense of place; it is a song that Stewart later said was about the phenomenon revealed in the statistic that most Americans marry people who grew up within five miles of them. "Some Lonesome Picker" is about the way the power of a particular song can bring comfort to people who encounter it long after it was written and originally recorded. In all, a spiritual sense hangs over the album. *California Bloodlines* matches the Americana Association's definition, but it also stands far out in front of American pop. It is original, simple in its structure, and complex in its ideas, an album that now, close to fifty years later, still brings new satisfaction and fresh insights when you listen to it.

To my mind, if we have to name a single album that started the movement, it would be *California Bloodlines*, if only because it was released before the Dirt Band's "Uncle Charlie and His Dog Teddy." As we will see later in the book, however, crediting a single album might be oversimplifying a complicated question.

If *California Bloodlines* was not called the album that started Americana, it's only because there was no perceived need for a genre called Americana in 1969, the year of its release. Unusual, boundary-crossing music could still be played on a number of free-form FM radio stations, the ones that billed themselves as underground. As long as the music was played, no one was interested in creating new genres.

Even though Stewart's solo albums never sold as well as his Kingston Trio records and he was relegated to cult status, he kept on, happy to be able to reach people with his music. And he did reach people. Buffy Ford remembers people telling him at concerts that his music had saved their lives. "His songs helped people get through," she said. "One time, we went to Scotland and played a club there. The whole audience knew the songs. They sang along with us, every song, every note. They were moved by the songs and we were moved by their response."

Like South, Stewart was not comfortable around lots of people. "John became a caveman," Ford says. "He dropped out. He was not a social guy. He was content, never lonely, though he was alone a lot. We lived in Malibu and were hanging out with people like Carole King and James Taylor when one night John said, 'I need solitude,' and we went home. He stayed there, fully content within himself."

Also like South, Stewart had a strong ambivalence toward the music industry. "He didn't care about being a celebrity. Said it was no big deal," Ford says. "He always said the work was important, not the guy that did the work." He did the show business things that were designed to sell records. He went on an all-music edition of *Hollywood Squares*; in a YouTube clip he looks very uncomfortable performing on the television show *Playboy after Dark*. "He didn't mind doing those things," Ford says. "He didn't love it, but he knew it was necessary."

His only hit single, "Gold," is about record companies who are out there "turning music into gold." He didn't particularly like the song; he said the record company demanded it of him.

> I did "Gold" for the money. It was the biggest hit I ever had, and it means nothing to me. It was just one of those things the record company wanted, and this time it worked. The song went to number five, and the album hit number four. I was in *People Magazine*, and I was doing interviews and I just cried. It meant nothing to me, nothing. I was doing these interviews and touring. And I was crying. What a great lesson I learned from that. Never go for the money.
>
> I toured with [the band] Chicago for three weeks and made eighty thousand dollars. Then I met with the record company, and I said, "What now?" and they said, "Now you do it again."[6]

But Stewart chose not to do it again. Instead, he would, again like South, write and sing meaningful music. His was music that, like most Americana, might not have been religious but had a strong spiritual foundation to it. He had visions, prophetic dreams, received communication in his dreams, and, again according to Buffy Ford, "traveled with real spirits." The guru Sri Swami Satchidananda was a major inspiration. "Every morning when we lived in Malibu, we'd read passages from *The Golden*

Present to each other," Stewart's widow, Buffy Ford, said in a series of interviews.

> And while we were in Malibu, our son was eight years old, and he was hanging out with celebrity kids and they were getting into some stuff. One day he came home and told us about his friend who had a gun under his bed, and I said, "That's it. We're out of here." So we moved to Virginia, where the Swami's ashram was, and enrolled our son in the Swami's school. We didn't live in the ashram but lived right down the road from it in our own place. We stayed there six years.

Buffy Ford remembers those years as a pleasant retreat from show business, the sort of retreat that always reinvigorated her husband's creative energies.

The members of Delta Rae also see Americana as spiritual music. "We seek the spiritual in the music but it's also a reflection of my core beliefs," says Ian Hölljes when I interviewed him. "I'm not a religious person. Neither are most of the members of the band, but we are spiritual, and that comes through in the music. I think the absence of religion can have an important way of helping us connect with a higher power."

"Music fills the void in some way. Music and art." Hölljes hesitates for a moment and then adds, "There are complicated feelings there. Whether the spiritual comes from the Deep South is an open question. Southern religion has always been complicated. We're in the Bible Belt here, and the religion is intense. It's changing, but it's still strong. So it might be direct, might be indirect, but certainly the southern music and literature reflects a spiritual search."

Stewart, born in Kentucky but raised in Southern California, didn't connect his spirituality to being raised in the Bible Belt. But it was definitely a part of his makeup and in his work. In fact, even as he used the secular tools of our time for inspiration, his entire approach to songwriting was spiritual. "John wrote with distractions," Buffy Ford declares. "Always had the TV on or some media going. He said it freed his mind. He was always creating, always writing. If he wasn't writing, he was painting or drawing."

His best songs were written while watching television. It was boring enough to let your mind wander, he believed. He'd get ideas from the History Channel. He also went to other media, finding a lot of his creative impulses in the newspaper. "Mother Country" began as a newspaper story. He dreamed a lot about songs. "Some Kind of Love," said Ford, came to him complete, in a dream. He was always writing down quotes that wound up in songs. Buffy Ford still has dozens of notebooks full of his quotes.

His mantra boiled down to a few aphorisms:

Never let anything interfere with an idea.
Don't wait. If you don't write it, somebody else will.
Never get tricky. That's when you lose it.
Your best writing partner is silence.

His favorite writers were Leonard Cohen, Shakespeare, and Rosanne Cash. He loved Joe South. He was also influenced by Mark Twain and the essays of Woody Allen, and he loved Jerry Seinfeld. Seinfeld does intelligent comedy and had no need to resort to foul language to get a cheap laugh. He appreciated that.

What did John Stewart contribute to Americana? It is quite possible that he is actually one of the founders of the form, with *Signals through the Glass* and *California Bloodlines* as his admission badges. Whether one believes that or not, we should all agree that he brought roots music, multigenre influences, a deep personal touch, a connection to American history, and American themes to the music, as well as a deep spiritual sense. Without songwriters such as Joe South and John Stewart, Americana would not be the richly written genre that it is, and the themes being explored would probably be much more narrow. In the formula-invention language of pop culture, these men both altered the formula and significantly raised the bar.

NOTES

1. When he hosts the Americana Awards show, Jim Lauderdale says, as each act leaves the stage, "Now, that's Americana," as an ironic comment on how difficult it is to define Americana (Kevin Welch, in conversation with author).

2. Jan Donkers, radio interview with Joe South, VPRO Radio, 1988, http://www.vpro.nl/.

3. John Stewart, interview, YouTube, http://www.youtube.com/.

4. Spencer Leigh, "Interview with an Angel," Bite My Foot, April 20, 1998, http://www.bitemyfoot.org.uk/.

5. William J. Bush, *Greenback Dollar: The Incredible Rise of the Kingston Trio* (Lanham, MD: Scarecrow, 2013).

6. Stewart, interview.

12

AMERICANA AS A SYMBOL OF MUSICAL ADULTHOOD

As the discussion of the songs of Joe South and John Stewart in the last chapter indicated, Americana is not geared toward a preteen audience. Most preteen music consists of mass-culture offerings, all formula and no invention. It can be entertaining and skillfully done, but its concerns are not those of adults. When the Strangeloves recorded "I Want Candy" in 1965, it was a song about the singer's lust for a girl named Candy. The record was given a lightweight Bo Diddley beat and a mix that emphasized the midrange so that it would sound good on AM radio, the preferred listening device of the young at the time. When the English New Wave band Bow Wow Wow covered it in 1982, however, it was about a guy who wanted to eat candy. In neither case, though, was it aimed at an adult audience, who would have found the song trivial.

Neither Joe South's "These Are Not My People" nor John Stewart's "You Can't Go Back to Kansas" can ever be described as trivial.

As varied as these songs are, one theme that all Americana music has in common is an adult orientation. Since the format was established by veteran music people, who had been around long enough to watch the music they loved disappear from the airwaves, the format has been aimed at a more mature audience. When Americana artists sing about love, it is generally an experienced love between a couple who have been kicked around by life.

In Kevin Welch's song "Anna Lisa, Please," the singer has been going through some hard times and his friends are worried about him, thinking that from the way he behaves, he must be cursed. They all give him a hard time about his drinking, but, he says, no one wonders about his thirst. In the song, he asks Anna Lisa to help him. It is a strong and powerful song that doesn't imply that love cures everything. Instead, it is about the desperate need for love and the false belief that our own redemption can come from another person.

When Americana artists write about lusting for a woman, the result is generally much more sophisticated than when the Strangeloves take on the same topic. In John Stewart's song, "July, You're a Woman," the singer is driving down the highway with the woman, July, at his side. He describes himself as drunk due to the mere fact of her being next to him. At this point, lust joins love as he says how tempted he is to pull over to the side of the road and make love to her. The song is about the intertwining of love and lust.

These songs have a serious intent, a desire to show the complexities of the topic at hand, and an intent and desire that commercial pop, which is simple music for undeveloped tastes, lacks. Commercial pop, like all mass art, is the common, stereotyped view of the young and uninitiated; when commercial pop singers sing about love, for example, they generally develop an overly romanticized and immature vision that has its origins in Barbie-doll role play instead of real life. The love songs of Americana artists reflect a mature, experienced view that is much more complex and recognizes that love can hurt as much as it can soothe.

Commercial pop is designed for a young audience, a crowd that prefers the performers to be in their own age range. After all, the most popular commercial pop artists, such as Ariana Grande and Taylor Swift, are in their early twenties and began recording while in their young teens. It has always been that way. In the 1950s, when Bill Haley and the Comets were hot, the band toured the United Kingdom. As they disembarked from the plane at London's Heathrow airport, they saw hundreds of teenaged British fans gathered to greet them. Haley and the band waved to the crowd, which was strangely silent. Finally, Haley's drummer said he heard a voice from the crowd say, "They're so old," and the fans quietly turned and walked away.[1]

From its very origins, rock and roll has been a young person's game. Buddy Holly began recording when he was nineteen and died eighteen months later, before his twenty-second birthday. During the dark days after Holly's death, when Frankie Avalon, Fabian, and Bobby Rydell were filling the rock charts, the mania for teen stars began, and rock went into a steep decline that helped to bring on the folk revival.

With few exceptions, rock became as simple as its audience. Only the British Invasion of the 1960s saved it. How did it do that? The invasion bands listened to and learned from American blues masters; Muddy Waters, Howlin' Wolf, Little Walter, and the rest of the men and women associated with Chess Records in the 1950s were their heroes. Van Morrison, the Kinks, Eric Clapton, the Yardbirds, and the Beatles all testified to the influence the Chicago bluesmen had on them. In an attempt to capture the Chicago blues sound, the Rolling Stones even went to the Chess Records studio to record.

These players rejected the trivial force that American rock had become, took American blues, cranked it up, and gave it back to us as rock. American bands picked up on what they were doing and adapted the roots music they were playing; a new creative era began as the music of the 1960s emerged. It was from this model that Americana eventually sprang.

The progression was simple. Sam Phillips's boys invented rockabilly, the bluesmen added their touch, and as Muddy Waters famously sang, "The blues had a baby and they named it rock and roll." But just at the moment when rock started to become everyone's music instead of teen music, Jerry Lee Lewis married his thirteen-year-old cousin, Elvis got drafted, and Buddy Holly died in the plane crash in Clear Lake, Iowa, on February 3, 1959, a date that Don McLean famously dubbed "the day the music died." All of these events left rock in the hands of Dick Clark, who gave us, in the name of rock 'n' roll, artists like Frankie Avalon, Fabian, Chubby Checker, and Bobby Rydell—all of whom recorded for companies he had a financial interest in and whose publishing was controlled by companies he owned. He even owned a piece of the plants that pressed their records. The music his artists gave us was to rock what *Schoolhouse Rock* was to education. As the more sophisticated audiences moved away, folk music took hold, and when the Beatles made electric music fun again, the folkies plugged in gave us folk rock. The music was moving ever closer to Americana.

American blues artists discovered they were very popular in Europe and began touring over there, where the British rockers heard them and were blown away with their music. Bands such as Them (with Van Morrison), the Animals, John Mayall's Bluesbreakers (with Eric Clapton), and the Rolling Stones all began playing blues-based rock. The British

Invasion sent this music back to America. The result was the underground music of the 1960s and the open-form FM radio of the day, which, ultimately, evolved into Americana.

Americana is much more sophisticated than pop. Its arrangements, its instrumentation, and its vocal approach are all more mature and complex than those of mainstream commercial pop. The songs, no matter what side of Americana they fall on, demand attention and focus from listeners. Taking each element in turn, we can study the arrangements of the songs and discover that even the simplest has a complexity that its more radio-friendly counterpart lacks.

For example, where pop might modulate, moving up one key at the end of the song, Americana is much more challenging: Johnny Cash's "I Walk the Line" puts each verse in a different key. It is a simple song, with its repetitive verse structure in which the singer pronounces himself true to his wife and closes each verse with the lines "because you're mine, I walk the line." Cash's vocal keeps the repetitive melody line tense and surprising by putting each verse in a different key.

Ray Charles once said that soloing is easy, but a good accompaniment is hard to write.[2] When the songs do not have a built-in knot of intricacy, the arranger has to provide one. When Charles recorded Melanie's "What Have They Done to My Song, Ma?" he took a straight-ahead verse-chorus song that Melanie added a quirky tension to by doing a chorus in French, and turned it into a big-band jazz number so that we heard exactly what they had done to Melanie's song.

That's the Americana invention. While the songs might be simple, consisting of three chords, artists such as Roger McGuinn make extensive use of passing chords, inversions, and substitutions, so that the final arrangement uses many variations of and additions to those three basic chords.

We will take a look at this process by examining the music of a solo artist and a band. Jennifer Knapp will serve as the solo artist, while Delta Rae will exemplify the band. Both are known for mature, idea-driven, theme-heavy music that has a profound spiritual undertone.

JENNIFER KNAPP BRINGS A DIFFERENT PERSPECTIVE TO CHRISTIAN MUSIC

Born in Chanute, Kansas, Jennifer Knapp discovered music early and credits it with getting her through a hard childhood. She attended Pittsburgh State University on a music scholarship and, while a student there, underwent a conversion experience and became first a Christian and then a contemporary Christian musician.

Instead of simple praise songs, though, Knapp's music reflected her own life, exploring not just the joy but also the hardships of the Christian life. From her own experience, Knapp recognized the difficulties inherent in living a religious life and made the exploration of those conflicting forces the centerpiece of her lyrics.

By her senior year in college, Knapp was working the church and coffeehouse circuit and, in an effort to extend her music, recorded an indie CD called *Wishing Well*. Over the next year, she sold three thousand copies of the CD and received attention from major Christian labels. In her autobiography, she speaks of those labels and why she believes she could never get signed to one of them:

> It didn't seem I was what the big labels were looking for. There were only a few guitar wielding chicks that I had ever heard of in CCM [contemporary Christian music] anyway and I didn't look or sound anything like them. I was used to playing in grungy little Christian coffeehouses for college students. When I heard artists like Amy Grant, Twila Paris, and Sandi Patti, I thought there was no way that CCM would consider me.[3]

She was correct in that assessment. The Christian music establishment passed her over, having no use for her music. However, the Christian hip-hop artist Toby McKeehan (better known as TobyMac) from the band DC Talk had started his own independent label, Gotee Records, and signed Knapp. McKeehan appreciated spiritual music that had strength, energy, and conviction so he didn't interfere with Knapp's vision. Her songs, propelled by hard-driving folk rock, bristled with power and emotion. McKeehan wasn't the only one who responded; her first album, *Kansas*, went gold, and her career appeared to be set.

The career, though, became all consuming. As Knapp writes, "From 1999 until I called it quits in 2002, things would move so fast, I would work almost nonstop, that I would call them my 'Heroin years' as I found that trying to remember the specifics of those years so hazy. If I want to remember what I did in any given year, I search Google instead of relying on my own memory."[4]

After three well-received albums and three years of constant touring, Knapp felt burned out, packed it all in, and went to Australia where she lived for seven years. Conflicted, she saw her career at an end until she visited a doctor who remembered her music and Knapp found herself explaining to him why she'd quit:

> "I gave my all. I wrote about my faith and my experience as a Christian. But I had to walk away from it." I found myself lamenting. "I was getting to the point where I didn't feel I could be myself." Apparently my plastic surgeon was becoming my therapist as well.
>
> Again, scratching behind his ear with meditation. "If you've done your work to the best of your ability, then you have no reason to be ashamed."
>
> In that moment, he uncorked the years of torment I had attempted to bottle up inside.[5]

Soon after that breakthrough, she returned to work. When she came back, she was writing and singing a more secular music, still powerful and painfully honest and still with a spiritual aspect to it but not overtly religious. She had moved from religious music to spiritual music.

RELIGION VERSUS SPIRITUALITY: THE NEW DICHOTOMY

To say that someone has shifted from religion to spirituality is an easy thing to write, but what does it mean? Is there really a distinction that both makes sense and clarifies? Half of the Americana artists I've interviewed have declared that their music is spiritual music but not religious. In fact, according to the Pew Research Center, 37 percent of Americans describe themselves as spiritual but not religious. If you add in the possibility of believing in God but not being religious, the percentage rises to 68 percent. When pressed to explain what they mean by those words, most people can't really explain them; the phrase has become a verbal shortcut that, like most shortcuts, doesn't lead anywhere.

When I asked Jennifer Knapp what she meant when she used the phrase, she agreed that the distinction was not easily grasped: "It took me twenty years to be able to answer that question, and I can only answer it in terms of the music. To me, contemporary Christian music is music made by Christians for Christians whose intent is to create more Christians. Spiritual music aims to share with the audience a spiritual feeling." The difference can be summed up in a question: "Am I trying to share with you a spiritual experience, or am I trying convince you to become a member of my religion?"

Bands like Creed walk that fine line between religious and spiritual music, she declares. And it is a line that she mostly walks herself. Even though she was fully committed to contemporary Christian music, she claims to have never felt fully comfortable in that genre. Her music was too dark. She wrote about the dark night of the soul instead of the bright light of the cross. In her songs, the spirit was something to search for, a force to fight for that could be easily lost, instead of a constant source of delight. She described the doubts every thinking person feels sometimes but that many members of churches can't admit to, even to themselves. When she discusses the deep and true feelings in her music, she says, "I have to take responsibility for that being true. I recognize there's a dark side too, and I wrote about the fight with the dark side. You always aim for truth in the writing. First you discover some empathy. I wrote a song about growing up in Kansas. My ignorance and youth made it true and made it fit in a marketplace." That song drove the sales of her debut album, winning her a gold record and a career in Christian music, but the very truth in her music prevented her from continuing in that genre.

Christian music was too constrictive, too narrowly focused, and Knapp's mind was too nimble and worked in too complicated a fashion for her to be thoroughly comfortable in that niche. She never felt she fully belonged there.

As she says, "I ran from a career in Christian music because I couldn't fit. I get thoughts like I don't want to hang out with God today, but I can't write that in Christian contemporary music."

WHEN THE STUDENT IS READY, AMERICANA APPEARS

Fortunately, it was around this time that an alternative entered Knapp's life. Americana music was breaking, and Jennifer Knapp was a natural fit in that genre. "In Americana," she says, "you can say anything."

The Americana Association's standard definition of the genre fits the music she was writing. Still, like most Americana artists, Knapp thrives on her own individuality; she does not easily accept labeling, so she does not feel totally comfortable with the label. "I think the definition of Americana has changed." In an interview, she said, "I'm in Nashville, and when I first heard the term twenty years ago, I felt it was going to rescue country music. Country music is beautiful. It's honest and beautiful, the music of everyday people. That's what I loved about it. But there was a gap between what people were living and what country music was about. Americana filled that gap. I wasn't sure that where I was musically."

The first Americana music she heard blew her away.

> When I was a teenager in Kansas and I heard Lyle Lovett, and Lucinda Williams, I was stunned. Here's Lyle Lovett, he wasn't pretty, but his music was amazing. His songs were wonderful and true and honest. So was Lucinda Williams. Think about k. d. lang. Without the freedom Americana gives, she couldn't even have had a career. She's so many genres at once. Mary Chapin Carpenter was another one. They were between folk and country. It's evolved. When I got lumped in, I remember thinking if I'm gong to be lumped in, why not with Mary Chapin Carpenter.
>
> I think of Lucinda Williams's *Car Wheels on a Gravel Road*. When I hear that record, I think she's been rode hard and put away wet. The Americana category gave her permission to do that, to go there. So the category is a good thing and a bad thing. It's a neighborhood. With most genres, we find one thing we don't like and complain about it being in the category. Americana is unique. It sets its own rules, and it is wide. I grew up on classical music. There are rules when you play Baroque music. You can't go from a one chord to an F minor 6. You can in Americana. You've got a lot more latitude in what you can do. So when people ask what I do, I say Americana.

Living in Nashville, the center of commercial country music, is one thing that causes her to question her membership in the Americana club.

> In Nashville, I never felt I was in my comfort zone. It's a little feeling, when you're not country but you don't go all the way over to Katy Perry. You're somewhere else from where everybody else is.
>
> When I'm home alone, writing songs, I try to be myself. I don't turn into anybody else. There's a place where I'm going to try to present music that people want to listen to. I'm always after a product people can buy.

But, she emphasizes, the sale has to be on her terms, and being an Americana artist helps her keep control of the transaction.

"Americana gives you confidence. It lets me be me. If I were pop, I'd have to dress like Taylor Swift or Madonna, lose forty pounds, get all glammed up, and sing like they do." That's a compromise she is not willing to make. Americana does not make the same demands that pop music does.

> I don't get too much pressure. There's a sense of community in Americana. It's like a club, and while I'm glad to be seen as a member, I have to say I haven't experienced that social circle. I'm not that famous. I'm wildly famous to the people who know me, but I'm unknown to all the others. I haven't been in the inner circles of that club. These are people who built the genre. I would distance myself from saying I had anything to do with that.

Knapp is a square peg and doesn't fit squarely within its round peg hole, but Americana is the genre for people who don't fit, either in round peg holes or in genres, which means the spiritual music Jennifer Knapp makes is able to live because of the freedom the category provides.

DELTA RAE LETS MUSIC FILL THE VOID

Delta Rae also embraces the spiritual in their music. Their songs, however, specifically embrace the spirituality of the South, whose music, as we saw earlier, has always embraced the spirit. This is because the South was and remains different from the rest of the country. It isn't simply located in the Bible Belt; it's the buckle.

As we saw in chapter 11, Delta Rae's music is spiritual but not religious, and Ian Hölljes finds southern religion complicated and intense.

There is a strong sense of the spiritual in Americana; it is one of the factors that give the music its grown-up dimension. Americana lyrics promote complexity; they embrace uncertainty and doubt. Even the love songs are complicated. One of Delta Rae's strongest ballads, "If I Loved You," takes as its theme the idea of how much easier and better the female singer's life would be if she was able to love her man without reservation, but she can't. So each morning she has to witness the way he watches her, and each night she has to break his heart.

Rather than celebrating the love between a man and a woman, it concentrates on the longing for love that causes so much suffering. It bypasses the conventional, leaping straight into the true and real, the uncomfortable. Religion would preach that she should commit fully to the man. Spirituality recognizes that the situation is not that simple.

The suffering and discomfort might come from the fact that Delta Rae is a southern Americana band. In 1941, an itinerant newspaperman named W. J. Cash published a weird little book, *The Mind of the South*, which explored exactly what it meant to be southern. In it, he pictured the South as an odd and strange place, a region as foreign to the rest of America as a British farm village is to New York City. He tried to explain the South to the rest of the nation.

To Cash, the South was an unusual place, "a tree with many age rings, with its limbs and trunk bent and twisted by all the winds of the years, but with the tap root in the Old South."[6] Exactly what Cash meant when he used the phrase "the Old South" has never been precisely nailed down. He never explains in detail what he means. Perhaps that's because he can't. Try to explain it and it sways in the intellectual breezes like a sail on a sinking ship, but according to Cash, the Old South has its own roots in literature, in the folktales and fairy tales, myths and mysteries, of the region and the dark spirituality that hangs over the area like fog over London.

You might argue that it was the mind of the South that created Delta Rae. Hölljes and his brother Eric—both born in Durham, North Carolina—attended Duke University, while their sister Brittany, a Berkeley grad, grew sick of California and returned to Durham to join her brothers in the band. Soon the trio recruited fellow southerners Elizabeth Hopkins, Mike McKee, and Grant Emerson.

Delta Rae was born.

Southern writers inform the band. As mentioned earlier, Hölljes says he learned a lot from southern literature, which led him to explore the southern tradition. "It's a tradition of a kind of beautiful, natural imagery," he says. "What you are is a tradition, a holding onto a southern tradition. I've always read the southern writers."

The literature of the South consists of folktales and fairy tales, romances instead of realism. Indeed, realism has little to do with the literature of the region. It is based more on regional myths and mysteries. In fact, in its mythology, the story of the South is the story of a sort of paradise lost, a land that had its own distinct sense of place and purpose, its own mores and folkways, and its own sense of honor and justice. It is also known as the Land of the Lost Cause. It was a land that existed outside of mainstream American while being physically a part of mainstream America.

In truth, the literature shows us a land that existed outside of reality itself. The myth that the South celebrated never really existed. As Cash recognizes, it was mostly a construct of fiction and, of course, being built on a slave class, the moral basis of the myth was compromised, but Cash feels that to judge the South purely on that basis is like judging a man by the size of his foot; there's much more to it than that.

It is also the land where American chivalry blossomed, where people took care of each other and where the sense of place, of home, was a central value. That's the part that spoke to Ian Hölljes.

When he started Delta Rae, it was only natural that he looked to the literature he loved for inspiration. It so pervades the music of the band that there has been some negative criticism. "We've been criticized for mythologizing the South, but the mythology is its biggest beauty. It's the story and the mystery of the place where we grew up. The literature of the South, myth loaded and folkloric, always spoke to me."

Hölljes's love of southern literature was undoubtedly deepened by his time studying with one of the South's finest writers and teachers, Reynolds Price. The novelist Anne Tyler, also a student of Price, once said of him, "You could not study with Reynolds Price and not become a writer." But Hölljes went beyond merely studying with Price.

Price, the author of thirty-eight novels, short stories, memoirs, poems, and plays, also attended Duke, winning a Rhodes scholarship that allowed him to do graduate work from Oxford University. When he finished at Oxford, he joined Duke's English department and taught there for more than thirty years.

In 1984, Price learned he had a cancerous tumor more than ten inches long curled around his spine. Surgery and radiation killed the tumor, but the treatment also destroyed his spine, costing him his ability to walk. He spent the last twenty-five years of his life confined to a wheelchair. Price, however, continued writing and teaching by hiring a graduate student every year to assist him.

One of those students was Ian Hölljes, and caring for Price had a great effect on him. During that year, Hölljes was beginning to find himself as an artist, and Reynolds Price was just the man to be around. "Reynolds was a songwriter as well as a novelist," Hölljes says. "He collaborated with James Taylor on some of Taylor's best songs." Price, for example, cowrote James Taylor's "Copperline," a top ten hit. Inspired by Price, Hölljes began to write Delta Rae songs during that year.

Within three years of Delta Rae's first rehearsals, they were signed to Sire Records, a division of Warner Brothers, which marketed Delta Rae in the Americana category, a branding that Hölljes disputes, not because he objects to it but more because he questions the idea of categories altogether. "It's a legitimate category, but I question whether we fit into a specific genre at all. If you're going to question Americana, you create the questioning of genre in general. I don't think we belong in any category at all. We're a band that loves all kinds of music. We draw on all kinds of music." That fact alone places them in Americana.

W. J. Cash summed up the South this way: "Proud, brave, honorable by its lights, courteous, personally generous, loyal, swift to act, often too swift, but signally effective, sometimes terrible in its action—such was the south at its best. And such at its best it remains today, despite the great falling away in some of its virtues."[7] Certainly these words describe not just a social and political quest but a spiritual one as well, a search for the best in us. It is this search that inspires Jennifer Knapp and Delta Rae.

NOTES

1. Otto Fuchs, *Bill Haley: The Father of Rock 'n' Roll* (London: Wagner, 2014), 361.

2. Ray Charles and David Ritz, *Brother Ray: Ray Charles' Own Story* (New York: Dial Press, 1978), 125–26.

3. Jennifer Knapp, *Facing the Music: My Life* (New York: Howard Books, 2014), 112.

4. Ibid., 113.

5. Ibid., 114.

6. W. J. Cash, *The Mind of the South* (New York: Vintage, 1972), 221.

7. Ibid., 226.

13

LET'S GO BACKWARD WHEN FORWARD FAILS

We've already established the importance of southern music to Americana. For the next movement in Americana's history, we'll stay in the South and see how southern rock became a part of Americana.

Henry Paul, the southern rock veteran musician and leader of three heavily influential bands, the Henry Paul Band, the Outlaws, and Blackhawk, says, "There was a vacuum after the rise of disco and LA Glam rock. Rock & Roll had a different musical persona in the mid-seventies." Disco and glam rock might have filled the airwaves and the TV screens, but just as many listeners rejected it as accepted it.

Both disco and glam rock were overproduced and trivial. The emphasis was not as much on the music as it was on the presentation. Disco continued the old practice of putting the producer in charge, rather than the musicians, and the whole scene revolved around the beat. Being able to dance to it was much more important than being able to listen to it. Beats per minute were measured in order to keep the dancers on the floor; disco must have between 120 and 128 beats per minute, while trance music can go up to 150, and bass and drum can reach 180. Not only does nearly every disco song have the same number of beats per minute, but also each song contains some of the same formula elements as the others. Unfamiliarity, in the form of too much invention, might cause dancers to leave the floor.

Glam rock relied on skin-tight spandex pants, arms covered with tattoos, huge blonde hair extensions piled up in mullets, and a persona for the artist that reeked of contrived strangeness. David Bowie changed personas with each album, going from androgynous to space oddity. The Los Angeles hair bands were nearly interchangeable in both their appearance and their music. Only a limited range of fans could respond.

Those who didn't respond to either disco or glam rock longed for the real thing. Paul says that "people have always sought out a real and authentic voice. When I was younger, folk filled that void. We'll always need that authentic musical personality that Americana has."

But in the 1970s that authentic voice was hard to find. Rock had abandoned it and so had middle-of-the road pop. "Sinatra, Dean Martin, and Andy Williams were all superficial and slick," Paul says, indicating that for a young musician to find his own way, discovering his own original voice in a world of imitations was difficult.

"I was a student of all that music. My goal as a young musician was to bring country into rock." To learn how, he listened to all of the pioneers. "I heard the Byrds, McGuinn's twelve-string Rickenbacker, the Buffalo Springfield, and when Richie Furay went off and formed Poco . . ." he pauses, letting the memory wash over him. "I was enormously influenced by them, and by Gordon Lightfoot—the Travis picking—Bob Dylan and Ian Tyson."

He could not study the music adequately from his native Florida so Paul did his sojourn in Greenwich Village.

> I went to the Village in the late 1960s, and I'd go to the record stores on Eighth Avenue and buy Woody Guthrie albums. I played the coffeehouses. The music got more media coverage then. Greenwich Village was a real bohemian paradise. It isn't any more, but it was then. It was a small town in the big city, and that's what I loved about it. It was a real fantasy land for me. I had an apartment, I played out, wrote songs, played in the streets.

Like most Americana musicians, Paul lived the folkie apprenticeship. But when the apprenticeship was up, he went back to Florida, joined the band that evolved into the Outlaws, and helped develop southern rock.

WHAT IS SOUTHERN ROCK, AND HOW DOES IT FIT INTO THE AMERICANA GENRE?

We've already seen how most genres of American music began in the South. Blues, rock, country, bluegrass, and folk all originated there, and those are the five categories that combine to form southern rock. Typical instrumentation for a southern rock band is up to three guitars. The All-man Brothers, the Outlaws, Lynyrd Skynyrd, and the Marshall Tucker Band all feature three guitars—two swapping leads and one playing rhythm—plus keyboards, and a rhythm section made up of a bass guitar, a drummer, and often a second drummer or percussionist. These instruments are frequently supplemented by fiddles (think of the Charlie Daniels Band) and mandolins, prominent in Blackhawk, while some groups, such as the Marshall Tucker Band, add a flute and a tenor sax to the mix. Regardless of the instrumentation, the music is characterized by driving, pulsating rhythms, improvised parts, and long jams.

In the early days, lyrics often concerned the life of young, southern, working-class people, expressing their hopes and dreams, their successes and failures. Today, as the band members have become older, their interests have shifted and the themes of the songs have, like Jennifer Knapp and Delta Rae, become more spiritual. Henry Paul puts it this way:

> As I grow older, I have the advantage of maturity. I have a more spiritual bent now, instead of being the roaring ambitious jerk I was when I was younger. It's the difference between having been to the party instead of wanting to get there. The party was different from what I thought it was going to be. I know better now than to make the party everything. My intentions are purer now. The honesty of Americana makes me want to be a better writer. I want to write a great song, put it out there, and let people hear it.

Thus, the themes of the songs have changed, as Blackhawk indicates in songs like "Down from the Mountain," which is about the need for individuality and personal honesty in creativity, and "Ships of Heaven," which is almost a straight gospel number. The Marshall Tucker Band's love songs take a unique view of love, showing its hardships and complexity as does "In My Own Way." The Outlaws have grown into social criticism with songs such as "Nothing Main about Main Street," which describes the death of small towns in America. The songs of the southern rock bands, then, have become more serious and more honest.

Also, like the best music of most of the southern Americana musicians such as Joe South, Johnny Cash, and Howlin' Wolf, the honesty Paul mentions is one of the things southern rock has contributed to the genre. Honesty has to be protected, he says, because it is so hard to come by. Too much of the music has a second agenda. "Honesty is a suggestion of quality," he says.

> Steve Earle's *Guitar Town* is honest, but it's also an attempt to be cool. Americana is like everything else; there's a whole lot of mediocrity around, but the honest, genuine writers and players resonate honesty and authentic moments. Take Dylan's *Blonde on Blonde* album. If you listen closely, it's a rewrite of Allen Ginsberg. Read *Howl* and then listen to *Blonde on Blonde*.

According to Paul, the honesty comes from the fact that Americana is a hybrid of styles. Drawing from all of those sources forces the musician to come up with something original and true, producing a quality that flies in the face of lavishly produced, synthesized pop. Americana sets aside the synthesizers, which are the most dishonest of musical instruments; they are programmed, not played.

And that honest, pure, and grown-up music is what Paul went back to Florida to play. It was already being played in Jacksonville bars by the Allman Brothers Band, the best-known and most influential of the southern rock bands. The key to the Allman Brothers sound was that in addition to the usual genres that made up Americana, they incorporated jazz into their sound. When an African American friend led Gregg Allman into soul music, the Allmans' formula was complete. They cut a couple of albums as the Hour Glass, but they didn't succeed, so Duane Allman took a job as a session musician in Muscle Shoals Studios.

It took Phil Walden to make them the force and power they became. Walden, who also managed Otis Redding, saw the Allmans as moneymakers and signed them to his brand-new label, Capricorn Records. They played a gig in Boston, opening for the Velvet Underground, and found the musical idea that would make them a force; lacking the material to play a full set, they began to jam, playing extended, improvised solos so that one song would take as much time as three.

Their first album, *The Allman Brothers Band*, was released in 1969 and sold a disappointing thirty-five thousand copies. The record company pressured them to move to New York, but they made another decision that would have a vast effect on southern rock: they decided to stay in Macon, Georgia. Staying in Georgia kept them far out of the range of influence of the major record companies and promotion people, who had definite ideas on how a rock band should be presented and marketed. Capricorn was distributed by Atlantic Records, and Atlantic wanted to present the Allmans with a rock-star image. The Allman Brothers Band was determined to be themselves, not anyone's idea of what rock stars should be. They succeeded by doing just that. Their next album, *At the Fillmore East*, became a huge hit and has been called one of the best live albums ever made. It was certainly one of the most influential; a case can be made that if it hadn't been for that album, southern rock would not have become the force that it did.

The Allman Brothers' values and attitude contributed to the rise of southern rock. In manifesting that independence, they modeled one of the major values of Americana music: that the image a band presented should be an accurate reflection of what the band is, rather than a pose. As Kevin Welch told me, "The interesting part of that is that all these people are fiercely independent. They are going to do any goddamn thing they want to." Welch seconds Henry Paul by adding, "If anything, Americana is honesty."

Southern rock is built on the roots of American music. It looks to the past for its building blocks, but it hasn't used those blocks to build a nineteenth-century log cabin. When you hear roots rock musicians from Los Angeles, for example, you hear them replicate the old sounds. It is as though they are content to play old music for new people. Their music is essentially nostalgic. The Brian Setzer Orchestra, for example, might as well be a jump blues band from the forties.

Southern rock had as its goal the use of old forms to build something new. The musicians did not simply play the blues, for example; in their hands, the blues became a foundation for self-expression. So did rocka-billy, the blues-based rock form pioneered by artists like Buddy Holly and Buddy Knox and the Sun Records fraternity. Instead of using straight major and minor scales as the rockabilly players did, the southern rockers use the pentatonic major scale and the Mixolydian scale to bring the music into the twenty-first century. From jazz, they took the idea of the extended solo and improvisation. All of these innovations—and more—created a new genre, which got subsumed into the Americana genre.

In all, we can think of southern rock as a musical TARDIS, Dr. Who's time machine. From the outside, the TARDIS looks like a typical British telephone booth, but on the inside it is infinitely bigger and different than its exterior physical dimensions would suggest, which is another way of saying that all of this musical time travel contributes to our dilemma over definition. The blues is a form of Americana, but so are folk, country, and bluegrass. And so also are jazz, polka, and klezmer. On the soundtrack from *O Brother Where Art Thou?* all of those forms are presented in an undiluted, unmixed form, and all are declared to be Americana. Southern rock, which blends all of those into a new type of protein shake, is also Americana. So, if each of the elements that combine to make the genre Americana is also Americana, how does that allow the overall form to qualify as something new?

Mumford & Sons and the Avett Brothers both play traditional music. Yet both bands play contemporary music also. And it is the same music. Like the southern rockers, they take the old forms, shake them up, add some seasoning, and serve them up to us as something new. They take the past into the future. As the Australian singer-songwriter and entertainer Peter Allen once put it in a pop song, "Everything Old Is New Again."

That's what southern rock has contributed to Americana; it has made everything old new again.

14

SWALLOWING OTHER GENRES

Since one of the stated purposes of Americana was to rescue genres that could no longer be heard on the radio, it is no wonder that the genre transformed some types, such as folk music and indie rock, and accepted others whole, as it did bluegrass, old time, and the blues.

As we said previously, many Americana artists and critics credit the soundtrack from the Coen brothers' film *O Brother, Where Art Thou?* as the turning point. The movie showed that roots music wasn't dead, just forgotten, proving Ian Tyson's often quoted statement: "Folk music never dies. It's always there. It can be hard to find sometimes but it's always there."[1] The music featured in the movie and on the album had always been there; it was as American as a Fender Stratocaster, but it had been largely forgotten, driven out of the popular consciousness by the corporate media's ubiquitous offerings; without free-form radio, it did not get played. The Coen brothers and producer T-Bone Burnett simply made us remember—even if many in the audience were literally too young to remember all of it.

The film and its soundtrack album propelled bluegrass and old-time music to a new level of popularity, adding years to the career of artists such as Ralph Stanley. In addition to the old-time sounds promoted by T-Bone Burnett's production of the movie's soundtrack, the strong reception to its release opened the gates for the classic country music of artists like Patsy Cline to be accepted fully into Americana. It also proved there was room in the Americana category as well for the R&B of Ray Charles and Roy Brown, the blues of Solomon Burke, John Lee Hooker, and

Muddy Waters, and the singer-songwriter artistry of James Taylor, Tom Rush, and Steve Earle.

By welcoming other endangered species genres, Americana created a wide tent that allowed all of roots music to come through the door. The factor that the artists had in common was that their music solidly reflected American life and values, which as it turns out, are the bedrock values of Western civilization and help account for Americana's popularity overseas.

PATSY CLINE LEARNS TO BE HERSELF AND SAVES COUNTRY MUSIC

When blacksmith Samuel Hensley was forty-one, he married sixteen-year-old Hilda who had three children before they split up. One of the children was Virginia Patterson Hensley, who later became famous as Patsy Cline. When she was sixteen, Virginia Hensley had to drop out of school to help support the family, taking jobs in a soda shop and in a poultry plant. She started singing wherever she could get a gig, determined to break out of a life of dead-end jobs.

In 1952, she got a break, joining a country dance band led by Bill Peer. She changed her name to Patsy for the band and, since most of their gigs were in the mid-Atlantic area, moved with her new husband, Gerald Cline, to Frederick, Maryland, to shorten the drive to her gigs.

In 1957, she caught her first big break, being invited to sing "Walkin' after Midnight" on *Arthur Godfrey's Talent Scouts*, a competitive singing show that was a type of *American Idol* program with a lower budget and fewer pretenses. She won the competition and signed with Decca Records, where she embarked on a string of hit singles produced by the same Owen Bradley who had failed to recognize the talent in Buddy Holly. Maybe he had a blind eye for rockabilly, but Bradley had a feel for traditional country music artists. Certainly, if you listen to the singles she cut early in her career and then to the Bradley-produced work, you can hear a huge difference.

Much of that difference came despite Cline's objections. From the moment he heard her sing, Bradley saw crossover potential; he thought he could successfully launch Cline as a pop artist, a move that Cline resisted out of insecurity. These days, crossing over is part of a country artist's career path, but in those days, it had rarely if ever been done. Certainly, Hank Williams's songs crossed over; they were widely recorded by pop artists such as Tony Bennett and Kay Starr, but Williams himself remained country. Even though Eddie Arnold, at his manager Colonel Tom Parker's insistence, put on a tuxedo and used string sections instead of fiddles, he remained primarily a country artist. Probably Cline's reluctance to go that route came from the fact that she had been struggling for nearly ten years to get a foothold in the industry. Now that she was becoming established, she didn't feel that Bradley understood her or her music. Despite her personal ambiguity, the power of her music and Decca Records' marketing efforts caused her to cross over to pop music anyway. The appearance on the Godfrey show began the process.

She wanted to sing the country weeper "A Poor Man's Riches," but since "Walkin' after Midnight" was about to be released, the producers insisted that she sing it instead. Cline wanted to wear her cowgirl outfit, but the Godfrey show insisted on a cocktail dress. When she won and was asked to become a regular on Godfrey's radio show (a gig she was, like Julius La Rosa and Archie Bleyer before her, fired from after a month because of "creative differences"), Cline saw that a more sophisticated presentation and a toning down of the traditional country elements in her songs would take her a long way. By incorporating pop elements and arrangements into her songs but without destroying the essential "countryness" of her music, she was able to make inroads into the pop market without losing her country audience. She remained a hugely influential artist, opening the doors for many more female singers, until her death in a plane crash on March 5, 1963.

Legendary though she was, we still have to wonder what makes her Americana. The answer is simple. She showed—and Owen Bradley deserves credit for this also— that country was not a niche music, that, rightly done, it belonged to everyone. She also pioneered the blending of genres. Cline was one of the artists who revealed the unity that underlies the different forms of music.

While Patsy Cline was reinventing country music, men like Ray Charles and Roy Brown were bringing R&B off the chitlin' circuit and into the wider arena of mainstream America, where it would eventually contribute to the creation of Americana. To understand how this happened, we have to take a short look at a turning point in American jazz.

LeRoi Jones reminds us that conventional history says jazz began in New Orleans and worked its way up the river to Chicago. That's the myth, and like all myths, it has become, over the years, more powerful than the truth. Jones points out that jazz, or purely instrumental blues, could no more have begun in one area of the country than could blues.[2]

Jazz originated in African American communities throughout the South and migrated toward New Orleans, which was a center for music of all types for one simple reason: it was, according to LeRoi Jones in *Blues People*, the only city in the new world that permitted slaves to own drums. These drums were central to keeping the strong beat and pounding out the frenetic rhythms that were featured in early jazz. The city was also important because of its mixed culture. In the nineteenth century, New Orleans was the home of many ethnicities: French, Spanish, Italian, Irish, German, and African—all of whom had their own music. European folk music and African elements were also present, along with mainstream American music. All of this was blended into a musical gumbo and came out as jazz. The most crucial elements of the emerging New Orleans jazz were blues, spirituals, marches, and ragtime.

BUDDY BOLDEN GETS PEOPLE UP AND DANCING

The city of New Orleans' first great jazz musician was Charles "Buddy" Bolden,[3] who formed his band in 1895 and quickly became the most popular musician in the city, playing with his band for dances all around New Orleans. The people of New Orleans loved to dance, and Bolden's success was based on his ability to get them out of their chairs and onto the dance floor. He took the string band instrumentation of the everyday dance band and combined it with the brass from the marching bands. By doing this, he established the instrumentation of the standard early jazz band: a front line of cornet, clarinet, and trombone against a rhythm section of guitar, drums, and bass—although the tuba often played the bass parts.

Establishing the instrumentation of a jazz band wasn't Bolden's only contribution. It wasn't even his biggest. Where the standard dance bands read their music off notated charts, the Bolden band improvised. Both dancers and musicians loved that aspect because improvisation was more spontaneous. After establishing the theme and the melody, players were free to play whatever they wanted to as long as they followed the song's chord structure. They could play extended solos and choruses to give the dancers more time to show off their moves as well as providing themselves with an opportunity to showcase their gifts on their instruments. Improvising made the evening a participatory experience.

Although Bolden became known as the first jazz musician, not everyone agrees. The ragtime piano player, Jelly Roll Morton, said, "It is evidently known, beyond contradiction, that New Orleans is the cradle of jazz and I myself happen to be the inventor in the year 1902."[4] Was Morton's statement true? Naming the first jazz musician is like identifying the first snowflake to fall in a blizzard, but the fact is Morton was there at the beginning. He had a different audience, though, playing as he did in the houses of prostitution in the city's Bourbon Street district.

Other bands formed to capture the segments of the audience that Bolden hadn't appealed to. When he collapsed while working a street parade and wound up institutionalized in a sanitarium for the rest of his life, these bands took over.

Trombone player Frankie Dusen wound up leading Bolden's band and renamed it the Eagle Band, but now, with the master dead, keeping the band on top was like trying to sell patrons a gourmet meal with no entree. Other bandleaders fought to be the main dish. Manuel Perez, like Bolden, a cornet player, led the Imperial Orchestra as well as a second band that played marches, the Onward Brass Band, and he introduced these two bands to improvisation. The man who emerged as the next king of New Orleans music, though, was Kid Ory.

Edward "Kid" Ory's father was a white trombone player of French ancestry named Ozell Ory, and his mother was a Creole from La Place, Louisiana. By 1907, he was leading a dance band in his native La Place, and by 1910, he had moved himself and his band to New Orleans. By 1918, he had discovered and hired Joe Oliver, Louis Armstrong, Johnny and Warren Dodds, and Jimmie Noone. He was the first black New Orleans jazz bandleader to make a recording, "Ory's Creole Trombone," in 1921.[5]

Why did all this happen in New Orleans? There are several reasons, beginning with the fact that of the slave cities, only New Orleans allowed open ownership of drums by slaves. What's more, New Orleans was a cosmopolitan city whose location at the base of the Mississippi River made it a trade center and brought people of all ethnicities, levels of socioeconomic status, and classes together. It was also a city that was built on a foundation of mysticism and the supernatural; voodoo rituals were common, accepted, and attended by everyone regardless of class or ethnicity. Citizens of the city routinely heard music from all cultures, and when they played, they tended not to separate it but to mash it all together into a new mixture that exploited the rhythms, tunes, and melodic structures of many lands leading to something new and original that belonged purely to them: the polyrhythms, syncopation, shuffle rhythms, looseness, experimentation, double-line rhythms, and group improvisations that became jazz. As African Americans spread out from the South, migrating to northern cities, they took the nascent jazz with them, and by the 1930s, the nation was dancing to big band swing.

The typical instrumentation of a swing band was a large horn section, which would include several saxes, trumpets, and trombones, so that it could be made up of a dozen or more players and a rhythm section, consisting of an acoustic rhythm guitar, a bass, piano, and drums. In size, these bands comprised twenty or more musicians, and they played primarily for dancing. They were also segregated; both white bands and African American bands were on the road, touring different circuits.

When World War II came along, the new economic realities made it impossible to keep a big band on the road. Most of them folded, and the musicians in them were forced to break into smaller units in order to keep working. These smaller bands took one of two forms: bop units, who took jazz in an intellectual and experimental direction, concentrating on the intellectual side of the music. Men like Charlie Parker, Dizzy Gillespie, Miles Davis, and Tadd Dameron were the formative forces in bop. Other musicians kept the dance tradition alive, forming units that resembled stripped-down versions of the big bands and, in their playing, concentrated on replicating the emotional side of jazz. With a maximum of seven players, the bands featured a small horn section, generally with a tenor and alto sax and a trumpet, and a rhythm section of piano, guitar, bass, and drums. Louis Jordan, Earl Bostic, Roy Brown, T-Bone Walker, and Ray Charles were jump blues bandleaders.

When Muddy Waters said the blues had a baby and they named it rock and roll, he recognized that the jump blues bands were the midwives. Jump blues led to R&B and on to rock and roll. The return of jump blues during the swing revival of the 1990s brought the form into Americana, where musicians gladly lifted elements from it to use in their music.

Jump blues led to a fresh appreciation of the urban blues, as played by people like John Lee Hooker, Muddy Waters, Buddy Guy, Little Milton, and others. Like Patsy Cline and like the jump blues artists before them, the electric blues musicians qualify as Americana because their music is so fully American. It reflects American values and shows the pain and the joy of being a citizen of this country, even if not a fully accepted citizen. Like the music of Muddy Waters—"Hoochie Coochie Man" and "Got My Mojo Working," for example—the electric blues also examines southern myth. Little Milton's "We're Going to Make It" is a tribute to the American upwardly mobile drive. Bo Diddley explores the braggadocio of the trickster figure that fills American folklore.

And not just the themes are American: Americana underlies much of the boogie rhythms that characterize rock and roll and southern rock. Like all Americana, the blues is our music.

TOM RUSH INVENTS THE SINGER-SONGWRITER GENRE

In 1968, after putting out four albums of traditional folk and blues material, folk singer Tom Rush released *The Circle Game*, a concept album whose songs traced a relationship, moving musically from its formation to its end. The album is made up of recently composed material, some written by Rush but most by such folkies as Joni Mitchell, Jackson Browne, and James Taylor. The software feature iTunes Preview has called *The Circle Game* the first singer-songwriter album. Whether that's the case or not, within a year of its release, all of the featured writers on the album had their own first discs released. Phil Ochs, Carole King, Cat Stevens, Dan Fogelberg, Carly Simon, Hoyt Axton, and Melanie were ruling the free-form FM radio stations. Some, like Stevens and Simon, could also be heard on the corporate stations.

Not everyone agrees that *Circle Game* began the singer-songwriter trend. Eric Andersen told an interviewer that the folkies were shamed into writing their own material by the beat poets. The folk singers played the bars and clubs where the beats read their work, and the poets belittled them for singing traditional music, saying that anyone could do that. What counted was being able to come up with your own material. The folk singers followed the lead of the poets and began composing their own songs.[6]

Regardless of where the truth lies, singer-songwriters led the way into Americana by staying true to folk music while opening up to rock, pop, the blues, and other influences.

Although he was born in the Boston area in 1948, James Taylor is a southern musician. When he was three, his family moved to Chapel Hill, North Carolina, where his father taught at the University of North Carolina School of Medicine. Taylor began studying guitar when he was twelve, concentrating on the Merle Travis style of fingerpicking. While still in his early teens, he met guitarist Danny Kortchmar on Martha's Vineyard, where the Taylor family vacationed every summer, and the two kids began playing coffeehouses around the island. In high school, he played in a band led by his brother Alex, but during his senior year, James Taylor went into a deep depression. In 1965, he signed himself into McLean Hospital, a treatment facility in Belmont, Massachusetts, where he remained for nine months until he checked himself out to go to New York City, where he formed a band, the Flying Machine, with Danny Kortchmar.

Though the Flying Machine worked regularly around Greenwich Village, the band never made it, and all Taylor got out of the experience was a heroin addiction. After going through treatment for drugs and depression, Taylor moved to London. There he eventually connected with producer Peter Asher, who was the A&R man for the Beatles' Apple Records. Taylor became the first American signed to the label. By the time Apple released *James Taylor*, he was back in drug treatment and unable to promote the album. Despite fine reviews, it failed to sell.

After his stint in detox, Taylor signed with Warner Records and recorded *Sweet Baby James*, the album that made him famous. He has remained famous for more than forty years. What accounts for this longevity? For one, Taylor has resolutely gone his own way throughout his career, making his own music the way he has wanted to and paying little attention to whether or not a market exists for his songs. When he released his 2015 album, *Before This World*, he told *Rolling Stone* he couldn't care less how many copies the album sold. "I have no idea what even releasing an album means anymore," he says. "Friends of mine say, 'James, you have to adjust your expectations. People don't buy these things.' Not to be presumptuous but Vincent Van Gogh sold just two paintings while he was alive. If that's what your medium is, you simply must do it."[7]

For another, Taylor is a master at mining his own life for material but making his personal discoveries relatable to everyone. Most of his songs have originated in some aspect of his biography that he has wanted to explore. "Carolina in My Mind," for example, is about the homesickness he felt while recording his first album in London. The way the longing is expressed, however, makes it about the need for home that we have all felt at times.

Mostly, though, Taylor's music falls into the Americana category. It sounds like folk music, but it isn't. It has elements of pop, but it doesn't fit there either. It has a superficial rock quality, but there is no way you can call it rock. It is James Taylor music, and only Taylor can write and perform it. The originality and honesty puts his material directly in the Americana category.

What all of these artists have in common is that they were known as writers before they became successful as performers.

Steve Earle was also around during those days. He has said he arrived at every folk scene just in time to kill it. Having no Tom Rush to champion his songs, he had to wait for his reputation to build until he was able to make his own albums. His first album, *Guitar Town*, spread awareness of his talent, but *Copperhead Road* made him an Americana darling.

Born in Fort Monroe, Virginia, in 1955, Earle grew up in San Antonio. A music-obsessed, lonely, and rebellious kid, like Jimmie Rodgers long before him, he ran away from home when he was fourteen intending to follow his idol Townes Van Zandt on tour. Caught and forced to return home, he waited until he was sixteen and then dropped out of school to go to Houston, where he lived with his nineteen-year-old uncle, also a musician. Both men were trying to get a musical career started. By 1974, he was in Nashville, playing bass in Guy Clark's band. (He is the bass player on Clark's breakthrough *Old No. 1* album.) After a couple of recording opportunities that went nowhere, Earle signed with MCA Records for whom he recorded *Guitar Town* and suddenly found himself in the center of the "new traditionalist" movement that was spreading through Nashville like a fever at that time; his name was coupled with artists such as Randy Travis, the O'Kanes, and Foster and Lloyd. Then came *Copperhead Road*, and Earle was being spoken of as an alternative, No Depression genius. At that point he suddenly disappeared. His drug use had spiraled out of control, and while he tried to hang onto his career, it slid out of his hands. He lost his MCA contract and for four years did nothing, issued no new records, and played very few shows.

In 1994, he was arrested and imprisoned on drug and weapon charges. After getting clean while serving time, he made a successful comeback. Overcoming his drug habit unleashed a new level of creativity. Even before his breakdown, he'd been experimenting with other musical forms. Now he looked upon all genres of music as Steve Earle music. His 1990 album, *The Hard Way*, had a strong rock underpinning, while *Train a Comin'* was nominated for a Grammy as Best Contemporary Folk album. Teaming up with the Del McCoury Band, he recorded the bluegrass disc *The Mountain* and then released the semi-psychedelic *Transcendental Blues*.

Earle has said that singer-songwriters such as himself practice a trade invented by Bob Dylan, bringing the reportorial style developed by Woody Guthrie into the twenty-first century. In practicing the reporter as songwriter model, Earle made two political albums in a row, *Jerusalem* and *The Revolution Starts Now*, which cemented his status as a left-wing critic of America's foreign policies. *Jerusalem* contained "John Walker's Blues," in which he tried to explain why a young American, John Walker Lindh, who was caught training with the Taliban when America invaded Afghanistan, wound up taking the path he did. Many people, both left and right, were angry because Earle didn't judge Lindh but instead tried to understand him. The Bush administration called Earle a traitor. Instead of backing down, Earle put out *The Revolution Starts Now*, an album that directly attacked the administration and its policies.

Yet just as he was becoming known as a political and protest singer, Earle turned 180 degrees and released *Washington Square Serenade*, an album of love songs celebrating his marriage to Allison Moorer and their move to New York City.

Since Earle is often characterized as an Americana artist, we must ask just what there is about his work that qualifies him as Americana. For one, there is his wide stylistic range. Earle is too restless to work in only one style. He plays folk, country, bluegrass, and rock, and has recently added blues to his palette. We also have to consider his lyrical sensibilities. Like Randy Newman, he writes from the point of view of the characters he creates for the songs. The concerns and themes are his and reflect his desires, dreams, and obsessions, but as often as not, the narrator in the song is a character. His instrumentation reflects the Americana

Music Association's description of what it means to be Americana. And, of course, there is the fact that his music cannot get airplay on most corporate radio.

Not everyone has leaped onto the Steve Earle bandwagon, however. A characteristic of Americana is that it is honest music. Americana songs are written with no ulterior motive; they are meant to convey the artist's specific truth, and while, of course, the artist hopes to use them to make a living, the music is forefront. Earle's honesty has been questioned. People have claimed to find his music fraudulent, to have nonmusical motives planted in it. Outlaws leader Henry Paul, for instance, says that the songs sound honest on the surface but that they have a secondary purpose, which is to create an aura of cool.

Whether Paul's criticism is valid is up to each listener, but the degree of honesty is an aspect of Americana music that we will speak of in more detail in later chapters. The major point of this chapter, though, is that Americana, by welcoming artists from nearly all genres into its folds, created a wide tent that allowed all roots music to dance through the doorway and down the aisle.

NOTES

1. Peter Feniak, "Ian Tyson: The Singing Cowboy," *Good Times*, March 2015.

2. LeRoi Jones, *Blues People: Negro Music in White America* (New York: HarperCollins, 2002).

3. New Orleans Jazz National Historic Park, "Buddy Bolden: Calling His Children Home, 1877–1931," November 13, 2013, http://www.nps.gov/; Donald M. Marquis, *In Search of Buddy Bolden: First Man of Jazz* (Baton Rouge: Louisiana University Press, 1978).

4. New Orleans Official Guide, "Music Greats: Jelly Roll Morton," accessed September 9, 2016, http://www.neworleansonline.com/.

5. Lewis Porter, Tim Wilkins, and Ted Gioia, "Kid [Edward] Ory," *Encyclopedia of Jazz Musicians*, http://www.jazz.com/, 2007.

6. "An Interview with Eric Andersen," *Performing Songwriter* 83 (January/February 2005).

7. Andy Greene, "James Taylor's Mellow Rebirth: Inside 'Before This World,'" *Rolling Stone*, March 27, 2015.

15

A SENSE OF COMMUNITY

In the first chapter of this book, Dennis Lord defined Americana as both a movement and a genre. So far, we have discussed the form mostly as a genre. It's time now to take a look at the other side: Americana as a movement. To do this, we have to ask what exactly a movement is. According to sociologists, social movements are group actions, which can be formal or informal. As they form, collections of individuals get together because of a common interest in order to execute, reject, or undo some thing, action, or idea that is currently happening. The beats, for example, were a group of avant-garde writers who banded together in order to break the stranglehold the major conservative and overly polite corporate publishers had on the literary world of the 1950s. The hippie movement came about when a group of 1960s kids felt abandoned by the postwar Eisenhower conformist society that the post–World War II move to the suburbs created. These kids banded together to assert their identity and create social change. The collection of rockabilly artists who gathered around Sam Phillips's Sun Records shared a similar mentality that was unable to find expression within the major-label recording system that dominated the times.

What conditions bring on movements? Sometimes, they are spontaneous, like the Occupy movement. Sometimes, like a political party, they are created to bring unity to a collection of actions that different people, largely independent of each other, are creating. Someone notices that a shared vision exists and feels it could be better brought to the fore by collective action than by individual acts. That's the story of the Americana Music Association.

It is widely believed that movements occur when people recognize that they are in some way repressed. The civil rights movement is often held up as an example. History, though, shows that movements happen not when people are down but when people's conditions are improving; that's when they can see hope. Feudalism fell, for example, only after the spread of literacy, which enabled the masses to perceive previously unseen possibilities.

For Americana, the movement became possible when the rise of technology allowed musicians to take control of their own destinies, when it became possible to make a record in a home studio set up in the artist's living room and edited and mixed on his or her personal computer. The resulting CD could be sold online through the artist's website and on sites such as CD Baby, as well as at personal appearances. It could also be uploaded to digital sellers such as iTunes. The individualization of technology removed the power from the major record companies and empowered the individual artists. Social media, then, changed everything, and a movement resulted.

Out of the movement came community. One of the defining factors of Americana is that it is as much a community as a genre of music. To many artists, Americana is a communal music, a movement that has created its own sense of being in this together. Cooperation trumps competition. Rising singer-songwriter sisters, the Hello Strangers, for example, have been welcomed into the Americana camp and have accepted membership in the category gladly but primarily for reasons that are secondary to their music; it gives them a like-minded group of artists to associate with. To them, Americana is a club, a place to go to find artists they can communicate with.

Larissa Chase Smith of the Hello Strangers defines Americana partially by its inclusiveness. "I would say there's an emphasis on folk music but we aren't just folk music. Lots of musicians extend the focus. Someone said Americana is people who can't get played on the radio. Maybe they can no longer be played on corporate commercial radio but it plays on radio. There are a lot of stations with an Americana format." She continues,

As much as anything else, it's an association. Americana is people you want to be associated with. It's a genre and it's also people we want to associate ourselves with. It's a label that gives us a group of artists to group ourselves with. We don't fit folk or country genres. We're a country-rock band, a roots rock band. We're not just folk. The fact that Americana ranges wide makes it comfortable to be a part of. We feel lucky we found our way into it. A stricter category would cause us problems: we're country in some ways but in other ways not at all.[1]

The Americana subculture is rooted in roots. Smith feels her band is fortunate to qualify for membership because Americana is not something you define; it's something you recognize. "It's a roots thing," she says.

You recognize Americana by the fact that it is roots music. When Bob Seger sings, you feel the roots. It's so down home, makes people feel, and John Hiatt. Classical roots musician. He makes you feel things. So Americana music is both a quality and an association. It makes you feel and it gives you a like-minded group of musicians to be a part of.

It's like a song I just wrote. It's a true story. My husband was doing some genealogy research and discovered one of his grandfathers was murdered, right on his farm. Now that's right up our alley. I don't know why but I got a sort of spaghetti Western feel. It fit the sound I heard in my head. I asked myself, do I want to be associated with that aspect of the music? That feel? If I'm a folkie, I don't. If I'm country, I don't. It's Americana.

Being a member of the Americana fraternity brings the support that creates the freedom to explore, to go beyond the limits that genre imposes.

Other artists agree that the sense of a group of like-minded artists is one of the strongest aspects of the field. Nora Jane Struthers has struggled to find her own way in the music business. Beginning as a folk singer in a duo with her father, she moved on to join a bluegrass band, left it to form a country-rock group, and is now moving into rock. She sees herself as an Americana artist because Americana is the only category that includes all of the types of music she has performed. Since Americana is "music drawn heavily from American styles: country, rock, folk, blues, jazz, but with something new added," it embraces the music she makes. "We have an electric guitar and a clawhammer banjo in the band. That's Americana."[2]

Self-identifying with this genre has given Struthers a place to feel comfortable, providing the acceptance she needed to grow as an artist. Genres are valuable and necessary because they create boundaries.

> We need genres because in order to process information, we need to put it in categories. So the emphasis on genre doesn't surprise me. As long as people listen with an open mind and don't reject an entire genre because they think they don't like it. I'm thankful the Americana category exists and that I'm a part of it. We're living in a commercial world. I make music that isn't country enough to be country or folky enough to be folk. Americana gives me a format. Its beauty is that it's a line-blurring genre. And the fact is, with Americana, people fit into other categories also. Springsteen is rock and Americana. Being in Americana gives you a sense of belonging to something bigger than you are and it makes you feel accepted. I feel like I'm not in this alone.

Many Americana musicians, no matter how different the music they play, buy into this community aspect. Trent Wagler of the old-time band the Steel Wheels describes the genre to me as

> a collective. It's a group of like-minded musicians who play very different music from each other. If you try to pin Americana down as a genre, the way pop is a genre, it's difficult. As a band, if you have a guitar, fiddle, mandolin and a standup bass and you stand around one microphone and sing, people call you bluegrass. We are more old-time than bluegrass, though. Americana is a collective. The community is bigger than the individual. I like using the medium of the string band to create a collective.

Most genres are restrictive; Americana, as we've seen, is inclusive. "It's as different from pop as a bicycle is from a Cadillac," Wagler says.

> What counts, though, is that there are many different types of bikes, which are Americana, but commercial pop is the Cadillac. Americana is an attempt to take back the heart of pop music. Commercial pop is about the bottom line. Americana is not about the bottom line. At its best, it's about the heart and soul of what a band can do. It's a group of musicians, playing music that has in common the fact that it is roots music but offers a wide variation.

It grants acceptance to many different kinds of musicians. Wagler explains,

> It's hard to get a handle on. If I'm going to an Americana show, am I going to see a string band or an electric band? As hard as it can be to pin down, I'm excited about hearing Willie Nelson, who isn't quite country enough, who plays standards, jazz, everything. Johnny Cash, who began as country and moved on from there, excited me also, especially as his music got more complex and stripped down. I love Americana both from a player and an audience standpoint. I love going to a festival and seeing a strong band and then a telecaster master.

All kinds of music can be found in Americana. As so many artists have noted, it is freeing, a quality Wagler is attracted to because "as a member of this community, I want to be able to draw from the Band; I want to pull from the best of Steve Earle."

Wagler believes genres are important and always will be.

> From the classic country of Patsy Cline to bro-country is quite a jump. They're different kinds of music altogether. Genre is designed to sell music, and Americana is the loosest, most open genre. Americana categorizes by association; if you like Alabama Shakes, you might like Alison Krauss. It's a grouping by attitude.
>
> In our own case, if you go to see us and you're expecting a bluegrass band, well, you're probably going to be disappointed because that's not what we are. I remember when I first heard of Mumford & Sons. Someone told me they were a British bluegrass band. When I saw the band, I thought, "That's not bluegrass. I loved what they were playing, but it wasn't bluegrass." If you have those kinds of expectations, you can be disappointed. If you have different expectations, though, we can satisfy them. Somebody in Charlottesville, Virginia, referred to us as an Americana roots band and we said, "yes." We can get behind that. Bluegrass has issues enough.

Another member of the community is Emmylou Harris, who declares she is not country anymore. She told Martin Farrer, "The people I know who are making music, they now have a name for us and they call it Americana. So it's Buddy Miller, Patty Griffin, Steve Earle and Shawn Colvin, Gillian Welch and Dave Rawlings and obviously, Rodney [Crowell]."[3]

How did Harris, who was labeled a country performer, become the Queen Mother of Americana? After dropping out of college to become a performer, she moved to New York and began playing the folk clubs in Greenwich Village. A quick marriage resulted in a daughter, and a quick divorce led her to move back to her parents' house in the Washington, D.C., suburbs, where she began playing. She started as a folkie, playing coffeehouses and clubs in the Washington, D.C., area. She once said that she was hiding out there until her option with Jubilee Records expired so that she wouldn't have to cut a second album for that company, which wanted to turn her into a Joni Mitchell clone. Even then, when she was barely out of her teens, Harris insisted on doing her own music and doing it her own way. In 1973, she got an opportunity to join her musical mentor and soul mate Gram Parsons in his Fallen Angels band, recording and touring with him until his death in 1973.

Parsons gave her a crash course in country music, and after his death, she signed with Warner Brothers Records and her first album for the label, *Pieces of the Sky*, was a hit. The album showcased her eclectic nature, eschewing pure country for a mixture of genres; she covered the Beatles, "For No One," and the Louvin Brothers' song "If I Could Only Win Your Love," done as a duet with Herb Pedersen, whose country-rock credentials were impeccable. He would go on to join the Dillards and the Desert Rose Band.

Warner wanted a "hot band" for her next album, so Harris formed the Hot Band, which consisted of Elvis Presley band veterans guitarist James Burton and pianist Glen Hardin, both of whom helped midwife the birth of rock and roll. Burton, while he was working with Dale Hawkins, played the famous guitar line and solo on Hawkins's original version of the roots rock classic "Suzy Q." Later, before joining Elvis, he became a member of Rick Nelson's band. Before he landed in Presley's band, Hardin was one of Buddy Holly's Crickets. Hank DeVito, John Ware, and Emory Gordy Jr. all came from Gram Parsons's band, while Harris discovered Rodney Crowell, who played rhythm guitar and sang backgrounds.

The Hot Band succeeded, and the albums Harris made with them are classics. What they have in common is a unique and solitary vision; they took a look at the direction country music was taking at the time and immediately rushed 180 degrees in the opposite direction. Harris recorded the Louvin Brothers at a time when their catalog was out of print.

She covered the forgotten singers Kitty Wells and Loretta Lynn and helped reestablish their reputations. Harris also helped Rodney Crowell, Vince Gill, Tony Brown, Barry Tashian, and many others become mainstream stars.

As the rising artists the Milk Carton Kids, a duo whose music has been described by *Acoustic Guitar* magazine as the Everly Brothers meet Simon and Garfunkel, said, "One of the best things about Emmylou is that she has an impressive and important way of staying current."[4] This need to stay current led her to win the Grammy for Best Americana album for her collaborative album with Rodney Crowell, *Old Yellow Moon*, in 2015. She also won the Americana Association's Album of the Year award for the same album. She and Crowell won again for vocal duo of the year. In fact, she shared in the award for the first Americana album honored by the Grammy association, *O Brother, Where Art Thou?* Asked about Americana at the ceremony, she said, "Rodney and I, maybe we're just arrogant, but we feel like we were Americana before it got a name."

In 2011, Harris told Fiona Sturges of England's *Independent* newspaper, "I've been bleeding outside the lines for some time," she notes. "I like to think I have my own category by now. I once said that I smoked country music but I didn't inhale. There is no more rural country music as it used to be. Country has to grow and change and evolve through the people who make it. Now I am often put in the category of contemporary folk, and thank God for that, because that's the only way I've been able to win Grammys."[5]

Her own category has turned out to be Americana, which has subsumed contemporary folk, and she has become known as the Queen of Americana, spending time and effort helping up-and-coming Americana acts, using the musicians in her bands and taking the new groups on tour with her. One reason the genre has as strong a sense of community as it does is because of Harris's work.

Mary Chapin Carpenter agrees that being in Americana offers a sense of belonging, a group of like-minded people to associate with. "What exactly is Americana?" she muses, in an interview with me conducted before one of her shows. "That's a question that has no answer. Music was never as compartmentalized as it was in the nineties. Everything was genre, and every radio station was carefully formatted. Americana broke that up. Now it includes blues, rock, country, folk, everything that has a base in roots music. That said, it's an umbrella term for anything that has a roots quality."

Carpenter spent a solid year playing complete reinterpretations of her classic songs, touring and playing with symphony orchestras in support of the album *Songs from the Movie*, which takes ten of her songs and reinterprets them for a symphony orchestra, arranged and conducted by Vince Mendoza.

"I wanted to do it for years and years," she says about the album,

> since I first heard Vince Mendoza's compositions. It took years to come together, and it's wonderful for me because he didn't just arrange the songs; he wrote new passages and wonderful arrangements. All of the new stuff on the record is a credit to Vince Mendoza.
>
> For me the great thing about the album is there's no shelf life to it. I can perform the album for the rest of my life.

Belonging to the Americana category allowed her to do the album. Its music is neither folk nor country, the two genres she has been associated with. It is, instead, original and new, though still connected to roots music. It is pure Americana, and that's an association Carpenter can accept. "It's very freeing. Why wouldn't I want to be associated with a form that allows me to be outside a box?" she asks.

Still, like many of the artists we'll discuss in the next chapter, Carpenter would rather not be categorized at all. "I don't know where people are going to categorize me," she says, "and I don't care."

NOTES

1. Quoted in Cameron Matthews, "Emmylou Harris and the Milk Carton Kids Reimagine Johnny Cash's 'Apache Tears' for New Compilation," Bluegrass Situation, August 12, 2014, http://www.bluegrasssituation.com/.

2. "Americana Awards Honor Emmylou Harris and Rodney Crowell," *CBS News*, September 19, 2013, http://www.cbsnews.com/.

3. Martin Farrer, "Emmylou Harris: 'I Don't Really Listen to New Country Music Anymore,'" *Guardian*, May 11, 2015, https://www.theguardian.com/.

4. Matthews, "Emmylou Harris."

5. Fiona Sturges, "Emmylou Harris: 'I Smoked Country but I Didn't Inhale,'" *Independent*, April 16, 2011.

16

IT MIGHT BE A GREAT BAG TO BE IN, BUT WHY MUST I BE IN A BAG AT ALL?

As wide open as the Americana category is, some artists such as Mary Chapin Carpenter, who have been dropped into it, simply don't want to be there. Not that they want to be in some other category. They see the whole idea of genre as limiting and believe that no category should confine them. The artists who reject categorization see themselves as wide ranging, adventurous, and original—or, at least, that's what they're striving to be. Though, as we've seen, Americana is a genre that ranges wide, rewards an adventurous spirit, and insists on originality; still, according to these artists, it promotes these values within limits. It's probably the biggest box, with the most flexible walls, but like any other box it still has walls, and while walls may be bent, they are still impossible to walk through. They stop you, and these artists do not want to be stopped.

Delta Rae is one of those groups that resist categorization. Promoted by their record label and publicists as Americana and, in fact, having headlined many Americana festivals, they recognize Americana as a legitimate category, even as they continue to question whether they belong there. Even though they see it as a valid genre, they're still reluctant to be associated with Americana, believing that being placed in this or any other genre limits them. They do not want their music classified into a category.

This chapter discusses why some artists see a possible down side to being placed in the Americana genre.

Ian Hölljes put it this way to me:

Americana? Sure, it is a legitimate category, but identifying ourselves as Americana immediately creates the question of genre in general. We're a band that loves all kinds of music. We draw on all kinds of music.

We attended the Americana Festival in Nashville last year. It was beautiful, with all kinds of styles represented. It was frustrating for a band like ours, though, who don't fit into a genre.

It is true that Delta Rae exceeds the limits of genre. Chart positions for their albums demonstrate this. Their 2015 release, *After the Fire*, hit number 152 on *Billboard*'s top two hundred chart, number 20 on the magazine's alternative chart, number 10 on the folk chart, number 3 on "heatseekers," and number 43 on rock airplay. This charting activity indicates that *Billboard* recognized the album as rock, pop, alternative, and folk, all at once.

Ironically, the Americana movement recognizes the blending of all of those musical types as one of the keys to the creation of Americana. That fact would appear to indicate that Delta Rae qualifies for the very reasons that seem to exempt them.

Maybe the diversity *Billboard* recognized stems from the band's writing and performing style. "When it comes to music," Hölljes declares, "there's two conflicting feelings: You want to create something that's transcendent and timeless, but at the same time you want to be the best." *Indy Weekly* declares the band to be interested in "musical forms both rustic and buffed, where call-and-response gospel vocals, string-band balladry and found percussion meet the close-harmony style of Fleetwood Mac, James Taylor and others from the family record collection. A less obvious component, but one that certainly adds to the band's ability to attract youthful ears, is the R&B inflections and vocal phrasings."[1]

Hölljes told me,

I think the Motown hits are probably the most soulful, nourishing music ever made. Songs like "Stand by Me" and "Midnight Train to Georgia" and so many of Michael Jackson's hits, they taught people to survive on those albums.[2] That's the kind of stuff I want to create. I just find them so stirring, and that's what I tend to go back to when I'm trying to write. I want the songs to feel like they came out of the sky.

Brittany Hölljes acknowledges that if Delta Rae is to be categorized, this one fits. "If you want to put it in a genre," she said to me, "I'd put it in Americana because it captures so much of American music, crosses all boundaries and time."

Her brother Ian reluctantly agrees. If Delta Rae must be categorized, he says, Americana is the one, since it "combines all the things I love about music: folklore, lyrical depth, imagery and a strong vocal quality." Still, the group is emphatic that they don't "want to be a single sound. They want to be a band." They want to make music. Without qualification.

As for being a genre band, Hölljes says, "We're all struggling with it. People who pick up our albums will hear all kinds of sounds: hip-hop, rock, folk, some soul . . ."

The Irish singer Maura O'Connell is also drawn to all sorts of songs and has long fought the idea of categorization, striving to be recognized as a singer who responds to any type of song that speaks to her. Indeed, she has T-shirts with her name on them and beneath her name the words "Just a Singer." O'Connell sees only the down side of being associated with a genre.

In fact, O'Connell announced her retirement from touring. Hers is a selective retirement, though. "I retired from the music business," she explains to me, "not from music. I won't go out and tour anymore, but if anybody wants me to come somewhere and sing a few songs, I'm delighted to do it." Why the retrenchment? "The music business has changed too much. You have to make your money touring now; record sales no longer do it. I can't carry a band out on tour anymore. The costs are too high, and the return is too low."

Part of the reason she finds herself in this awkward situation is the very quality that made her career and her music so interesting: her versatility. "I never fully integrated into one group. I was never this or that. It's too expensive now to do it if you're outside the system."

One reason artists are assigned to categories, even if they don't think they fit in them and even if they do not want to be categorized, is economic. As we saw earlier, touring costs are way up and returns have shrunk. Everything from gas and lodging to van rental and food on the road and to venue costs and electricity is up. Clubs can't afford to put up guarantees anymore, and tickets have priced themselves out so that audiences are having to be more selective in the shows they attend; where in better days they might have gone to monthly or biweekly shows, they can no longer afford to attend concerts that frequently. They've cut back. Most people are aware of how rising prices affect audiences, but they don't think of the impact they have on artists also, especially those who like Maura O'Connell don't fit easily into one category and are forced as a result to work outside the major show business system.

O'Connell has spent most of her career outside the system. Born in the town of Ennis, in County Clare, Ireland, she worked as a child in the family fish shop, growing up hearing the music her parents loved: opera on her mother's side, Irish rebel ballads on her father's. When she discovered her own gift for singing, she began working local folk clubs as half a duet with Mike Hanrahan, who later became the leader of Stockton's Wing.

Then she got a break; she joined De Dannan as their first vocalist. The timing could not have been better.

> In the early seventies, traditional Irish music was like rock 'n' roll in Ireland. It was everywhere, all over the radio. De Dannan asked me to join, and I told them I didn't really do that kind of music—and I didn't. I didn't think I could do that. But I joined them and became known as a folk singer. Now, it's a frustrating thing. I still get put in that category, and I've never really belonged there. Now I joke about it: What kind of singer are you? A good one. What kind of songs do you do? Good songs.

She sang on De Dannan's *Star Spangled Molly* album, which became a huge hit, and its reception nailed the lid on her public identification as a folkie. While touring with De Dannan, she met the members of New Grass Revival, who were busy reinventing bluegrass, adding elements of rock and jazz and jam-band improvisational freedom to the traditional driving string-band sound. She became so enthralled with their music that she moved to Nashville so she could work with them and the nucleus of musicians that made up the then thriving New Grass movement: Sam Bush, Béla Fleck, Jerry Douglas, Edgar Meyer, and others. A string of major albums for Philo, Warner Brothers, and Sugar Hill Records followed.

The musicians she associated with were known for pushing boundaries, blasting away at genres, deliberately transcending all of the established limits. O'Connell felt right at home in their company. Their musical philosophy matched hers. "I'm still mostly considered a folk singer," she says, continuing her argument against categorization, "although I'm not, and I mostly work at folk clubs. But any song has the potential to be a folk song. If it's an American standard, a pop song, anything, it can be a folk song."

Show business economics kept her in the clubs. "I've mostly worked folk clubs and shows because I couldn't afford to take a band on the road."

Being labeled a folk singer also kept O'Connell in the folk clubs. Once you're placed in a particular bag, that's the way bookers think of you. "Whatever category is hot, they try to fit you into," she says. "Lately it's been Americana. The last time I was nominated for a Grammy, it was in the Americana category, and there was only one other folk person nominated. Categorization is music business stuff. It's a business. I've been put into one category after another, and I've fought not to be categorized through my whole career."

If she ever had a chance of breaking out of a category, that chance was erased forever by her participation in the album *A Woman's Heart*, a group album containing cuts by many wonderful female Irish singers. Eleanor McEvoy, Dolores Keane, Francis Black, Mary Black, Sharon Shannon, and O'Connell all performed a couple of songs each, and the resulting album was such a massive hit that it has been said everybody in Ireland—and elsewhere—owns a copy. Its success shocked everybody, including the participants. Nobody expected the album to become the force it did, and no one knows why it happened.

Asked why it was so big, O'Connell laughs and says, "I don't know. If I knew, I'd use it. Maybe it's because it was the celebration of the singer."

Whatever else the album accomplished, it cemented her into the folk category.

Her professional life has not been just an attempt to break out of the folk category; it's been an effort to transcend all categories, to get the public and the industry to recognize that she is, in her own words, "Just a singer." Rather than simply performing folk material, Maura O'Connell sings whatever songs appeal to her, looking for the celebratory moments, the rare times on stage and in the studio when magic happens.

And the possibility of that magic is why she fights being categorized, even going so far as advertising the fact that she is not, in her own eyes, a folk singer, an Americana singer, or any other genre-clad singer. When she proclaims herself to be just a singer, she is not denigrating herself in any way. To Maura O'Connell, a singer is an artist who penetrates one's own soul, as well as the soul of the song. She told the variety show *Music City Roots*, "A lot of people think every singer is someone's puppet. That they are not fully invested in the song—that they are at the whim of a producer or a songwriter or a band. Singing has been denigrated like that for too long."

Many singers are actually the puppets of a producer. In fact, a Nashville session musician told me that in most cases, the band gets together with the producer and arranges the song before the singer arrives. Sometimes, when they know the key she's going to sing it in, they'll lay down the basic tracks before she even appears. The idea of finding the soul of the song or touching the singer's own soul doesn't enter into the equation.

Maura O'Connell has never been and says she never will be that kind of singer. She says she has not been in the superficial pop song business, declaring that she was in the business of touching souls, her own and the audience's. Being confined to a single genre deadens the soul.

Mary Black is another Irish singer who has been widely influenced by Americana musicians and has been cast in the bronze of Americana. Although mostly thought of as a folk singer, she says that from her very first public performances, she had her eyes on a wider prize. Being from the city of Dublin, rather than from rural Ireland, she was exposed to a wide variety of music and always wanted to sing all of it. She says being categorized as folk first and then Americana has limited her opportunities.

Black says she never had a chance to be anything other than a singer. She was born into a musical family; her father was a fiddler, her mother was a singer, and her three brothers and younger sister were all performers.

"From the time I was a little girl, I sang with my older brothers," she told me. "They dragged me along to sing at places where you just signed up and sang at clubs. We never thought of it as a career. We were doing it for the love of it, for the joy of the music. Then I got a big break. The singer Christy Moore, who was very well known in Ireland, invited me to sing on his TV show. I didn't have an album out or anything. That was the starting point."

From that start, Black built a thirty-year international career, with eleven released albums and the title of the Voice of Ireland. With her retirement from touring in 2015, that career has come to an end. Like Maura O'Connell, Black has given up the road. Again, like O'Connell, she emphasizes that she did not retire, just "gave up the road. I've been doing it for thirty years. I feel the time is right. My life is pointing that way. Still, I can't imagine not singing. I'll do some things at home. I want to travel, though, to see parts of the world I haven't seen. I want to take up painting again."

Considering the career she's had, the drive to live a normal life is understandable. Christy Moore's show led to her joining the folk band General Humbert, with whom she made two albums and toured for two years before going out on her own and recording her first solo album, *Mary Black*, which became a hit. Invited to replace Maura O'Connell when O'Connell left De Dannan, Black accepted on one condition: she insisted that she be able to continue her solo career while still being a member of the group.

They agreed, and she stayed with them until 1986, leaving after winning Ireland's Entertainer of the Year award. In 1987 and 1988, Black was named Ireland's Best Female Artist, and by the 1990s she had become an international superstar. All of her albums have gone platinum; several are multiplatinum.

Billboard has called Black "a firm favorite to join the heavy hitting ranks of such Irish artists as Enya, Sinead O'Connor and Clannad's Maire Brennan in the international marketplace."[3]

The unique quality of Black's voice is a major reason her career has lasted so long. The editors of *What Hi-Fi?* magazine feel her voice is so pure that they use it to compare the sound of stereo systems, and music critic Michael Leahy said, "Over the years, Mary Black has come to define what many people see as the essence of Irish women singers: profound, slightly ethereal and beyond the reaches of trends."[4]

Black's ability to find great songs has also kept her in the forefront. Originally known as a folk singer, she deliberately tried to break out of that category by seeking out and recording the music of the up-and-coming songwriters of Ireland, a move that caused some critics to accuse her of deserting the traditional folk music that made her famous. "I don't see it that way," she says. "From my first solo album, I did some traditional folk, but also newer material. I lived in Dublin, not the rural areas, so I was exposed to a lot more influences from the beginning. I wanted to explore, wanted a wide range of songs. When I discovered all the great new Irish writers, I had an opportunity to record their work. A lot of them are not performers." Her reasoning for the variety is simple: "I don't like to put music in boxes." About the wide variety of music she has recorded, she says, "I started in folk music but never felt there should be any boundaries in music. Fortunately here in Ireland there's an openness about music that allows you to step outside of categories."

That openness might exist in Ireland, but it certainly hasn't spread to the music industry in the United States. Here, she has never overcome the folk singer identification, although it has expanded to become a subset of Americana. So, even if she would rather not be put in a box at all, she is resigned to that categorization: "The folk singer images used to drive me crazy. Although folk and traditional have had a huge influence on me and I would never turn my back on that, I didn't want to be confined to one area of music. I wanted to explore."

Ironically, it is that confinement to a single area that has allowed Black's music to be heard worldwide. So, even if the artists discussed here would rather not be thrown into a category, the commercial side of the industry insists that they be grouped so that their music can be broadcast, promoted, and marketed. As Al Moss, the record promoter who is the only person to have served on the Americana Association's board of directors from its beginning, says, the concept of Americana is a marketing tool, but at least it markets these performers as artists, not as sellers of plastic wares. By being associated with Americana, Delta Rae, Maura O'Connell, Mary Black, and many others are able to be taken seriously, on close to their own terms. In no other genre would they be free to make the music they have given to the public.

NOTES

1. David Klein, "Will Durham's Delta Rae Again Polish Americana for the Masses," *Indy Weekly*, July 25, 2012, http://www.indyweek.com/.

2. Technically, "Midnight Train to Georgia" and "Stand by Me" are not Motown songs. Hölljes is categorizing by mood rather than literalism.

3. Carolyn Andre, "Mary Black," Carolyn's House of Music, accessed September 18, 2016, http://house-of-music.com/.

4. Michael Leahy, "Mary Black: A Woman's Voice," A-Lyric.com, accessed September 18, 2016, http://www.a-lyric.com/.

Interlude: Jim Lauderdale:
The Face of America

Jim Lauderdale did not turn to Americana from another genre; he was already there. An accomplished folk, country, soul, bluegrass, rock, R&B, and blues singer, he is also a first-rate songwriter and a record producer. Lauderdale appears to excel at all things roots, and since the rise of Americana, he has tossed his hat into that ring, operating a radio show with Buddy Miller on satellite radio and serving as emcee at most of the Americana Awards shows.

Another thing that places him in the center of Americana is what Kim Richey named "the Jim Lauderdale Phenomenon,"[1] which refers ironically to the fact that as soon as he was nominated for a Grammy, his record company dropped him. He was also dropped by three other major labels even as he was winning accolades. He has found success on small independent labels, including his own Sky Crunch Records, releasing most of his more than twenty-five albums that way. He has also been successful as a writer, with hundreds of songs recorded by country, pop, and soul singers.

Music and the church have been circulating in Lauderdale's blood since birth. His mother, a piano teacher, served as music director, choir director, and organist in the Presbyterian churches around their South Carolina home, while his father was a minister. Both of them sang. Growing up in that atmosphere put musical instruments in Lauderdale's fingers at an early age. He was playing drums at the age of eleven and by the time he was fifteen had added harmonica and five-string banjo to his repertoire. Guitar was added in college. He performed in bluegrass bands, rock bands, and folk groups through his teenage years.

After college, he, like so many budding musicians and songwriters, moved to Nashville where he hustled unsuccessfully long enough to come to believe that his future lay elsewhere, maybe New York City. There he met the legendary guitarist Buddy Miller and played in a band with him, beginning a friendship and musical collaboration that lasts to this day.

Ever restless, anxious for success, Lauderdale relocated to Los Angeles, where in 1989, he recorded an album for CBS Records, which wasn't released until 2001. He also landed a publishing deal with Blue Water Music and made another album, which has never been released.

Landing a better publishing deal with Reprise, he moved back to Nashville and released *Planet of Love* in 1991, an album that was produced by Rodney Crowell and John Leventhal. He told *Rolling Stone*, "It was a long road for me. I was 35 when my first record came out."[2] The record tanked as another victim of the station manager's favorite cliché: too country for rock, too rock for country. Eight of the ten songs on *Planet of Love* were recorded by other artists, a fact that led to the idea that Lauderdale's albums were actually collections of demos for other artists to choose songs from.

He followed this one with *Lost in the Lonesome Pines*, a bluegrass collaboration with Ralph Stanley that won the 2002 Grammy Award for Best Bluegrass album. That leaping around in genres, the movement from country rock to bluegrass that those albums represented, set the pattern for Lauderdale's recording career; he has made albums with groups like the jam band Donna the Buffalo, acoustic blues group Hot Tuna, the North Mississippi All-Stars, and guitar wizard Buddy Miller. In 2015, he released a two-record set, *Soul Searching*. Volume 1 was recorded in Memphis and explores the soul music made famous by that city's musical scene, while volume 2 does the same for Nashville.

Lauderdale's brilliance is that he sees the future in the past and is holding it aloft so that everyone can see it, and reminding his audience where it came from. Where other singers come to Nashville with visions of Blake Shelton or Tim McGraw in their heads, Lauderdale carried a mental image of George Jones as the man he wanted to model himself after. He has also spoken admiringly of Johnnie and Jack, a harmony duo from the late 1950s and early 1960s, and is a great admirer of the triad of

Johnny Cash, Merle Haggard, and Buck Owens. His own music is rooted in the soil of early country; his album, *I'm a Song*, is a road trip through country music history, offering up songs in the Bakersfield tradition of Buck Owens, western swing tunes, classic country weepers, and the Nashville sound. Lauderdale, in this album, touches on all country styles and makes them his own.

Lauderdale maintains control over his music. He makes no compromises and maintains his artistic autonomy. He has never written to formula or to order; he writes what is meaningful to him. For that he pays a price: no airplay on country radio.

Twang Nation, the Nashville-based online Americana magazine, reported on Sony Music Nashville CEO Gary Overton's 2016 statement to the Nashville *Tennessean*: "If you're not on country radio, you don't exist." Those words sound callous and unfeeling. Overton was criticized for saying those words, but *Twang Nation* went on to point out that Overton made the controversial comment at the Country Radio Seminar Convention where a couple thousand attendees got together to discuss the future of country radio. In that context, says *Twang Nation*, Overton's words make sense: "As with any trade convention, quality was not the focus, unless there is a direct line between it and profits. It's about return on investment. Period."[3]

Jim Lauderdale is not played on country radio. As far as country radio is concerned, he does not even exist. He is not invested in the world of contemporary country music, so far as commercial radio goes; they see no return in playing his songs. He very definitely exists in the Americana world, though. A cross-genre singer, musician, and singer, he has a stack of awards to his name—Grammies and Americana Association prizes— as high as his chest and has emceed the Americana Association Awards since 2002, the year he won both Artist of the Year and Song of the Year.

Lauderdale made a deliberate choice early on to write and play his own kind of music, instead of commercial mass-culture songs, and he has lived up to that commitment. After his early experiences, he has gone so far as to avoid signing again with a major label, preferring instead to release his records on small independent labels, including his own. That way he can maintain full artistic control over what he does and can remain independent himself.

All of that has made him the face of Americana.

NOTES

1. Peter Cooper, "Without 'Star-Level' Clout, Lauderdale Released from RCA," *Tennessean*, February 21, 2001.

2. Daniel Durchholz, "Jim Lauderdale Reflects on Legendary, 'Left-of-Center' Career," *Rolling Stone*, September 29, 2014.

3. "Sony Music Nashville CEO Gary Overton Is Right (And So What?)," *Twang Nation*, accessed September 18, 2016, http://www.twangnation.com/.

17

THE ARCHETYPES OF AMERICANA

On February 13, 2011, the Americana field had what might be described as the gathering of the archetypes: at the annual Grammy Awards show, where Mumford & Sons and the Avett Brothers sang "Maggie's Farm" along with its composer Bob Dylan. At that time, the worldwide viewing audience saw one of the veteran founders of the movement welcome those who would carry the flag along when he stepped down. In other words, they saw new archetypes being born.

It was that night that new fans flocked to the format like bats leaving a cave at sundown, and it was that night that millions of viewers both here and abroad had all of their doubts about Americana as a medium erased. Everyone who saw that show—or saw the video on YouTube—now knew what Americana both looked and sounded like. They had a model, an archetype, to follow.

And they saw that it was international. Mumford & Sons are English and were formed in London in 2007 by four musicians who had been playing in other people's bands. When they formed their own band, the characteristics of the music they played appeared to be deceptively artless and homogenized: simple arrangements played on folk instruments with a rock-styled five-string banjo played "incorrectly." Instead of the old-time clawhammer style or either the standard bluegrass or melodic three-finger picking, the banjo is primarily strummed loudly and aggressively. The voices feature complex harmonies, and at odd times during the song, the band shifts the tempo, exploding in a violent stream of sound before returning to the original tempo. In lesser hands the sound would be too formulaic, but Mumford & Sons make it work.

Island Records liked what they heard but held off on signing the band, wanting to be sure that the band was ready to play in the big leagues. By 2009, Mumford & Sons determined themselves ready but, rather than sign with Island, decided to handle their recording themselves. They signed a licensing deal with Island Records. To cover the Australian and New Zealand market, they signed with Dew Process, while in the United States Glassnote Records got the deal. Ownership remained with the Mumfords' company, Gentlemen of the Road.

When they went to record their first album, they did not own any instruments or equipment. They showed up at the studio empty-handed and were turned away by the producer. Using bluegrass and folk instruments found in the studio, a core instrumentation of guitar, banjo, piano, and double bass, the band played in an aggressive alternative-rock style that they adapted from Old Crow Medicine Show. As Marcus Mumford says, "I first heard Old Crow's music when I was, like, 16, 17, and that really got me into, like, folk music, bluegrass. I mean, I'd listened to a lot of Dylan, but I hadn't really ventured into the country world so much. So Old Crow were the band that made me fall in love with country music."[1]

It was that band that made Mumford & Sons add the banjo to the mix and start the country nights in London that led to their recognition. Had it not been for Old Crow Medicine Show, Mumford feels, the band would not have been led to the old-time sounds.[2] The first album was promoted as bluegrass, but as Trent Wagler told me, as soon as anyone heard it, it was obvious that it wasn't bluegrass. It was something new, something unique and different that grew organically out of the old and the familiar. Mumford & Sons did not play bluegrass. They changed it.

But after the band ended the tour with their second album, *Babel*, Winston Marshall, the band's banjo player, told *Vulture* magazine that they were breaking up. Mumford & Sons, he said, was over.[3] Keyboardist Ben Lovett told *Rolling Stone*, "There won't be any Mumford & Sons activities for the near future."[4] Marshall, though, reached out to *Vulture* once more and insisted this was no sabbatical; the band was through. "It was a good time," he said. "It's over."[5]

The band's management, however, insisted the parting was not permanent, which turned out to be accurate. After a two-year layoff, the group announced a third album and a tour. This time it would be different, however: no banjo. Speaking once more to his favorite outlet, Winston Marshall said that Mumford & Sons had not just killed the banjo; they murdered it. "We let it yeah—fuck the banjo. I fucking hate the banjo."[6] So the new album, *Wilder Mind*, would not only be totally free of the sound of the banjo but also have no acoustic instruments on it at all. All of the guitars and the bass were electric, and the cello was dumped along with the standup bass.

The question that pops into everyone's mind immediately is this: why would a band that had a platinum hit their first time out and a multiplatinum hit with their follow-up album suddenly change everything for their third album? In the case of Mumford & Sons, the change was due to the archetypal status that they held and took so seriously. Archetypal bands change and grow. They try different approaches, different sounds, and as Jimmie Fadden said about the Dirt Band's collective approach to the music, there's a lot of failure, but then, there's a lot of success also.

A band that models itself after the archetype will stay in the same groove. The archetypal band will grow and change, and will experiment and fail as much as it succeeds in reaching its artistic goals, but it will continue to take chances, which is what Mumford & Sons did with *Wilder Mind*.

The growth and development of the Avett Brothers matches that of Mumford & Sons. From North Carolina, they are the only band I know of that has posted a video on YouTube explaining how to pronounce their name.

Like Mumford & Sons, the Avetts played in a bunch of bands while establishing themselves, but their success began when they joined forces in the rock band Nemo. While playing in Nemo they began writing and playing acoustic music, and upon discovering that the acoustic stuff went over with audiences, in 2000, they released the self-titled EP, *The Avett Brothers*. When Nemo folded, they decided to concentrate on acoustic music and, after recruiting a bassist, recorded the first full-length Avett Brothers disc, *Country Was*.

This album caught the attention of local label owner Dolph Ramseur, who signed them to Ramseur Records and released *A Carolina Jubilee*, a turning-point record for them. It was the first of their records to hint at what the Avett Brothers would become; it was a blend of bluegrass, punk, country, pop, folk, rock honky-tonk, and ragtime, all put through a blender that created an intoxicating mixture that few people had imagined before they came along.

A steady release schedule of albums followed, building on the foundation they had laid down with *A Carolina Jubilee*, culminating in the band's winning the Americana Music Association's Duo/Group of the Year and New/Emerging Artist of the Year award for 2007. At about this time, they also announced that they had signed with Rick Rubin's American Recordings label and that he would produce their next album. Rubin was their ideal producer because, as he had shown in his work with Johnny Cash late in that artist's career, Rubin was interested in integrity and authenticity in an artist and had a way of drawing those qualities out. Working with Rubin, the band recorded *I Love You and You*, a CD that pointed to them as the American version of Mumford & Sons.

It got them their shot on the Grammy program singing with Dylan and Mumford & Sons, a night that made them archetypal and sent them beyond the notion of being a mere band into legendary status, a status their last few Rick Rubin–produced albums have built on.

WHY ARE MUMFORD & SONS AND THE AVETT BROTHERS IMPORTANT?

Eric Sunderman, an associate editor at the website Noisey, posted on August 6, 2013, a piece in Noisey called "Don't Let Mumford & Sons Trick You into Liking Them" in which he argues that the music of the band is "very bad. It's overtly sincere folk rock. It's more earnest than a sophomore in college who discovered Walt Whitman's *Leaves of Grass* for the first time and quotes it regularly. It's more pretentious than tattooing 'Live, laugh, love' on your leg." He also claims that their folk-stompy style has become so common that it's practically a cliché. In all, to sum up Sunderman's argument in his own words, it is "stupid music" and Mumford & Sons is a "terrible, terrible, terrible band."[7]

We can point out immediately that an attack this strong on a band, an all-out assault that depends entirely on negative judgments and is almost completely without factual content, reveals not simply a dislike but an active fear. His title suggests that if you listen to Mumford & Sons, you'll get somehow hornswoggled into liking them, and you must not under any circumstances let yourself enjoy the self-awareness, courage, humor, or the way their music taps into "a side of humanity that we all must appreciate and engage with in order to learn about ourselves, about why we think the way we do and about what it all means"—all qualities that can be found, the author says, in the terrible, terrible, terrible music of Mumford & Sons.[8]

Sunderman may have a point: Mumford & Sons' songs do exhibit self-awareness, courage, and humor, but I maintain that these very qualities help us learn about ourselves. It teaches us who we are and why, and that is what is archetypal about it.

And that is why we need it—with or without acoustic instruments.

As for the Avett Brothers, they offer the same archetypal qualities of Mumford & Sons, except instead of being personally attacked by critics, they have been used as a tool to attack other North Carolina bands, such as Delta Rae.

Although they are thought of as an old-timey, bluegrass-inflected band, the Avett Brothers described their 2016 album, *True Sadness*, as being inspired by Queen, Sister Rosetta Thorpe, Jimmie Rodgers, Tom Petty, Nine Inch Nails, Gillian Welch, Aretha Franklin, and Pink Floyd.

Their relationship with their fans allows the Avetts to draw on so many influences on the same album. "For us, we're very connected to our audience and we feel a great responsibility to keep it honest with them and to take responsibility for what we release and so instead of taking a more safe route, I think we want to be even more honest and less concerned with image or being cool," Scott Avett told the *Huffington Post*.[9]

That's the magic with the Avett Brothers; that's what makes them archetypal: they and their audience are one. Like the Carter Family before them, they don't need to project an image that the mass audience will find favorable. Simply being themselves, like the Carters, they have proven to be a positive influence on their audience because there is very little distance between them and the crowd. They are their audience. As long as they maintain their honesty, integrity, and, like Mumford & Sons, their self-awareness, then their archetypal authenticity will shine through.

And that authenticity has driven every band or performer who has become identified with Americana. Realness is the stuff that creates and propels Americana, and as was the case with Jimmie Rodgers and the Carter Family, these bands are real.

NOTES

1. Marissa Moss, "Mumford & Company Case the American Dream in Big Easy Express," *American Songwriter*, April 27, 2012.

2. Ibid.

3. Caroline Bankoff, "Mumford & Sons Is Going on Hiatus," *Vulture*, September 21, 2013, http://www.vulture.com/.

4. "Mumford & Sons Taking a Break for a Considerable Amount of Time," *Huffington Post*, September 21, 2013, http://www.huffingtonpost.com/.

5. Bankoff, "Mumford & Sons."

6. Anna Silman, "Mumford & Sons' Winston Marshall F*cking Hates the Banjo, Says the Band Is Done for Good," *Vulture*, March 26, 2014, http://www.vulture.com/

7. Eric Sunderman, "Don't Let Mumford & Sons Trick You into Liking Them," Noisey, August 8, 2014, http://www.noisey.com/.

8. Ibid.

9. Lauren Moraski, "The Avett Brothers Don't Care If You Think They're Cool," *Huffington Post*, June 22, 2016, http://www.huffingtonpost.com/.

18

BACK TO THE QUESTION

Do We Have Any Idea What Americana Is?

In order to come to grips with the rise of Americana, we're going to have to take a little walk through the changes in technology that have altered the paradigm of our society. As far back as 1982, the futurist John Naisbitt identified a core concept that has contributed greatly to the rise of Americana: he devoted a chapter in his paradigm-changing book *Megatrends* to an idea he called high tech, high touch. (In 1999, he followed up with a full book on the topic.)[1]

High tech refers to the technology we have surrounded ourselves with: personal computers, smartphones, video games, interactive books, e-books, music downloads, e-mail, texting, and virtual reality—all of the things that inundate us daily, a twenty-four-hour immersion into a world that only truly exists in cyberspace. Naisbitt saw the high-tech world as a "technologically intoxicated zone"[2] that causes all of us to live in it to look for instant solutions and to live lives that are "distanced and distracted."[3] The ultimate cost of living in a high-tech world is a loss of the important values and abstractions that once guided our lives: love, hope, fear, longing, forgiveness, authenticity, nature, and spirituality. It is no coincidence that those abstractions are exactly what Americana songs are about. In a high-tech world, we need to be able to interact with each other and our technology in a human way; we need to be able to touch and use it, to be a partner with our technological advances, instead of victims of them. The high-tech world isolates us from each other, physically and mentally; it destroys community. We need the high-touch world to keep a sense of belonging together.

What does this have to do with Americana music? The answer is as simple as it is obvious: Americana is high-touch music. Played on mainly acoustic instruments, with little or no use for high-tech programmed instruments such as synthesizers, it presents a simple surface, one that is accessible and comprehensible, and carries a message that has been in danger of becoming lost in our high-tech world. It unites us, gives us a sense of belonging; not only are fans close to each other, but also many times the artists are close to the fans; there is little distance between them. Carolyn Hester said once that a concert is often a reunion with old friends. "People come that you've gotten to know from speaking to them at other shows. We talk about each other's kids, catch up on our lives. Some of them are learning the songs and talk about that." At the time she said those words, we were sitting at an empty table after a show, doing just that.

Often, as is the case with house concerts, fans are promoting the shows. Networks build. Facebook pages spring up, devoted to the work of a particular artist or to the use of an instrument or even discussions of the whole movement. Americana, then, is a high-touch genre in a high-tech world. It is a way of getting beyond our alienation, of cutting the distance between ourselves and our world.

This is not to overlook the role of our high-tech world in the creation of the music. As noted earlier, small, inexpensive, high-touch home-recording studios and personal computers make the music possible and, certainly, computers make promotion and sale possible, but to use technology does not mean to be victimized by it. Americana is careful to stay human and accessible.

WHEN WE LISTEN, HOW DO WE KNOW IT'S AMERICANA WE'RE LISTENING TO?

At this writing, the Americana chart at *The Alternate Root Magazine* has listed the top one hundred Americana albums of 2015. Among their choices are such diverse artists as Australian folk-rocker Kasey Chambers, former bluegrass singer Chris Stapleton, jazz- and classical-influenced bluegrass band the Punch Brothers, chameleon Steve Earle (this time with his roots-rock band, the Dukes), progressive country singer Kacey Musgraves, R&B masters Barrence Whitfield and the Savages, Texas troubadour Ray Wylie Hubbard, chart regulars Emmylou Harris and Rodney Crowell, and bluesman Joe Louis Walker.

This is one diverse group. On the surface, it would appear that many of them have nothing in common. If we examine their common factors, however, including factors we identified in earlier chapters, we might find some generalizations that can be said to be true of the entire Americana genre. This examination will be primarily a review of the qualities we have already identified as being building blocks of Americana, a summing up, if you will. Then we will move into interpretation.

THEY WORK OUTSIDE THE MAINSTREAM

Like all Americana, these artists have careers that are largely outside the mainstream of contemporary popular music. Even though Kasey Chambers and Kacey Musgraves are country singers, it is safe to assume that most fans who depend on contemporary country radio to discover new music have never heard them on their radios or on record. Their names may be vaguely familiar but not their music. They do not get much mainstream radio play and are ignored by radio programmers because their records do not fit current formulas. Neither Ray Wiley Hubbard nor Steve Earle has gotten regular play on country radio since the 1990s, and both tolerated very spotty play even back then. And, according to record promoter Al Moss, both Chris Stapleton and Kacey Musgraves received more airplay on Americana stations than country stations. They also rose higher on Americana charts than on mainstream country charts.

What this all means is that Americana can "break" an artist, that is, get him or her the exposure needed to become known. Americana stations propelled both Musgraves and Stapleton to Grammy nominations, where they joined other Americana favorites such as Florence and the Machine, Bob Dylan, and James Taylor. This level of acceptance would indicate that promotion as an Americana artist can cut significant time off an artist's apprenticeship.

THEY ARE MORE INTERESTED IN ROOTS THAN CURRENT MUSIC

Steve Earle's albums with the Dukes have little to do with current country rock, or for that matter, contemporary rock. Instead of the current rock band Apache Relay, its model is Chuck Berry. The songs are mostly blues based, shuffle riffs that strike the listener as familiar because they have been heard for so long in the rock and R&B of the 1950s. Earle, who has a deserved reputation for spreading his musical net unpredictably wide, goes to the past to illuminate the future.

The country of Chris Stapleton is reflective of the outlaw era that Willie Nelson, Waylon Jennings, Tompal Glaser, and David Allan Coe developed back in the 1970s. In fact, his biggest song, "Tennessee Whiskey," previously a number one hit for George Jones, was also covered by Coe. Stapleton, who first came to prominence as the lead singer for the bluegrass band the SteelDrivers, was discovered by country radio but deemed acceptable after Americana stations broke the album. Upon seeing the reception his album *Traveler* got on Americana radio, the Country Music Association invited him to appear on its awards show. The result was a new country star being born, a new star that Americana followers had known of for months. Mercury Records vice president of promotion Damon Moberly told *Billboard*, "His performance was obviously a watershed moment that we needed to take advantage of. He was unknown to many until the show. Since then, there's just been an on-going discovery. . . . With radio, I think a lot of programmers wanted to play him previously and felt a little more confident after the CMAs."[4] The result was that an album that had lingered as though buried in the upper reaches of the *Billboard* charts for months suddenly springboarded to number one and also spent twelve weeks at number one on the Top Country Charts. In 2015, Stapleton was nominated for four Grammy Awards and won two, for best country album and best country vocal performance for its title song. All of this was for an album that has its roots in the 1960s and 1970s. And, of course, Joe Louis Walker's music is not simply connected to the past; it is, like that of Barrett Whitfield, the past.

THEY ARE AUTHENTIC

Al Moss considers authenticity to be the hallmark of Americana. Most people would agree that it is a major distinction between Americana and mainstream pop. If I am listening to Americana, I want to hear the lyrics, and I want to believe them. I want to hear and feel the singers' deepest feelings expressed and reflected in their songs.

Kasey Chambers has always been her own woman, following her own muse and recording what was important to her, rather than what would bring her a large audience. Her songs, such as "The Captain," the title song of her first album and still her signature song, often explore politically incorrect subjects. "The Captain," for example, is the lament of a young girl who wants only to belong to the man she addresses, the captain of her body and soul. It expresses her willingness to give herself to him entirely, sacrificing her autonomy and self-esteem for the sake of her love. Hearing it, listeners feel compassion for the girl, even as we find her actions frightening and a little repulsive.

Chambers, however, delights in the unexpected. Of her album *Bittersweet*, she said, "I wanted to have the experience of making a record that I had never had before. I wanted to challenge myself and I wanted to be excited." AllMusic says the album "confirms that she can move in any number of different directions and still offer her listeners something remarkable." Her love of the unexpected and her delight in musical shapeshifting are authentically her and have caused the *Huffington Post* to call her the "best Americana singer since Lucinda [Williams]" while praising her "near-delirious joy in singing to us."[5]

But what precisely do we mean by authentic? Superficially, the word means genuine, so an authentic song would be one that rings true, and an authentic performance would be one that reveals the real thing. If the performance, the song, the CD, or whatever product is being discussed has an aura of truth to it, then we can call it genuine. Certainly the best Americana offerings fit that definition. But we don't have to be content with genuineness. We can go a little deeper. *Webster*'s dictionary does and claims that authentic refers to originality of authorship. When Kasey Chambers says she wants to make an album that she's never made before, she means that she wants to own it; she wants to be its author.

And whether or not you write something has little to do with whether you are its author or not. Linda Ronstadt did not write songs, but there are dozens that she has made her own. Piano Red did not write many of the ragtime blues and hollers that he recorded, but he proved ownership of them in his passion and his performance. So authenticity means to make a thing your own, to become its author.

Perhaps a negative example will clarify the situation. When Justin Timberlake played a folk singer in the film *Inside Llewyn Davis*, many critics and viewers did not find him credible in the role. He was never able to transcend the fact that he was acting; he failed to create a sense that he had become the folkie he was pretending to be. He never stopped being Justin Timberlake, movie star and pop music performer. It is not difficult to understand why he had trouble channeling the authenticity of the role. Known as a mainstream R&B performer, he built his reputation on Michael Jackson's, coming of musical age and being perhaps a little too influenced by Jackson. His model, then, was not inside himself but outside. That lacks authenticity.

Steve Earle can wander from genre to genre as if he were playing hopscotch and be authentic in all of them. That's because there is a core performer within him that owns all of the genres in which he plays.

WE HEAR BEYOND THE LYRICS WHEN THEY SING

Americana promoters and stations got many people to listen to Chris Stapleton, and consequently, Stapleton became a star. Yet everyday, Americana promoters get stations to play promising records by artists we should all know about, and yet the albums wind up rejected by the larger public. What makes the difference? A large part of it is that Stapleton had a long apprenticeship as a performer and songwriter that turned him into a communicator. He is able to not just get people to pay attention to what he is singing but also get them to pay attention to him as a person as well as a performer.

He can communicate.

We think of communication as the ability to get your point across. That's part of it, but the whole thing is much more complicated than that. In truth, communication is the act of transmitting a verbal, written, or implied message through a common system of symbols, signs, or actions that create a personal rapport between the person who initiates the attempt at communication and the person he or she intends to communicate with.

Every attempt at communication involves three factors: (1) a sender, the person initiating the communication; (2) a message, which is the thing the sender wants to get across; and (3) the receiver, which is of course the person receiving the message. So, with a musical performance, the singer is the sender, the song is the message, and the listener is the receiver. And here is the major point: unless the message gets through to the receiver, communication has not taken place. Therefore, when you hear a song and your response is to shrug your shoulders, no communication has happened.

When Chris Stapleton sells, as he has so far, 830,000 copies of an album that didn't do that well upon its initial release, he has not simply made a product acceptable; he has created a personal rapport with the audience that causes them to want to own the symbols, images, and metaphors that are present in his album.

Americana audiences took country stars Johnny Cash, Waylon Jennings, and Willie Nelson to heart because they could sense their authenticity; perhaps these artists had public personas at the beginnings of their careers, but by the time they matured, they had become their authentic selves and had the personal power to communicate that to an audience.

Americana encourages authenticity. When Jennifer Knapp was discussing with me why she preferred being in this genre rather than mainstream pop, she said, "Americana gives you confidence. It lets me be me. If I were pop, I'd have to dress like Taylor Swift or Madonna, lose forty pounds, get all glammed up, and sing like they do." Americana not only does not require that sort of transformation but also does not honor it. Instead, it demands that you be yourself. People who trade in a show business image are rejected by the field. When he appeared on the Dirt Band's *Will the Circle Be Unbroken* album, for example, Roy Acuff was a welcome visitor but remained, both by circumstance and temperament, a visitor. He was the archetype of 1940s and 1950s country, and his music would not change as the decades did. A 1990s rerecording of a song he originally did in the 1930s would sound remarkably like the original. The biggest change would be a cleaner sound due to the advances in studio equipment.

Long after his contemporaries had given up the Nudie-made cowboy suits, huge belt buckles, and ten-gallon hats, Acuff continued to wear them. He was his image and did not choose to be anything other than that. As such he communicated very well with his audience but not with the young and hip crowd that the Dirt Band and the Scruggs sons were playing for. What he sang and played was wonderful, but because of his decision to remain anchored in the past, both his authenticity and his ability to communicate beyond his immediate audience were limited.

ROOTS AND BRANCHES

The fact that Americana is roots music is important. What is more important, though, is that in Americana, the roots are pulled out, twisted, turned, curled up, and replanted as something entirely different; they are transformed into a personal vision by the artist.

To use Ernest Tubb as an example, you can listen to any of his records and not know what decade they are from. "Drivin' Nails in My Coffin" is a Western swing shuffle that was written by Gerald Irby in 1945 and recorded by Tubb in 1946, and it sounds exactly the same when rerecorded in the 1960s as it did in the 1940s. No transformation takes place when Tubb gets hold of a song. In fact, his vocal claim to fame is that he really couldn't sing.

After releasing two records in Jimmie Rodgers style that went nowhere, Tubb underwent a tonsillectomy that destroyed his voice and wrecked his ability to sing. He left the performing business to become a songwriter. After getting an opportunity to sign with Decca Records, he began singing again but never really sounded good again. He was flat and nasal and had very little control over his voice. An eight-bar line could become ten or twelve bars when he sang it. Yet, when he had the right song for his voice, the effect, if not pretty, could be powerful. A good entertainer and smart enough to surround himself with a fine band, Tubb succeeded despite the fact that he lacked the vocal dexterity to transform material. Tubb remains an important figure in country music, both historically and artistically, but he never transcends the genre; no transformation happens.

THEY DON'T FIT IN ANY OTHER GENRE

Ernest Tubb fits naturally and organically in country music. So do his contemporaries, Roy Acuff, Red Foley, Kitty Wells, Jack Green, and Lefty Frizzell. It is impossible to think of them in any other category. Among pop artists, Justin Timberlake failed playing a folk singer because he is too closely connected with pop music. One reason audiences have never fully accepted Justin Bieber as a hip-hop artist is because he cannot help but be pop. That is his natural category. Similarly, Katy Perry could go from contemporary Christian, where she was managed by Jennifer Knapp, to pop in a seamless transition because pop music was a natural fit for her.

Similarly, Americana artists might have been lumped into other categories before Americana came into existence, but it was always an uneasy fit. Emmylou Harris was ushered into the country field. She was lumped into that genre by her record company who saw the biggest chance to sell records that way. When she was chosen as the reigning queen of Americana, she felt much more at home. It is the same with other Americana artists. James Taylor was originally promoted as a folkie and then became known as a singer-songwriter before finding his home in Americana. Solomon Burke labored for decades in soul music, while his music, though soul and blues based, was always more at home in Americana.

Americana artists can cross genres. Other artists cannot. When they try, the effort always feels contrived, inauthentic.

THE TECHNOLOGICAL EXPLOSION

New technology made Americana possible.

It is no accident that Americana rose as the record industry collapsed. As folk singer Tom Paxton once said, "New recording technology changed everything. You used to have to wait till you got signed by a record company and then you did what they wanted. Now, you can take charge of everything. You can put together your own studio, do your own recording and marketing. You can take charge of everything."[6] As the major labels lost their grip on the industry, home-recording gear became smaller, less expensive, and easier to use. Personal computers had recording and editing programs, and with digital recording, artists were able to play directly into their computers and store their music there, so tape was no longer needed. CD pressing plants were plentiful by this time; there were enough of them to make their prices competitive. Artists could have small runs of their CDs professionally designed, pressed, and packaged, and could hire promotion and publicity people to handle radio, review sources, and record stores. Performers could sell CDs at their shows.

The do-it-yourself attitude became pervasive. Even artists who were offered deals with record labels, such as John Prine, sometimes preferred to remain on their own labels, where they had absolute artistic freedom.

NEVER MAINSTREAM, ALWAYS ALTERNATIVE

What this means is that Americana music is alternative music. If mainstream music is controlled by the major record companies, and Americana is for the most part overlooked by the majors, then Americana will not be mainstream. It has an outsider status and will continue to have it.

As an example, listen to the music Melanie made when she was signed to the mini-major Buddah Records and then listen to what she has recorded since becoming independent. Her corporate recordings were good, but they rarely reflected the full extent of her talents and abilities. Even though they were produced by her husband, a professional mainstream record producer, they were always corporate controlled and most of the time showed some tendency to compromise. "Brand New Key," for example, one of her most famous songs, was written with a type of Dr. John–Louisiana swamp rock feel but was turned by her producer husband, in an attempt to get a hit single, into a bubblegum song.

In an attempt to get control, Melanie and her husband formed their own label, Neighborhood Records, where they could record freely, without record company interference. The quality of her records immediately improved. The adventurous and deeper side of her writing was allowed to flourish. The result was a major and important body of work that has not, at this writing, been fully appreciated. Her music is unique, creative, and authentic, speaking to the listener's soul as it reveals Melanie's.

It is also alternative music. Melanie has spent the last thirty years as a steadily working singer-songwriter, appreciated by her peers and with a worldwide cult following but little mainstream recognition or acceptance. Given a choice between art and business, Melanie has, like most Americana artists, chosen art.

IS A DEFINITION EVEN POSSIBLE?

The Americana Association's definition is based, as previously noted, on the surface aspects of the genre: the instruments used, the sources, and so on. As such it does the job, but it overlooks the inner qualities that make the genre what it is.

Those qualities are almost impossible to define. Americana is so many things at once. Getting a grip on it is almost like getting a grip on Newtonian physics and quantum physics.

Granted we are oversimplifying a little, but for our purposes Newtonian physics can be said to have four guiding principles:

1. Knowing the parts gives you knowledge about the whole. Everything is predictable because everything is linear.
2. Logic and mathematics are the tools we use to understand everything. These tools will reveal the basic processes that guide the universe and will permit us to make predictions.
3. The principles are absolute. Everything is made of matter and the forces acting upon that matter. No matter how small the parts the matter can be divided into, they will follow the basic laws of Newtonian physics.
4. Reality is what you can perceive through your senses. If a thing cannot be apprehended on a sensory level, it does not exist.

Because quantum mechanics is much more complicated, it has eight basic assumptions:

1. The fundamental building block of the universe is energy, which can take many forms. The electrons orbiting the nucleus of an atom, for example, can exist as particles or waves. Whichever form they take at the moment, they are still energy.
2. While Newtonian physics is linear, quantum is not. Electrons, for example, do not orbit a nucleus in a fixed path. They are instead electron clouds.

3. An electron can exist in more than one place at the same time.

4. This is because everything exists as potential or possibilities. They remain possibilities until they are observed. The "observer effect" kicks in and the potential becomes a reality. Therefore, nothing exists until it is observed.

5. When electrons move to a different energy level, they don't move linearly, like climbing a ladder. In fact, they don't literally move at all; they just change from one state to another. There is no movement through time and space.

6. The laws of quantum physics do not simply apply to our world. They apply to us also. We are vibrating frequencies, energy creatures. We have Newtonian existence, that is, we displace space and utilize time, and have an existence as physical creatures, but we also have another existence as energy. Quantum physicists claim our energy existence is our primary existence, even though we are largely unaware of it.

7. We are all connected. We all exist in the same energy field but with different frequencies, which means our experiences will be different, but at the core we are the same.

8. We exist as both particles and energy. The articles collect into bodies. At our core, however, we are simply energy.

In what ways are Newtonian physics and quantum mechanics metaphors for mainstream and Americana music? There are many, ranging from the songs themselves to the relationship between artists and audience and to the way we as audience receive the songs.

Mainstream pop is linear. There is a certainty to it, a feeling that the makers of the music have found the way and know what an audience wants. Artistic expression, inner satisfaction for the musicians, is not as important as that straight line from performer to listener. The main sign of artistic quality is popularity; if it draws a big audience, then the song is good. If he or she maintains that big audience, then he or she is an important artist.

Logic dictates what is acceptable and what is not. The operating rules of the genre create the logical framework that must be followed. When John Hiatt laments in "Drive South" that he doesn't believe Ronnie Milsap is ever going to record this song, he means that he has written outside of the standard logical framework for the country genre, of which Milsap was a prime practitioner. To be outside the logical framework is to be outside the genre. When the Americana singer-songwriter Mark Germino told Kevin Welch that they needed a new name because otherwise people would assume they were writing Nashville music, he meant that they were writing outside of the logical framework. In a linear structure, to be outside is to miss, like an arrow that misses the target completely.

Since the principles are absolute, there can be no variation in their application. A country song can be a recitation, for example, but only if it is either a spiritual or a trucking song. When the Flying Burrito Brothers released "Hippie Boy," a recitation about a young boy hired to deliver a package of drugs, the record was solid country in its writing, performance, and arrangement, but it violated the logical framework and was strongly rejected by the Nashville establishment. Similarly, when Garth Brooks was at his peak and had more power than any singer in Nashville, he decided to cover Todd Snyder's song "All Right Guy," a song that contained references to drunkenness, insolence toward the police, and masturbation. His record company would not let him record it. The song violated the absolute principles of Nashville country, principles that declared drinking songs were fine, but drunkenness and harassing the cops was not, that lusting after women in bars was fine but pleasuring yourself while reading Madonna's sex book was over the line. The reference was over the line in terms of good taste, but Snyder's purpose was satirical to attack the speaker in the song in a humorous way, not to necessarily endorse his actions.

If a thing cannot be apprehended by our five senses, it does not exist. Companies such as Clear Channel make it clear that, in their eyes, only a small part of the possible musical landscape can exist. And each part must exist in a separate category. Just as Monday can't be Tuesday, light jazz can't be hard bop and the two can't be blended together. The result would be confusing. An audience expects to hear a variation on what it has just heard. Take them outside their comfort zone and they might abandon your station for another one. Say there's not another station in your area? That fact doesn't make you safe. There's still Pandora, iTunes, YouTube, and all of the other streaming services. These services are taking 25 percent of radio's audience every year, so their danger is real. And that danger is all that the corporations can see; therefore, for them, it is all that exists.

In a linear system, when what you are doing isn't working, you do more of it, harder. The results, of course, will not be different. That's why, no matter how many units of the big hits are being sold, the mainstream is shrinking, while Americana is growing.

We still have the problem of defining exactly what it is that's growing. Kevin Welch insists that it can't be defined, that it is too many things, and claims that the fact that it is so many things is what gives it its durability. "When we were at that New Orleans conference, and I saw all those different guys there, country, blues, rock, everything, I smiled and thought, 'this one might last for a while. They can't buy this one. It's too many things.'"

Still, by looking at its energetic qualities, we can come closer to figuring out what this movement is. If the mainstream is linear physics, then Americana is quantum mechanics.

Americana is energy. It can exist as more than one thing. Chris Stapleton's *Traveler*, for example, is an album that exists simultaneously in the country and Americana genres. Americana built the album, and country provided a means for it winning a Grammy. Yet, whether the album is called country or Americana, it still has the same energy. The fact that energy does not change is due to the fact that, like electrons, Americana records do not take a normal, fixed, and predictable path to their goal, and like electrons, Americana records can exist in more than one category at a time. That's one reason it's so hard to define; it's not limited to any one thing. Muddy Waters is solidly blues; for most of his career, he was ghettoized in the blues category, locked in a Newtonian linear path that did not permit him to get off the chitlin' circuit. Then, as more people discovered his music, the observer effect kicked in, and while Waters's music stayed the same, its larger possibilities became reality and he became an Americana artist while remaining a blues artist.

Again, like electrons, Waters moved to a different energy level without any movement in his music. The movement to the new level was accomplished without movement through time and space. Waters did not move to Los Angeles, nor did he begin dressing differently or add synthesizers to his band. He did what he had done all his life, but the public saw him differently.

In mainstream pop, when performers want to alter their presentation, they change their image and bring in hotshot producers. Miley Cyrus tries to be heard through a program of selective nudity and the utilization of currently hot producers on her records. Ariana Grande decides to signal that she has grown up by dressing and behaving like Madonna and using rappers on her records. It is linear change and consists of doing what has been done before.

In Americana, quantum effects are created. The artists are true to themselves and to their music. The musicians have a linear presence that causes them to displace time and space, but the quantum reality of vibrating frequencies is more important because it connects artist to artist and artist to audience. We should consider Robert Earl Keen's statement that now he has someplace to belong. By emphasizing the quantum connection, Americana creates a community; there is closeness between artist and audience that came to Americana through folk music. The artists are not distant archetypes, as linear mainstream performers attempt to be, but are instead real, genuine, and authentic people.

What then is Americana? It is a type of music that fits the Americana Association's definition but that, like quantum reality, cannot be pinned down to any singular thing. Because it is both particles and energy, outside of us and inside us; because we give it life by perceiving it individually, knowing no two people perceive exactly the same way; and because it connects us, joins us into one large being, perhaps it should not be defined at all.

Maybe it should be sensed rather than stated.

Americana, then, is one more thing that we can't pin down but that we recognize when we encounter it.

NOTES

1. Chuck Armstrong, "In Conversation with Tom Paxton," Diffuser, March 16, 2015, http://diffuser.fm/.

2. Jim Asker, "Chris Stapleton Logs 12th Week Atop Country Chart, Next Up: Grammys." *Billboard*, February 10, 2016.

3. John Naisbitt, *Megatrends: Ten New Directions Shaping Our Lives*, New York: Warner Books, 1982, 26.

4. Jim Asker, "Chris Stapleton Travels to Top of Country Charts without Strong Support from Radio," *Billboard*, November 10, 2015, http://www.billboard.com/.

5. "Kasey Chambers' Bittersweet Tour," *Huffington Post*, October 22, 2015, http://www.huffingtonpost.com/.

6. Chuck Armstrong, "In Conversation with Tom Paxton," Diffuser, March 16, 2015, http://diffuser.fm/.

CODA

Annotated List of Recommended Recordings

Here, for readers who want a guide to the essential recordings of the artists discussed in these pages, is a starter list. I've only chosen one or two major recordings from each performer, enough to give interested parties a place to begin. It is highly recommended that you go beyond this list and sample widely from the available works of these and other Americana artists. The recommendations are listed in the order they are mentioned in the text.

Nitty Gritty Dirt Band. They have fifty years of albums to select from, but for our purposes, the two most essential are *Uncle Charlie and His Dog Teddy* and *Will the Circle Be Unbroken*. Both have been named albums that started the Americana Revolution, and while that may be overstating the case, it can't be denied that they were and remain very influential.

Jimmie Rodgers. Germany's Bear Family label has reissued all of Rodgers's work in handsome, beautifully done editions, but for those who simply want to sample, *My Rough and Rowdy Ways* and *Never No Mo' Blues* contain a good portion of his most popular work. Add to them the compilation *Train Whistle Blues*, and you have more than enough selections to give you a working knowledge of Rodgers's music.

The Carter Family. Rounder Records is the best source for Carter Family material. That firm has reissued all of the original Carter Family's recordings from 1927 to 1941 on nine compact discs. Bear Family and JSP Records have both issued boxed sets of their complete works.

O Brother, Where Art Thou? soundtrack album. This record, produced and assembled by the ubiquitous T-Bone Burnett, started the modern movement toward the recognition of Americana. Burnett put together a movie soundtrack that featured old-time music, bluegrass, folk, blues, and country, mixing older-generation artists (Ralph Stanley) with contemporary artists (Gillian Welch and Alison Krauss). The album became a mainstream success and piqued listener's curiosity about what came to be known as Americana music.

Robert Johnson. He only recorded twenty-nine songs in his lifetime, so his complete recorded output, including outtakes and alternate takes, is included in the two CD set *Robert Johnson: The Complete Recordings*. Heard for the first time, you'll be amazed at how primitive he sounds. Heard for a second time, you'll be amazed at how modern he sounds.

Mississippi John Hurt. The major songs of the rediscovered Mississippi John Hurt can be found on the three-CD set *The Complete Vanguard Recordings*. In these albums, Hurt was put together with a sympathetic producer, Patrick Sky, who knew his music and also knew how to keep Hurt relaxed and happy in the uncomfortable studio setting. The results are masterful.

Muddy Waters. Chess Records, his label for the most creative parts of his career, has reissued every scrap that Waters put on tape. The major recordings, though, can be found on the Muddy Waters boxed set, a three-CD package that contains representative Waters work from his beginning on the label up to his departure. It wisely avoids the *Blue Sky* albums that Johnny Winters produced and played most of the lead guitar on. If you're listening to Muddy Waters, you want to hear his guitar.

The Byrds. The first two albums, *Mr. Tambourine Man* and *Turn, Turn, Turn*, are the ones in which the Byrds perfected folk rock and put it on the charts. *Sweethearts of the Rodeo* invented West Coast country rock, and the sadly overlooked *Untitled, Unreleased* showed Roger McGuinn's mastery at mixing genres. Listened to from a historical perspective, these albums show how huge the Byrds' contribution to Americana was. Listened to from a contemporary perspective, they still provide a fine listening experience.

Sun Records. Sun was a singles-oriented company; albums were an afterthought. A rounded picture of what they did can be found on *Sun*

Record Company: Where Rock & Roll Was Born, a four-CD boxed set that contains representative singles by Johnny Cash, Roy Orbison, Carl Perkins, Jerry Lee Lewis, Warren Smith, Charlie Feathers, and all of the rest of Sun's talent pool. Probably because of contractual problems, Elvis is absent.

Buddy Holly. Again, every scrap Buddy Holly recorded has been issued and reissued, sometimes literal scraps: after Holly's death, Norman Petty found little abandoned pieces of tape, some as short as eighty seconds. He brought in a band he produced and managed, the Fireballs, had them write arrangements, and then, by puttering with the tape, created new Buddy Holly releases. "Peggy Sue Got Married" was one of these constructions after the fact. So, MCA was not always as careful as they could be with the reissues; they once put out *Buddy Holly: A Rock 'n' Roll Collection*, an album that contained a version of "Love's Made a Fool of You" that Holly did not sing on. Taken from the original master tapes, the music is reliable.

The Everly Brothers. The *Complete Cadence Recordings* is exactly what it claims to be: all of the Everly Brothers earlier recordings, including the complete *Songs Our Father Taught Us*, their collection of traditional folk material. Couple that with *The Complete Warner Brothers Recordings* and you have pretty much of all the Brothers' recordings up until they broke up. They made a few albums after their comeback, but they are not essential.

Rosanne Cash. When he saw she was serious about making music, Rosanne Cash's father gave her a list of the one hundred essential songs that she would have to study if she wanted to understand American music. Years later, she picked a dozen off the list and recorded them. The result is one of her most important albums, *The List*. Couple that with *Black Cadillac* and her Americana award–winning *The River and the Thread*, and you've got a picture of the Americana Rosanne Cash. Her *Greatest Hits* will show you country Rosanne.

Eileen Ivers. *Eileen Ivers* contains the best of her traditional Irish fiddle tunes, along with her audience-killing performance piece "Pachelbel's Frolics," which starts out as a well-played version of the "Canon" but goes on to alter the original, bringing in loops and variations that eventually work it into a Irish jig. It's a masterful piece of work. *Beyond the Bog Road* is a concept album about the Irish experience in America. Both albums are, as is all of her work, wonderful.

The Clancy Brothers and Tommy Makem. Their early albums on Tradition Records show their laid-back, relaxed, and informal approach to Irish music. *Come Fill Your Glass with Us* is a set of drinking songs recorded around the back table in the White Horse Tavern, which Liam described in his autobiography as four men singing unison while drinking beer. *The Rising of the Moon* is an album of war songs recorded under the same circumstances. After they performed on *The Ed Sullivan Show* and found themselves famous, they signed with Columbia Records and their albums became a little more formal, though in no way less fun. The Columbia albums have more of a beat and a higher energy level than the Tradition ones. The brothers are at their best live and fortunately have a lot of live albums in their oeuvre.

The Blind Boys of Alabama. To get a sampling of the Blind Boys' past, try one of their best-of packages: 1973's *Best of the Five Blind Boys of Alabama* is one of the most complete, as is 1998's *Have Faith: The Very Best of the Five Blind Boys of Alabama*. For the contemporary Blind Boys, *Higher Ground*, *Down in New Orleans*, *Take the High Road*, and *I'll Find a Way* show what the group has been up to for the past decade and show them with some fine guest artists.

The Steel Wheels. This is an old-time string band and not a bluegrass band. They are also a performing band, for whom recording is secondary. For that reason, their live recordings provide valuable insights into who the band is. I recommend *Live at Goose Creek*. Of their studio records, *Red Wing* and *No More Rain* show the band's range and versatility.

Kris Kristofferson. Most of the great and greatly popular early songs are found on his first two albums, *Kristofferson* (reissued as *Me and Bobby McGee*) and *The Silver Tongued Devil and I*. His recent songs, which lean toward the social and political, emphasizing even more his notion of freedom as a burden, can be found on *This Old Road* and *Closer to the Bone*.

Joe South. When South's first big hit, "Games People Play," raced up the charts, the album that contained it, *Introspect*, had already been declared a loser by Capitol Records and stripped from the catalog. It was hastily repackaged and issued again as *Games People Play*. Along with *Don't It Make You Want to Go Home* and *A Look Inside*, it contains most of the songs South is known for. Those albums can be hard to find, however. A good greatest-hits package is the best approach to Joe South's body of work at the moment. Of the several that are on the market,

Anthology: A Mirror of His Mind ranges widest over his body of work. It contains all of the hits and several fine songs that were not hits but in a just world would have been.

John Stewart. Among Stewart's solo work—his work with the Cumberland Three and the Kingston Trio is outside the scope of this book—the two albums that are credited with starting Americana have to be heard. Whether or not they are the first, *Signals through the Glass* and *California Bloodlines* are audio-operational definitions of Americana. Two fine albums, *Cannons in the Rain* and *Wingless Angels*, have been issued on a single CD, and between those and the rock trilogy, *Bombs Away Dream Babies*, *Dream Babies Go Hollywood*, and *Blondes*, you have a good overview of this important musician.

Jennifer Knapp. Knapp's contemporary Christian music is gathered on her first three albums, *Kansas*, *Lay It Down*, and *The Way I Am*. None of them are the soft, superficial praise music without substance that so many associate the genre with. They are tough, substantial albums that explore the personal relationship between people and their gods. Since her comeback, she has released two Americana albums, *Letting Go* and *Set Me Free*, both of which explore the type of issues often raised by Americana artists, such as Kristofferson's burden-of-freedom idea, from a religious feminist perspective.

Delta Rae. This band has consistently fought against categorization on the grounds that their music draws from too many different influences to be easily placed in one bag. A listen to their two albums *Carry the Fire* and *After It All* makes a pretty good case for their argument. Delta Rae draws inspiration from all over the map and adds to their various musical influences a healthy dose of southern mythology and folklore. Do they not fit in a single category? How fortunate that Americana is the genre for music that can't be placed in a genre.

Henry Paul. Paul states that he is proud to have been a part of three successful bands, the Henry Paul Band, Blackhawk, and the Outlaws. To sample his work, it is necessary to listen to all three. Of the three, the Henry Paul Band is the most traditional southern rock band. It features the Mixolydian scales, the lyrics celebrating southern life and extended jams. Their self-titled *Henry Paul Band* album provides a good overview. Blackhawk falls more into the country-rock field; it is the Outlaws with acoustic guitar and a mandolin, while the current version of the Outlaws features two lead guitars, a third playing rhythm, and fine three- and four-part harmonies. Blackhawk and the Outlaws songs have a spiritual under-pinning that reflects Paul's musical and social maturity. He has been around the music industry, he says, long enough to have outgrown the ego factors that attracted him to the music in the first place and is now in a place where he can explore deeper ideas.

The Allman Brothers. Considered the band that invented southern rock, the Allman Brothers Band created a fusion of rock, jazz, blues, and soul that changed the way we listened to rock 'n' roll. *At Fillmore East* has been consistently named one of the best live rock albums ever made, and after nearly fifty years it still holds up. So does *Eat a Peach*, which is part live and part studio recording. Of the pure studio records, *Idlewild South* shows the band's range well.

Patsy Cline. Cline was country's first real crossover artist, which makes her the first real and genuine country singer accepted by main-stream America. Although Owen Bradley, her producer, certainly tried, he could not remove the country from her voice and her personality. Her second major label album, *Showcase*, not only contains her major hits, "I Fall to Pieces," "I Love You So Much It Hurts," "Crazy," and "Walkin' After Midnight," but also has a cover of Gogi Grant's "The Wayward Wind," a tricked-out "South of the Border," and a couple of other pop-oriented tunes that show how Bradley tries to make the crossover easier for her. If you want to stick with the tried and true, several best-of pack-ages are available.

James Taylor. Very few people need to be introduced to the music of James Taylor. If you're among the few, begin with *Sweet Baby James*, which has the hits "Sweet Baby James," "Country Road," and "Fire and Rain" on it, along with some good selections that are not as familiar. If you want a good overview of the hits, a few best-of packages are avail-able. Easily the best is *The Essential James Taylor*, a two-record set that contains all of the hits and a few tracks that should have hit.

Steve Earle. The problem with buying Steve Earle albums is that you never know what you're going to get. Will this one be by the folkie Steve Earle, the rocker, the bluegrass guy, the love balladeer, or the political radical? If you want to sample all of the personalities on a single record, begin with *I Feel Alright*, which blends country, rock, and old-time Sun Records rockabilly. *Jerusalem* and *The Revolution Starts Now* are politi-cal albums. A wide variety of Steve Earle can be found on *Transcendental Blues*, an album that he deliberately packed with every style he could think of because he had been making an album a year and wanted to slow down; Earle figured if he got it all on this one album, he wouldn't feel compelled to go into the studio again so soon. *Guitar Town*, the CD that brought Earle to public attention, is a must.

Emmylou Harris. You can find two Emmylou Harrises on records. The Warner albums feature mostly the woman who smoked country but didn't inhale; they are usually country rock with a smattering of bluegrass and are mostly excellent. Of these, the first few, *Pieces of the Sky*, *Elite Hotel*, and *Luxury Liner*, show listeners who she is. But no matter what, there's an Americana artist in there trying to get out, and when she leaves Warner Brothers for Electra/Nonesuch, the Americana finally breaks free and surfaces. *Wrecking Ball*, *Red Dirt Girl*, and *Stumble into Grace* bring Harris deeper into focus.

Maura O'Connell. O'Connell has never made a bad album, so it is safe to start anywhere, but among the best are the ones she made with Dobro artist Jerry Douglas, banjo master Béla Fleck, and other members of the New Grass Revival. Try *Western Highway*, *A Real Life Story*, and *Blue Is the Colour of Hope*. Again, those seeking a best-of album are directed to *The View from Here*. *Naked with Friends* is an a cappella album loaded with guest singers.

Mary Black. Her first album, *Mary Black*, is the one that got her typecast as a folk singer because it is primarily made up of Irish folk songs. It does have a lot of recently composed songs on it, but they sound traditional so that their placement on the album tends to create an impression of folkiness. *Without the Fanfare* sees her committing more to the music of a new generation of Irish songwriters, a practice she continued throughout her recording career. In a ten-year period from 1998 to 2008, three best-of collections were issued: *Song for Ireland*, *The Best of Mary Black, 1999–2001*, and *Twenty-Five Years, Twenty-Five Songs*. *Down the Crooked Road*, another best-of set, was issued as a "soundtrack" to her autobiography.

Jim Lauderdale. Lauderdale is another of those prolific artists who have released far too many albums to keep up with. Many were on small or fugitive labels and can be hard to find, but enough of his work is available to please everyone but completists. You may not have heard his records, but you know his music; he has written for artists such as Elvis Costello, the Dixie Chicks, Vince Gill, Patty Loveless, and Lee Ann Womack and has produced albums for everyone from Ralph Stanley to the North Mississippi All-Stars. The best introduction to his work is probably *Soul Searching*, a two-album set with one record centered on the soul music of Memphis and the other exploring Nashville's soul.

Mumford & Sons. Americana fans are probably going to go for Mumford & Sons' first two albums, *Sigh No More* and *Babel*. *Sigh No More*, their first and biggest hit, produced four hit singles and wound up selling over four million copies, 3.2 million in the United States alone. It features the banjo-crazed sound that the band is famous for. *Babel* lightens up on the banjo and brings the piano forward. It sold fewer copies, one million in the United Kingdom and 2.7 million in America. After this release, the band abandoned the banjo, along with their acoustic instruments, and issued their third album, *Wilder Mind*, on electric instruments. When they did not provide the type of music their followers had gotten used to, their fans abandoned them; *Wilder Mind*'s numbers were far below those of the band's previous albums: 107,000 in the United Kingdom, 542,000 in the states. The sudden change in style is something Americana fans are accustomed to; musicians are mercurial and so is the music they make.

The Avett Brothers. Virtually every stage of the Avett Brothers' development can be traced on records: they've issued eighteen of them over the sixteen years they've been a recording act. Most fans, though, are most interested in the discs that Rick Rubin produced for his American label. These began with *I and Love and You*, their breakthrough album, from 2009. Rubin helped the band get the discipline they needed to put their sound across without imposing himself or his favored ideas on their music. Rubin's genius is to see what's inside the artist and help him or her free it. The difference between the albums he produced and the ones that appeared earlier on Ramseur Records is remarkable. *I and Love and You* hit number sixteen on the *Billboard* charts. A second breakthrough was achieved by *The Carpenter*, the brothers' 2012 album. Again, it was produced by Rick Rubin. *The Carpenter* has a strong spiritual impulse beneath it; you come away from a listening feeling you've been given a peek at something you haven't quite been able to get a good look at.

SELECTED BIBLIOGRAPHY

"An Interview with Eric Andersen." *Performing Songwriter* 83 (January/February 2005).

Bush, William J. *Greenback Dollar: The Incredible Rise of the Kingston Trio.* Lanham, MD: Scarecrow, 2013.

Cain, Michael Scott. "Kevin Welch Keeps on Writing Songs." *Rambles*, November 18, 2006. http://www.rambles.net/.

Caligiuri, Jim. "Carrie Elkins and Danny Schmidt Sell Out: Betrothed Songwriters Ready a Wild Weekend at Wyldwood." *Austin Chronicle*, June 19, 2013.

Cash, Rosanne. *Composed: A Memoir.* New York: Penguin, 2010.

Cash, W. J. *The Mind of the South.* New York: Vintage, 1972.

Cawelti, John. *The Six-Gun Mystique.* New York: Popular Press, 1972.

CBS News. "Americana Awards Honor Emmylou Harris and Rodney Crowell." September 19, 2013. http://www.cbsnews.com/.

Charles, Ray, and David Ritz. *Brother Ray: Ray Charles' Own Story.* New York: Dial Press, 1978.

Clancy, Liam. *The Mountain of the Women: Memoirs of an Irish Troubadour.* New York: Doubleday, 2002.

Cooper, Peter. "Without 'Star-Level' Clout, Lauderdale Released from RCA." *Tennessean*, February 21, 2001.

Darden, Robert. *People Get Ready! A New History of Black Gospel Music.* New York: Bloomsbury Academic, 2005.

Donkers, Jan. Radio interview with Joe South. VPRO Radio, 1988. http://www.vpro.nl/.

Dorson, Richard M. *Folklore and Folklife: An Introduction.* Chicago: University of Chicago Press, 1982.

Federman, Raymond. "The Real Begins Where the Spectacle Ends." Raymond Federman, 1996. http://www.federman.com/.

Feniak, Peter. "Ian Tyson: The Singing Cowboy." *Good Times*, March 2015.

Fowler, Gene, and Bill Crawford. *Border Radio: Quacks, Yodelers, Pitchmen, Psychics, and Other Amazing Broadcasters of the American Airwaves.* Austin: University of Texas Press, 2002.

Fuchs, Otto. *Bill Haley: The Father of Rock 'n' Roll.* London: Wagner, 2014.

Georgia Radio Museum and Hall of Fame. "Zenas Sears, 1914–1988." Accessed September 9, 2016. http://www.grhof.com/.

Goldrosen, John. *The Buddy Holly Story.* Madison, WI: Popular Press, 1978.

Greene, Andy. "James Taylor's Mellow Rebirth: Inside 'Before This World.'" *Rolling Stone*, March 27, 2015.

Guralnick, Peter. *Sam Phillips: The Man Who Invented Rock 'n' Roll*. New York: Little, Brown, 2015.

Harrington, Beth. *The History of Christianity*. DVD. London: BBC, 2010.

———. *The Winding Stream: An Oral History of the Carter and Cash Family*. Georgetown, MA: PFP, 2014.

Hurd, Mary G. *Kris Kristofferson: Country Highwayman*. Lanham, MD: Rowman & Littlefield, 2015.

John Stewart Memorial. Tales from the Tavern, 2006. YouTube. http://www.youtube.com/.

Jones, LeRoi. *Blues People: Negro Music in White America*. New York: HarperCollins, 2002.

"Kasey Chambers Teams with Nick DiDia for Bittersweet." http://www.noise11.com/news/kasey-chambers-teams-with-nick-didia-for-bittersweet-20140703, July 3, 2014.

Klein, Joe. *Woody Guthrie: A Life*. New York: Delta, 1999.

Knapp, Jennifer. *Facing the Music: My Life*. New York: Howard Books, 2014.

Korzybski, Alfred. *Science and Sanity: An Introduction to Non-Aristotelian Systems and General Semantics*. New York: Institute of General Semantics, 2003.

Leigh, Spencer. "Interview with an Angel." Bite My Foot, April 20, 1998. http://www.bitemyfoot.org.uk/.

Marquis, Donald M. *In Search of Buddy Bolden: First Man of Jazz*. Baton Rouge: Louisiana University Press, 1978.

Maryland Public Television. *American Roots Music*. Aired October 2001. http://pbs.org/.

Matthews, Cameron. "Emmylou Harris and the Milk Carton Kids Reimagine Johnny Cash's 'Apache Tears' for New Compilation." Bluegrass Situation, August 12, 2014. http://www.bluegrasssituation.com/.

Mazor, Barry. *Ralph Peer and the Making of Popular Roots Music*. Chicago: Chicago Review Press, 2014.

Miller, Stephen. *Kristofferson: The Wild American*. New York: Omnibus, 2010.

Miller, Zell. *They Heard Georgia Singing*. Macon, GA: Mercer University Press, 1996.

New Orleans Jazz National Historic Park. "Buddy Bolden: Calling His Children Home, 1877–1931." November 13, 2013. http://www.nps.gov/.

New Orleans Official Guide. "Music Greats: Jelly Roll Morton." Accessed September 9, 2016. http://www.neworleansonline.com/.

Niles, John Jacob. *The Ballad Book of John Jacob Niles*. New York: Dover, 1981.

Ownby, Ted. "Jimmie Rodgers: The Father of Country Music." *Mississippi History Now*, July 2004. http://mshistorynow.mdah.state.ms.us/.

Porter, Lewis, Tim Wilkins, and Ted Gioia. "Kid [Edward] Ory." *Encyclopedia of Jazz Musicians*. http://www.jazz.com/.

Rock and Roll Hall of Fame. *The Roots of Rock and Roll: Blues, Gospel, Country, Folk, Bluegrass, and R&B*. Exhibit catalog. Cleveland: Author, 2016.

San Antonio Express-News. "Blues Wizard's S.A. Legacy." November 30, 1986.

The Search for Robert Johnson. Directed by Chris Hunt. London: Iambic Productions, 1992.

Smith, Harry. *Anthology of American Folk Music*. New York: Folkways Records, 1952.

Wald, Elijah. *Escaping the Delta: Robert Johnson and the Invention of the Blues*. New York: Amistad, 2004.

Welding, Pete. "Robert Johnson: Hellhound on his Trail." *DownBeat Magazine* 66 (1966).

Wynn, Ben. *In Tune: Charley Patton, Jimmie Rodgers, and the Roots of American Music*. Baton Rouge: Louisiana State University Press, 2014.

Zwonitzer, Mark, and Charles Hirshberg. *Will You Miss Me When I'm Gone? The Carter Family and Their Legacy in American Music*. New York: Simon & Schuster, 2004.

INDEX

a cappella, 88
Acuff, Roy, 199
adult orientation. *See* maturity
African American music, xxx; the Allman
    Brothers Band and, 150; churches and,
    91; gospel music and, 89–91; played by
    DJs, 51, 52, 53; Sears and popularity of,
    in South, 50–51; vaudeville and, 68–69.
    *See also specific African American
    musicians*
age. *See* maturity
alcohol, 110
Allman Brothers Band, 150–151, 214
The Allman Brothers Band (the Allman
    Brothers Band), 151
"All Right Guy" (Snyder), 205
alt-country. *See* alternative country
The Alternate Root Magazine, 194–195
alternative country (alt-country), xxix,
    19–20, 21–23
alternative to mainstream, 202
AMA. *See* Americana Music Association
Americana. *See specific topics*
Americana Awards show, 131n1
Americana Music Association (AMA),
    xxix, 1–3, 6; CMA compared with, 6–7;
    commerce and, 7; genre definition by,
    58, 61, 203; Holly and, 58; as
    infrastructure, 8
amplification, electrical, 37–38, 159
Andersen, Eric, 159–160

"Anna Lisa, Please" (Welch), 133–134
Anthology of American Folk Music (Smith,
    H.), 14, 16, 35
Appalachian folk music, 10, 11, 84–85
Apple Records, 160
A&R. *See* artists and repertoire
archetypes of genre, 187–188, 189–190;
    the Avett Brothers as, 187, 191; Cash,
    R., as, 77–78; Dylan and, 187;
    Mumford & Sons as, 187, 189, 191
arrangement: complexity of, 136; of
    "Games People Play", 124; symphonic,
    xxii, 117–118, 172
art, xxiii, 23–24, 101
Arthur Godfrey's Talent Scouts (television
    show), 154, 155
artists and repertoire (A&R), 101–102
Asch, Moses, 34–35
Asher, Peter, 160
Atlantic Records, 151
At the Fillmore East (the Allman Brothers
    Band), 151, 214
audiences, 133, 134, 191
authenticity, xxxi, 115, 197; authorship
    and, 197–198; the Avett Brothers and,
    191; Chambers and, 197;
    communication, country music and,
    199; Earle and, 163, 198; folklore,
    fakelore and, 24; of genre, 120, 163,
    197; in lyrics of Holly, 58; in *O
    Brother, Where Art Thou?*, 22;

ABOUT THE AUTHOR

Michael Scott Cain was born in East Point, Georgia, and grew up commuting between there and New York City. In both cities he was exposed to the finest Americana music ever played—folk, jazz, and blues in New York City; and country, rhythm, blues, and gospel in the Atlanta area. He started his record collection buying Ray Charles singles for five cents each when they were taken down from juke boxes and has remained a lifetime fan and student of roots music.

He taught literature, creative writing, and pop culture on the community college level for most of his adult life and was perhaps the first person to build a course around the music of the Outlaw Movement led by Tom Paul Glazer, Waylon Jennings, Willie Nelson, and David Allen Coe. A musician himself, he plays six and twelve string guitars. He has written three novels, most recently *Midnight Train*, and seven books of poetry, including *East Point Poems*. Among his other nonfiction books is *The Community College in the Twenty-First Century*. He is currently at work on a new book exploring the symbiotic relationship between folk music and the New Left political movement in the sixties. Cain writes regularly about Americana for the online cultural journal, Rambles (www.rambles.net)

CPSIA information can be obtained
at www.ICGtesting.com
Printed in the USA
BVOW03*1359270317
479021BV00001B/1/P

Lead Belly

p. 31